China's Strategic Competition with the United States

This book examines the transformation and the multifaceted nature of the relationship between the US and China in the post-Cold War era, and the implications of their strategic competition in military, political and economic terms, as well as in relation to Taiwan, Japan, the Korean peninsula and Central Asia. The author argues that both powers compete in virtually every sphere in the international system; their relationship is overall competitive rather than co-operative, even in areas that are amenable to co-operation such as trade and nuclear non-proliferation.

The book addresses important questions, including: does China's growing power and influence unavoidably come at the expense of the US or the wider world? It also asks, to what extent do the national interests and policies of the US and China coincide or diverge on a host of regional issues? It covers all the important issues including politics, security, nuclear deterrence, military modernization, energy, trade and economic interaction, and Asia-Pacific power reconfiguration.

Russell Ong is a Lecturer in the School of Government and Public Policy, University of Strathclyde, UK. He is the author of *China's Security Interests in the post-Cold War era* and *China's Security Interests in the 21st Century* (both published by Routledge).

Routledge security in Asia series

1 **Taiwan's Security and Air Power**
  Taiwan's defense against the air threat from mainland China
  Edited by Martin Edmonds and Michael M. Tsai

2 **Asia Pacific Security – Values and Identity**
  Leszek Buszynski

3 **Taiwan's Defense Reform**
  Edited by Martin Edmonds and Michael M. Tsai

4 **Maritime Security in Southeast Asia**
  Edited by Kwa Chong Guan and John K. Skogan

5 **China's Security Interests in the 21st Century**
  Russell Ong

6 **China's Rise – Threat or Opportunity?**
  Edited by Herbert S. Yee

7 **India and the South Asian Strategic Triangle**
  Ashok Kapur

8 **Southeast Asia and the Rise of China**
  The search for security
  Ian Storey

9 **China's Strategic Competition with the United States**
  Russell Ong

China's Strategic Competition with the United States

Russell Ong

LONDON AND NEW YORK

First published 2012
by Routledge
711 Third Avenue, New York, NY 10017

Simultaneously published in the UK
by Routledge
2 Park Square, Milton Park, Abingdon, Oxon OX14 4RN

Routledge is an imprint of the Taylor & Francis Group, an informa business

First issued in paperback 2013

© 2012 Russell Ong

The right of Russell Ong to be identified as author of this work has been asserted by him in accordance with sections 77 and 78 of the Copyright, Designs and Patents Act 1988.

All rights reserved. No part of this book may be reprinted or reproduced or utilised in any form or by any electronic, mechanical, or other means, now known or hereafter invented, including photocopying and recording, or in any information storage or retrieval system, without permission in writing from the publishers.

Trademark notice: Product or corporate names may be trademarks or registered trademarks, and are used only for identification and explanation without intent to infringe.

British Library Cataloguing in Publication Data
A catalogue record for this book is available from the British Library

Library of Congress Cataloging-in-Publication Data
Ong, Russell.
  China's strategic competition with the United States/Russell Ong.
  p. cm. – (Routledge security in Asia series; 9)
  Includes bibliographical references and index.
  1. United States–Foreign relations–China. 2. China–Foreign relations–United States. I. Title. II. Series: Routledge security in Asia series; 9.
  E183.8.C5O54 2012
  327.73051–dc23
                                                                    2011018444

ISBN: 978-0-415-56107-5 (hbk)
ISBN: 978-0-415-72594-1 (pbk)
ISBN: 978-0-203-22223-2 (ebk)

Typeset in Times
by Wearset Ltd, Boldon, Tyne and Wear

To my parents

Contents

Acknowledgements	viii
List of abbreviations	ix
Introduction	1
1 The US's global supremacy	9
2 The US and liberal values	25
3 The US and the international economic system	42
4 The US and the Taiwan issue	59
5 The US and Japan	76
6 The US and North Korea	93
7 The US and South Korea	110
8 The US and Central Asia	126
9 Conclusions	141
Notes	147
Selected bibliography	162
Index	169

Acknowledgements

I would like to thank Noel O'Sullivan, Christopher Coker, Eric Grove, Rosemary Gosling, Inderjeet Parmar and David Judge for their assistance over the years. Special thanks must also be given to the IT support and library staff at the University of Strathclyde, who have provided the necessary facilities to carry out my research.

Abbreviations

APEC	Asia-Pacific Economic Co-operation
ARF	ASEAN Regional Forum
BWC	Biological Weapons Convention
CCP	Chinese Communist Party
CentrasBat	Central Asian Battalion
CIS	Commonwealth of Independent States
CPSU	Communist Party of the Soviet Union
CSCAP	Council on Security Co-operation in the Asia-Pacific
CSTO	Collective Security Treaty Organisation
CTBT	Comprehensive Test Ban Treaty
CWC	Chemical Weapons Convention
DPP	Democratic Progressive Party
EEZ	Exclusive Economic Zones
EU	European Union
G-8	Group of Eight
GCC	China-Gulf Co-operation Council
GDP	Gross Domestic Product
GNP	Gross National Product
IAEA	International Atomic Energy Agency
IISS	International Institute for Strategic Studies
IMF	International Monetary Fund
IPR	Intellectual Property Rights
ISAF	International Security Assistance Force
KEDO	Korean Peninsula Energy Development Organization
KMT	Kuomintang
KWP	Korean Workers' Party
LWRs	Light Nuclear Reactors
MTCR	Missiles Technology Control Regime
NAFTA	North American Free Trade Area
NATO	North Atlantic Treaty Organisation
NDPO	National Defence Programme Outline
NIEO	New International Economic Order
NPC	National People's Congress

NPT	Non-Proliferation Treaty
NUC	National Unification Council
ODA	Official Development Assistance
P5	Permanent Five
PFP	Partnership for Peace
PFP	People's First Party
PLA	People's Liberation Army
PNTR	Permanent Normal Trade Relations
PRC	People's Republic of China
PSI	Proliferation Security Initiative
RMA	Revolution in Military Affairs
SCC	Security Consultative Committee
SCO	Shanghai Co-operation Organisation
SDF	Self Defence Forces
SEZ	Special Economic Zone
SPR	Strategic Petroleum Reserve
TMD	Theatre Missile Defence
TRA	Taiwan Relations Act
TSU	Taiwan Solidarity Union
ULO	Uighur Liberation Organisation
UN	United Nations
WMD	Weapons of Mass Destruction
WTO	World Trade Organisation
XPCC	Xinjiang Production and Construction Corps

Introduction

The aim of this book is to analyse China's strategic competition with the US in the post-Cold War era. It seeks to examine the intensity of this strategic competition but also explores to what extent avenues for co-operation exist. A corollary is that this central question has policy implications, namely, how do the Western powers manage the ascendancy of China? Certainly, China's strategic competition with the US has implications for both regional and international security. At the same time, it must be noted that strategic competition does not imply the inevitability of military conflict. The book focuses on China, although the US's perspective will be discussed insofar as it sheds light on the analysis. This introductory chapter is divided into two sections. The first section provides the theoretical background for China's strategic competition with the US. The second section explains the link between China's status as a great power and its strategic competition with the US.

The basis for strategic competition

With reference to the question of how far China competes with the US, the answer lies in the theoretical perspective of Structural Realism. The theory of Structural Realism depicts the world as anarchy – a domain without a sovereign, although one might argue that the US comes close to being one today. In that domain, states must look to themselves to survive – self-help is paramount, both to China and the US. Speaking of the anarchical condition of international politics, Kenneth Waltz observes:

> A self-help system is one in which those who do not help themselves, or who do so less effectively than others, will fail to prosper, will lay themselves open to dangers, will suffer. Fear of such unwanted consequences stimulates states to behave in ways that tend toward the creation of balances of power.[1]

Given that no state can prevent others from doing what they are able to, such as using force to achieve certain national security objectives in international politics, war is always possible. This applies to both China and its strategic competitor, the US.

Despite changes brought about by technological advances, the key to survival in war is still primarily military power. This can be generated either internally or through alliances, usually by both. In China's case, it wants to build itself up and it is worth noting that the only alliance it ever had was the Treaty of Friendship, Alliance and Mutual Assistance with the Soviet Union in the 1950s. Hence, in the international system, states in general pay attention to their relative power position because power is the key to survival – both in a physical sense and in a political sense of the continued exercise of sovereignty, especially in the case of China, as it has always emphasised this Westphalian concept. Moreover, power is not only relative but is also the key to increasing influence in the international system; it enables defence and offence as well as deterrence and coercion. Therefore, states will try to increase their power when they believe they can do so without too much risk. They will also try especially hard to preserve the power they have. This applies in particular to the case of the US, China's strategic competitor.

At the same time, a country's position in the international hierarchy can deteriorate due to another's domestic or foreign success. For example, China's security improved with the collapse of the Soviet Union in 1991 as Moscow had been a persistent northern threat to Beijing since the Sino-Soviet schism. When another state increases its capacities through either internal or external efforts, it must be noted that others have incentives to reassess their own positions. States behave in this manner not because they do understand the intentions of other states but because they do not. Anarchy permits exploitation of the weak by the strong, making international politics a competitive realm. Therefore, states do not wish to be weak relative to others nor do they wish to depend on them.[2] If one state improves its relative power position – by vanquishing an old enemy, finding new allies, building more military power, achieving and demonstrating qualitative improvements in its military capacity, purposefully improving its ability to generate military capability, or endeavouring to dominate critical strategic geography or resources abroad – others are likely to take note and respond in an appropriate manner. They will tend to find their own allies, mobilise their own capabilities, and emulate the successful competitive practices of other powerful states, including military and diplomatic practices.[3] This is balancing behaviour predicted in the Structural Realist variant of balance of power theory. The purpose of our analysis, is to answer the question, to what extent China as well as other states in the international system balance against the US.

The theory of Structural Realism predicts both a general pattern of competitive behaviour that ultimately leads to balances and deliberate balancing against particular powers, usually the most powerful states in the international system. Both constitute balancing and elements of both types are present in post-Cold War era. Structural Realism does not predict all powers will behave this way all the time; however, those who do are more likely to thrive, and those who do not are likely to suffer in the long run. In this regard, most Chinese analysts still point to the enduring wisdom of Structural Realism; in addition, they continue to regard the nation-state as the dominant actor in the international system, despite the increasing importance of transnational actors today.[4] Hence, in general, adopting the perspective of Structural Realism leads one to the notion of strategic competition between great powers. In particular, it will be argued in this book that China and the US compete in virtually every arena of international politics for strategic gains today.

For the purpose of our analysis, the term "strategic" relates to key national security interests, with Chinese planners often using a more inclusive term "comprehensive national strength" in discussions on their country's long-term strategy.[5] These national security interests are often separated into three interrelated aspects for analytical purposes. The first is military security, which is foremost in the minds of defence planners and the traditional concern in international relations and security studies. From a Chinese viewpoint, "the military force shoulders the important mission of defending the state's territorial sovereignty and integrity, resisting foreign aggression and safeguarding state unification".[6] Accordingly, it is necessary to develop strong military capabilities in order to achieve this mission. This Chinese formulation is quite similar to the conventional concept of military security employed in Western strategic thought; the focus is on the interplay of military threats and mutual perceptions of military intentions. For China, direct military threats have on the whole diminished following the disintegration of the Soviet Union in 1991. More important today will be meeting new military challenges from a resurgent Japan and of course, the US. The latter's military prowess is currently unmatched in the world and this has raised acute concerns for Chinese defence planners.

The second element of national security interests is political security, with the preservation of a state's ideology, values and political system being high on the agenda. China often emphasises that its political system must not be undermined and that its sovereignty must not be encroached; Beijing is adamant that "no country shall meddle in the internal affairs of another country" and has stated that "the superpowers should not be allowed to order other countries about, pursue power politics and impose their values on others."[7] Essentially, political security relates to the organisation and process of government, and the ideology that gives the rulers of a particular country legitimacy. In China's case, the ruling communist ideology – no matter how irrelevant it may seem today – is severely under threat as Beijing becomes increasing drawn to the capitalist orbit in the search for economic resources for its national development. Although one might even argue that there is little meaning to the term "communism" in China today as market reforms continue to accelerate and spread throughout the country, the point is that the potential collapse of communism in China is linked to the perceived Western strategy of peaceful evolution (*heping yanbian*).[8] At a wider level, one might argue that China's political security, or more specifically, the security of the current Communist regime, is very much related to the wider global contest between the remaining communist and Western-style political systems. This contest is particularly relevant to China as it had witnessed a major defeat for communist political systems when the Soviet Union and the Eastern European states abandoned communism. To be more accurate, China is determined to defend its authoritarian political system in an era when the US has embarked on a mission to spread liberal values worldwide.

The third aspect of national security relates to the economic dimension. Chinese worldviews have already incorporated Marxism and Realism, which, as materialist theories, give prominence to the role of economics in both international relations and security thinking.[9] Compared to Western strategists, it is fair to say that Chinese analysts tend to give more weight to development issues on the national security agenda. This is primarily because China is still a developing country; since 1949, a top national priority is to catch up with the world's industrialised powers, and more importantly, rapid economic development is deemed as the basis for achieving truly global power status. The cases of Britain and the US achieving global hegemony in the nineteenth and twentieth centuries, respectively, serve as valuable lessons for Chinese strategic thinkers. Underpinned by unrivalled economic strength, Britain and the US were able to become the dominant force in international system at different periods in time. Essentially, economic security today includes the promotion of fast-paced growth, unfettered access to global markets and guaranteed supply of natural resources such as oil. It is increasingly important, not only to China, but to every state in the international capitalist system. In the twenty-first century, economic issues are sometimes seen as taking precedence over political ones, and it can be argued that, in general, the dichotomy of "high politics" (military) and "low politics" (economics) in international relations has proved to be a false one. Energy security is a case in point and it occupies the substantial attention of Chinese security planners today; this is primarily because China became a net importer of oil in 1993, following three decades of energy self-sufficiency. China is set to become the world's second largest consumer of oil after the US. Currently, China has to rely on imports, with about 60 per cent coming from the Middle East. Therefore, it will be affected by global oil price volatility and supply disruptions; it is also worth noting that developing countries tend to suffer more from oil price volatility than developed ones. In sum, strategic competition as defined in this book relates to three elements of power: military, political and economic.

Great power status

The fact that China engages in strategic competition with the US is partly linked to China's drive to truly global power status. This is in turn reinforced by historical traditions. Due to its supremacy in Asia and its sheer size, China was once at the top of the regional hierarchy and the smaller neighbouring states often had to conduct their relations with Beijing in a deferential manner. Before the arrival of Western powers in Asia, China's security was as at a maximum as its smaller neighbours never came close to challenging Beijing in military, political or economic terms.[10] Basically, the Chinese empire regarded itself as the centre of the universe; all states had to revolve around it insofar as they paid tributes to the Chinese emperor.[11] Historically, this was especially the case with adjoining vassal states such as Korea and Vietnam. To a certain extent, this type of Sino-centric thinking is still evident and influences the Chinese security policies in areas such as the Korean peninsula.

One of the features of the Sino-centric world order is hierarchy – as opposed to anarchy – whereby "political actors are formally differentiated according to degrees of their authority."[12] In many ways, this hierarchical structure derives from the workings of political and social relations within China, whereby inequality exists in relationships such as those between the ruler and its subjects, or a father and his son. In effect, the practice of such hierarchical relationships has been extended to the realm of foreign relations over the previous centuries. Essentially, China views itself as the most powerful state in Asia and it demands that smaller neighbouring countries acknowledge this in some form; this thinking continues to serve as the basis for the classification of China as a regional power. Generally, it is useful to distinguish between four kinds of hierarchical structures in international relations: spheres of influence, protectorates, informal empires and formal empires.[13] China has always regarded Northeast Asia as its sphere of influence. It had established protectorates in certain regions of Central Asia in the past. The tributary system might be regarded as some sort of informal empire. The most interesting point is whether China has the intention to establish a formal empire in the long run as this could represent one way for states to achieve comprehensive security. If that is the aim, then China will have to challenge the US presence in Asia more directly.

Another feature of the Sino-centric world order is the notion of moral superiority, which is supported by the fact that China is a civilisation going back over some 4,000 years. There is a connotation that the Chinese ruler had duties toward his counterparts in the periphery, who were regarded as his inferiors.[14] The surrounding states were regarded as equal to each other; the Chinese rulers did not discriminate against them but they were all deemed to be beneath the Son of Heaven, the Chinese emperor.[15] To a certain extent, this stands in sharp contrast to the European states system that emerged following the Treaty of Westphalia in 1648, where each nation-state was regarded as equal in sovereignty and mutually independent. In certain areas of Chinese foreign policy, one can still detect a moral tone whereby insistence on principles reflects a political culture that long prized ethics over law; moral consensus over the judicial process and benevolent government over checks and balances. For example, China had helped socialist regimes in Africa in economic development in the 1960s and it continues to give aid to other smaller developing nations today. Another case in point would be the 1997–1998 Asian currency crisis. Deeply shaken by the suddenness and scope of the crisis, China argued that it acted responsibly by not devaluing its currency, and by offering aid packages and low-interest loans to several Southeast Asian states. These actions were not only appreciated in Asia in general but also stood in stark contrast to the dictatorial posture taken by the International Monetary Fund (IMF) and international creditors in response to the crisis. To a certain extent, China's stance modified the prevailing image of itself in the region as a hegemon and portended the notion of China as a responsible power. The key question is how much this Chinese policy was driven by morality rather than strategic interests in relation to Southeast Asia.

In general, China achieved comprehensive security under the Sino-centric world order until this world order collapsed under the challenge of the Western powers and Japan. Subsequently, it took China about a century – roughly from the 1840s to the 1940s – before it could reassert itself in the international system. During the Cold War, China's rise as a communist giant even led to rivalry with the Soviet Union from the 1960s onwards. Although significantly weaker than either of the two superpowers, China was adept at playing its role in the great power triangle and even managed to extend its influence considerably in global affairs during the Cold War era. This fact unmistakably points towards China's global power ambitions and the implication is that those ambitions must be fulfilled today. In short, China aims to achieve truly global power status in the twenty-first century and this also represents a way to achieve comprehensive security. In this sense, strategic competition with the US, the lone superpower, will occur although the intensity of this competition is more debatable.

Drawing on its long civilisation, Chinese strategic thought can at times be linked to the Confucian emphasis on peace as the best option (*yihe weigui*) and taking the middle path to avoid extremes (*zhongyong zidao*). At times, this implies that China has no desire to challenge another great power or another power bloc. In reality, one might argue that China still lacks the actual military muscle to challenge the global status quo. In regional terms, a good neighbourliness policy (*mulin*) seems to be the best option in the short term. China currently calls for peaceful development, with the aim of using economic growth to achieve parity with the Western industrialised nations, including the US. This in many ways vindicates the salience of economics in China's security policy formulation today.

At the same time, China has called for a new security concept, which has the key characteristics of "comprehensiveness, equality, mutual trust, mutual benefit and co-ordination"; the first indication of it being applied, according to the Chinese, is the major security agreement signed with Russia and other Central Asian states in 1997 and the announcement of a unilateral disarmament in the same year whereby China would further cut its border troops.[16] According to Beijing, the core purpose of the new security concept is "to conduct dialogue, consultation, and negotiation on an equal footing", which then helps "solve disputes and safeguard peace". It is argued that "only by developing a new security concept and establishing a fair and reasonable new international order can world peace and security be fundamentally guaranteed."[17] It is evident that any new international order would involve the US, China's strategic competitor.

In reality, it must be pointed out that China's new security concept is not really innovative. It is, in essence, a repackaged version of the Five Principles of Peaceful Coexistence that were first enunciated by then premier Zhou Enlai at the Afro-Asian People's Solidarity Conference in Bandung, Indonesia, in 1955. Those Five Principles are: mutual respect for territorial integrity and sovereignty, non-aggression, non-interference in each other's internal affairs, equality and mutual benefit, and peaceful coexistence. One can discern that today, given the salience of economics, Chinese foreign policy thinking has gradually shifted from peaceful co-existence (*heping gongchu*) to peaceful development (*heping fazhen*).[18] Peaceful co-existence was advocated during certain periods in the Cold War era because China was relatively weak regarding the US-led capitalist bloc. On the whole, China did not wish to instigate a direct military confrontation with the West. It calculated that a period of peace would be useful as a breathing space to catch up with the world's most industrialised nations; the idea was to wait for the forces of socialism to become stronger so that China could then defeat and replace capitalism. Obviously, the blurring of capitalism and socialism since the introduction of market reforms in 1978 has modified much of this Chinese strategic thinking.

At a wider level, one can detect a slight shift away from a strictly zero-sum approach to international relations, which was apparent during the Cold War, to a more co-operative one today. This is certainly the case of China as a great power. It is important to realise that great powers can play constructive roles in a regional system. Generally, great powers are powers recognised by others as well as conceived by their own leaders and citizens to have special rights and duties in the international system.[19] These powers "assert the right, and are accorded the right, to play a part in determining issues that affect the peace and security of the international system as a whole"; they do so "by managing their affairs relations with one another, and by exploiting their preponderance in such as a way as to impart a degree of central direction to the affairs of international society as a whole."[20] Implicit here is the international society approach. In an international society,

> a group of states ... not merely form a system, in the sense that the behaviour of each is a necessary factor in the calculations of the others, but also have established by dialogue and consent common rules and institutions for the conduct of their relations, and recognise their common interests in maintaining these arrangements.[21]

In a society of states, the consensus among great powers such as China and the US on certain issues often serves as a kind of norm, upon which international behaviour will be judged. This could then place certain constraints on the foreign behaviour of all states involved in a particular security issue such as the North Korean nuclear issue.

Unfortunately, such an international society has not yet existed in China's backyard of Northeast Asia due to reasons such as the lack of a long history of Westphalian-style international relations, the paucity of democratic states and the existence of territorial disputes there.[22] If such an international society does not exist or count much in Northeast Asia, then it is even more important for the great powers such as China and the US to set some norms and then maintain them. At the initial stage, those norms could come from shared interests such as maintaining the status quo, preventing nuclear proliferation and enhancing trade. Here the emphasis is on China matching its interests with the US's, although the aspirations of other great powers such as Russia and Japan should not be totally ignored either.

Structure of this book

We can now turn to the structure of this book: Chapter 1 focuses on how China perceives and deals with US global supremacy, Chapter 2 explores how China counters the US export of liberal democracy and human rights, Chapter 3 deals with how China competes with the US in the international economic system. Chapter 4 examines Taiwan as a case of strategic competition between China and the US. Chapter 5 analyses how China views and counters the US–Japanese alliance, which is the lynchpin of American strategy in East Asia. Chapter 6 explores the interaction of Chinese and US security interests in relation to North Korea. Chapter 7 evaluates China's policies towards South Korea, a US ally in East Asia. Chapter 8 looks at Sino-US strategic competition in Central Asia. The final chapter restates the main arguments stemming from the various chapters. It is hoped that this book will encourage further research and debate on the evolution of China's relations with the US, which will undoubtedly have a major impact on international politics in the twenty-first century.

1 The US's global supremacy

In this chapter, the aim is to examine how China perceives and copes with US preponderance in the post-Cold War international system. Basically, the disappearance of a direct strategic competitor since the Soviet collapse has led to a certain degree of US leadership in international politics. In addition, the emergence of transnational terrorism as a challenge to American national security has inadvertently provided the US with the rationale to pursue a war against terrorists. This ongoing war to eliminate terrorism – an international security threat – has in turn given Washington an opportunity to exercise its military and political leadership in the global arena to a large degree. The important thing to note is that these recent developments reinforce the traditional Chinese fear of unbridled US unilateralism.

In terms of structure, this chapter first considers the implications of unipolarity for China. It then considers the notion of US hegemony and how this is perceived by China. In addition, US military prowess is eliciting concerns for Chinese defence planners and this will be analysed. Finally, the case for Sino-US co-operation in world affairs, which is centred on the shared aim to maintain international stability, is assessed. We begin by examining China's concerns over unipolarity.

Unipolarity

First and foremost, a unipolar world where American leadership in the international system is inadequately challenged has implications for China's national interests. In International Relations, polarity refers to the distribution of power in the international system at a given period of time. In a unipolar system, there is a dominant state and this state can often shape the global order to its advantage. This means that under such circumstances, China's national interests could be threatened as America seeks to redefine a new world order following the end of bipolarity in 1991. Given the conflictual nature of Sino-US relations, it is expected that China has consistently advocated a multipolar world structure where America should ideally be just one of several poles of powers.

In fact, China's preference for multipolarity can be traced further back to its experiences since joining the international system, after the collapse of the

Sino-centric world order. In the age of imperialism, China often manoeuvred between various Western imperial powers by playing one aggressor off against another with some degree of success, in order to maintain its territorial integrity and sovereignty.[1] At the same time, this was a strategy of the weak as it was premised on the basis that the Western powers would not collude on their encroachments into Chinese territories. From China's perspective, the task of keeping Western imperial powers at bay was highly challenging in the age of European expansionism. Nonetheless, in such a multipolar system, China had more strategic choices in maintaining its national security interests; it could shift from one European power to another, depending on the international power structure at a given point in time.

In the era of bipolarity from 1945 to 1991, China had less strategic choices as the number of poles in the international system was narrowed down to two – the Soviet Union and the US. After the Second World War, China viewed the US in the context of an international system that was largely defined by a bipolar world of East–West conflict, with Beijing's military and political security considerably entwined with this structure. From an ideological perspective, Communist China naturally leaned towards the Soviet Union in the 1950s in order to counter the US offensive against the Communist bloc. At the same time, it is important to note that national survival was arguably the main reason for the conclusion of the Sino-Soviet military alliance in 1950 as a young People's Republic of China (PRC) sought to ensure its very own survival in an anarchic international system. However, the Sino-Soviet split in the 1960s led to China regarding the Soviet Union as a "social imperialist". At this point in time, China had to face two hostile superpowers on its own simultaneously. Accordingly, the solution for China was to count on the moral and ideological support of Third World countries, especially Marxist ones, to counter the threat posed by both the Soviet Union and the US. Again, this was a challenging task as the two superpowers carve out their spheres of influence on a global scale and this was a limitation to China's strategy.

Gradually, during the 1970s, China's attitudes towards the US changed and parallel concerns about Soviet global power became more pertinent. The result was China tilting to the US to counter the Soviet threat, which was regarded as more menacing at that time. In fact, China fought a border war against the Soviet Union on the Ussuri River in 1969. From about 1979 onwards, China essentially manoeuvred between the US and the Soviet Union. Within the strategic triangle, Beijing oscillated from one superpower to another, depending on which one was regarded as the more dangerous threat to its national security at a given point in time. At the time, some analysts have contemplated a notion of tripolarity in the international system as China was becoming a more powerful country by the 1980s. However, it must be pointed out that if one argues that the international system was indeed tripolar, then China was clearly a distant third behind the two superpowers. In short, a stronger argument is that the Cold War system was essentially bipolar and China had to work within such a structure, like any other major country such as France or Britain.

From the above historical analysis, the important point is that in a non-unipolar world, Beijing has more room to manoeuvre. From China's perspective, multipolarity is the best because it allows for the most number of strategic options in seeking alliances, for example. Historically, the next best option is bipolarity, where the options for forming alliances – formal or informal – are reduced to two. Clearly, the worst-case scenario is one where there are no options but to balance against the hegemon.[2] In short, a key Chinese concern today is that the US no longer faces a direct strategic competitor following the collapse of the Soviet Union in 1991. As such, China has to face the US very much on its own with little realistic option of balancing against the US together with another great power. The point is that currently, Russian influence in international politics is not at the level of the Soviet era and hence there is no adequate balance to American power. As for the notion of a united European bloc, the national interests of the key countries there have yet to diverge too radically from those of the US, attesting to the enduring nature of the Atlantic Alliance.[3] In the absence of a direct strategic competitor, it appears that the US is free to pursue its national interests and shape the international system to a large extent, which will have implications for China.

From China's perspective, the US grand strategy is to completely replace the East–West bipolar system with an American-led unipolar structure in the twenty-first century. Accordingly, a key problem is how to stop the single superpower from aligning closely with the advanced industrialised democratic states in western Europe and regional rival Japan. Although the US is far ahead of other states in terms of national power, it still needs the support of key allies to maintain the international order. The key issue here is the sustainability of a US-led world order. In the long run, one may argue that US unilateralism is difficult to sustain for two reasons. First, non-traditional security factors such as terrorism, energy shortages, financial crises and global diseases require multilateral solutions. Second, and perhaps more importantly, US unilateralism has been rebuffed to some extent by some of its European allies. In particular, during the Bush administration, the adoption of a strong unilateralist posture has led to disharmony with European allies such as Germany and France.[4] From China's perspective, the possibility of certain European states and Russia offering a higher degree of counterbalance to US preponderance in the international system in the forthcoming decades is a good sign. In general, the various scenarios of the US's relations with its European allies and Russia have implications for China's national security strategies in the twenty-first century.

In the meantime, from China's perspective, one common tactic is to exploit the differences between the US and its closest allies. For instance, the US continues to pressurise its western European allies to maintain the arms embargo that was imposed on China after the 1989 Tiananmen event, even warning that lifting the embargo could have a negative impact on bilateral defence cooperation. From the US perspective, the embargo should be maintained for three reasons: serious human rights abuses persist in China (see Chapter 2), ending the embargo would have a negative impact on cross-Taiwan Strait and Asian stability (see Chapter 5), and no mechanisms are currently in place to prevent China from transferring technology and lethal weaponry to other, less stable regions of the world or to use it for internal repression. Compared to its European allies, the US is definitely more forceful in demanding that China improve its human rights record. Hence, it is in China's interests to highlight the importance of bilateral ties, especially economic ones, with European states in the hope of winning more diplomatic support there. At the same time, this task has become more pressing given that the US can affect China's military security, albeit marginally, by insisting that its European allies do not sell China specific types of weapons.

In general, one of China's fundamental goals in the current era is to replace unipolarity with, ideally, multipolarity. The classic Structuralist argument in international relations is that states can do relatively little to affect the international system; in other words, the onus is on states to devise appropriate national security strategies largely in reaction to systemic forces. At the same time, this does not necessarily imply a passive acceptance of the existing status quo; rather, it entails states employing resources effectively in order to facilitate a certain degree of favourable change in the international structure. For China, this basically means working towards eroding the US's status as the lone superpower in the world and pre-empting the possible negative American impacts or pressures on itself. In the medium to long term, the US is likely to maintain its position as the lone superpower in the international system. For a considerable period of time, America will continue to be a major influencing factor in international relations and also China's relations with other great powers such as Russia. In this sense, China's room for manoeuvre is somewhat limited and, accordingly, it needs to address the relationship with the US strategically, in the hope that multipolarity would soon ensue.

At the same time, it must be stressed that China's active promotion of multipolarity does not equal an anti-American position, although the actual effect will weaken the position of the US as the lone superpower. Interestingly, a common conclusion today is that China will emerge as the most likely direct strategic competitor to the US in the foreseeable future. The other potential strategic competitors to the US include a resurgent Russia or a more united Europe, as noted earlier. Although China has the potential to challenge the US in the long run, it must be stressed that, at the moment, a considerable power gap still exists between itself and the US. Hence, the biggest challenge for China is closing this gap in the shortest possible time span by building a strong economic base to enhance comprehensive national strength.

Currently, China cannot afford to oppose the US openly on every international security issue because of the current capability gap between the US and itself as well as between the US and other great powers. Moreover, open opposition to the US risks alienating potential supporters such as France and many developing countries; for China, a better option is to invest more resources in winning recognition and support from countries that share some concerns over unipolarity. The general Chinese argument is that multipolarity is a natural and inevitable requirement of a globalised world where countries are increasingly interdependent one another; such an argument is in line with the themes of globalisation as well as with the domestic emphasis on rapid modernisation. At the same time, it must be noted that Chinese analysts still largely adhere to a Realist approach to international relations whereby great power competition is deemed as central and inevitable; to a large extent, they see the US now taking steps to prevent another powerful foe, like the Soviet Union had once been, from challenging American hegemony.[5] In this sense, China is right that the US will use all its resources to maintain its hegemony in the international system.

US hegemony

In this section, we move from the international structure to focus specifically on the implications of US hegemony for China. As a key concept in international relations, hegemony refers to the dominance of one great power over other states in the international system through military, political, economic or other means. Given that the concept of hegemony encompasses various aspects of international relations, it is worth noting that Realist and Marxist strands in Chinese strategic thought have accordingly converged in the interpretation of this concept. Chinese realists worry about a hegemon's ability to impose its political will on others while Chinese Marxists interpret American efforts to expand the community of market democracies as a new form of hegemony. Both the realist and Marxist perspectives give grounds for concerns that the US will use its power to seek hegemony with possible negative consequences for China. Hence, opposing any form of US hegemony in the current era is regarded as an important principle and vital to China's national security.

Importantly, China has its own usage of the hegemony concept and this is in many ways linked to its modern history in general and experience of Western imperialism in particular. As noted in the Introduction, before the arrival of the Western powers, China was the regional hegemon and it could impose its will on smaller neighbouring Asian states via the tributary system. Tracing the roots of the Chinese concept of hegemony further reveals that this concept actually dates back to ancient times. The character *ba*, the term from which *baquan zhuyi* (hegemony) is derived, can be found in Chinese political thought and has appeared in a variety of records beginning from the Warring States period.[6] In short, the concept of hegemony is not alien to China's rulers because they have actually pursued it and imposed it upon neighbouring states when they had the chance to do so. It was the arrival of the Western powers in the nineteenth century that led to China losing its hegemonic role in Asia. To be more specific, China's own security was directly threatened by those powers and neighbouring Japan.

To a certain extent, the loss of its traditional hegemonic role in Asia has led to China emphasising the hegemonic tendencies of other great powers, be it the US or the Soviet Union in the era of superpower rivalry. In other words, given that China could not become the dominant power in Asia during the Cold War, it adopted the stance of denouncing the hegemonic ambitions of the US, as well as the Soviet Union. In the post-Cold War era, China's task has become more specific as US hegemony is now the sole target of criticism. Specifically, undermining US hegemony in the international system today can only strengthen China's own position regarding America. From China's perspective, the worrying thing is that the events of September 11, 2001 have provided the rationale for the US to sustain its hegemony since the Soviet collapse. In other words, the war to eliminate terrorism has provided the US with further impetus to reinforce the notion of a new world order, whereby American military strength will preserve international security through, among other things, defeating terrorists.

In particular, the US mission to defeat rogue states, which often provide military, financial and moral support for transnational terrorist networks, has implications for China. The definition of a rogue state varies but is generally understood to mean states that develop weapons of mass destruction (WMD), defy international norms and support terrorism.[7] Inevitably, these states have become more obvious military targets for the US after the events of September 11, 2001. Specifically, the US's plans for drastic action against the "axis of evil" – North Korea, Iraq and Iran – have implications for China.[8] To date, the US has eliminated the Saddam Hussein regime in Iraq and American efforts have been focused on dealing with the remaining two states. Specifically, it must be emphasised that the Bush doctrine has left its mark on how China perceives the US.[9] The previous US administration's attempt to draw a dividing line has forced China to make a strategic choice, whether to join or oppose US efforts in the war against terrorists. The point is that China accepts the need to eliminate terrorism, but a specific concern is that the US might violate the sovereignty of other states and intervene in their domestic affairs under the pretext of eradicating transnational terrorism. Through operations against terrorists, the US has in effect intervened in the affairs of some sovereign states. Such behaviour is typical from a hegemon and in fact, China had itself intervened in the affairs of other states when it was at the top of the Asian hierarchy. Intervention in the domestic affairs of the vassal state of Korea in an earlier age is a case in point. However, today, as an ardent advocate of the Westphalian concepts of sovereignty and non-intervention, China sees waging the war on terrorism as smokescreen for pursuing US hegemony.

Moreover, there is a general Chinese perception that the US leads military actions in the name of humanitarian intervention and peacekeeping in order to create an international order under its control today. To Beijing, this is a pursuit of hegemony that needs to be opposed. For instance, whereas the US saw humanitarian motivations for organising a North Atlantic Treaty Organisation (NATO)-led coalition force to intervene in Kosovo, China discerned a dangerous precedent that could later be used to oppose Beijing's designs on Taiwan and control of dissident ethnic areas such as Tibet. Knowing that, as permanent members of the UN Security Council, both Russia and China could, and probably would veto military interventions in Kosovo, it must be pointed out that the Clinton administration was shrewd in working through NATO in 1999.

At the same time, this gave the Beijing leadership yet another grievance: the other members of NATO had conspired with the US to ensure the Atlantic Alliance's dominance in Europe in general and the Balkans in particular. Basically, China does not view US military preponderance as the only the condition for preserving international security and has in fact called for the abrogation of alliances such as NATO, arguing that they are often not the best means for maintaining peace.[10] With the overall concern over US assertiveness, it is clear that China is unwilling to give unqualified endorsement to American-led military interventions in any parts of the world as these actions generally have the result of reinforcing US hegemony.

Overall, the war on terrorism has provided the US with the chance assert its preponderance in Asia as well as in the international system. For instance, the ongoing hunt for terrorists has enabled the US to establish its presence in Central Asia, a key geopolitical region that was once part of the Soviet empire (see Chapter 8). Specifically, the US was able to set up military bases in the region with vast energy resource potential. In other parts of Asia, the war against terrorism has provided the US with the rationale to regain its military presence; for instance, in the Philippines America regained its bases that abandoned in the early 1990s. At a regional level, China is clearly concerned about US hegemony in its sphere. Furthermore, to a certain extent, the US's alliances in the Asia-Pacific region are still viewed as a way to contain China. This is certainly true of Beijing's perceptions of the US–Japan alliance and the extension of North Atlantic Treaty Organisation's (NATO) Partnership for Peace (PfP) proposal for Central Asia. In addition, the US has security ties with South Korea, Australia, Thailand, the Philippines and Singapore. In other words, America definitely has potential instruments at its disposal to adopt a strategy of containing and encircling China. To a certain extent, the deployment of American forces in Central Asia and East Asia is perceived by China as the first stage of an encirclement process directed at itself.[11] In fact, such concerns of US encirclement are not entirely new: China had seen the US deploy this strategy with a string of alliances in Northeast Asia, Southeast Asia and South Asia during the Cold War against primarily against the Soviet Union but also at itself. From the Chinese perspective, the concern is that US hegemony in these regions will become harder to erode the longer the war on terrorism continues.

From China's perspective, its short-term strategy is to avoid challenging US hegemony directly due to the huge capability gap between the two states. One can also argue that doing so will not match China's growing international status and its international responsibilities. In the long run, when the capability gap between China and the US has been narrowed, confronting the US directly would become a more realistic option. In this sense, such a stance reflects the essence of the idiom *taoguang yanghui*.[12] This idiom dates back almost 3,000 years and has been drawn upon by Chinese leaders such as the late Deng Xiaoping. Translated into English, it literally means "to put one's brightness in the quiver behind one's back and to nourish one's capabilities secretly". Put into practice, this strategy entails biding one's time and building up one's capabilities discreetly; the key point is that a rising power must not show its true capabilities too readily on the international stage.

Hence, unlike the US display of military might in Iraq and Afghanistan, China prefers to keep a low profile as it modernises its military. The key point of the *taoguang yanghui* strategy is that a country should only display its comprehensive national strength when the time is ripe. In other words, it is a strategy emphasising a patient and cautious build-up of comprehensive national strength. At the same time, it is a strategy of a weaker player in the international system as it can ill afford to confront the stronger powers directly in the short term. Above all, the *taoguang yanghui* strategy is one of survival, tailor-made for an anarchic international system: a rising power employing this strategy is less likely to elicit opposing balancing coalitions and hence ensure the continuous accumulation of its comprehensive national strength. This resonates with theoretical arguments on the provocations of balancing coalitions if a country builds itself up rapidly and then displays its increased national power, especially military prowess, too explicitly.[13]

US military strength

To a large extent, it is clear that the US's dominant position in international politics is backed by its military strength. The central tenet of realist international relations theories is that military strength holds the key to national power. In military terms, one of China's concerns is the US's unassailable gap over other great powers in the international system. This concern was already evident in the early 1990s when America scored an easy victory over Iraq in the 1990–1991 Gulf War. Moreover, Washington's success in mobilising a broad international coalition during the war suggested that Beijing simply could not afford to oppose the US – at least not directly – in the global arena, without risking international isolation or marginalisation. It must be noted that on that occasion, international pressure was largely the key to China's public pledge to cease arms transfers to Iraq and China's positive vote on the first United Nations (UN) Security Council resolution calling for Iraq's withdrawal from Kuwait.

Subsequently, in the 1999 Kosovo war, Chinese anxieties over US military prowess were further fuelled when America and its allies in the NATO coalition defeated Serbia; the point is that the degree of Western military sophistication on display went beyond that evinced during the 1990–1991 Gulf War.[14] More recently, the US's wars against terrorists and rogue states have been successful – at least in the military sphere; the US won two battles – in Afghanistan and Iraq.[15] At the same time, it must be noted that the two wars that the US had been involved in did not result in total victory; in this sense, achieving military operational victory is more correctly seen as the first step towards achieving US strategic objectives.[16] The implication for China is that these US activities, including the ongoing hunt for Al-Qaeda in Central Asia and indeed worldwide, further validate the sheer might of the American military machine, albeit against lesser adversaries. The prowess of the US military machine, as demonstrated through those missions described earlier, elicits concerns for China's defence planners. Linked with the lone superpower's unilateralist tendencies, this portends unstoppable US dominance in the international system that China will find difficult to cope with for the foreseeable future.

Furthermore, the use of force by the US in the post-Cold War era raises critical issues for China. In particular, China views the US strategy of pre-emption (*xianfa zhiren*), which entails using force to respond to an imminent threat, with grave concern.[17] This concept of pre-emption is perhaps the most controversial of all US military doctrines, simply because its entails encroaching on the sovereignty of other states in the international system in the name of self-defence. The US argues that the existing legal right of pre-emption rests on the existence of such a threat – "most often a visible mobilisation of armies, navies and air forces preparing to attack" – but it also advocates broadening the concept of imminent threat to better reflect the capabilities and objectives of today's adversaries because, quite simply, rogue states and terrorists do not seek to attack the US with conventional means.[18] Hence, the US argues that it needs to adapt its military strategies to fight these new adversaries. Washington's argument is that terrorists groups like Al Qaeda are "irregular" threats because they employ "unconventional" methods to counter the "traditional" advantages of stronger opponents; these groups also pose "catastrophic" challenges because they seek to acquire and use weapons of mass destruction.[19]

Hence, the US aims to forestall or prevent hostile acts by rogue states, terrorists-linked states and terrorists groups by, amongst other means, attacking them first before they have the chance to strike or use their weapons of mass destruction. To this effect, China watched the US succeed in forestalling the threat posed by Saddam Hussein but more notably, it criticised Washington's occupation of Iraq, notwithstanding a joint undertaking to denounce terrorism and terrorist-linked states. Currently, nuclear aspirants Iran and North Korea are the possible next targets for the US strategy of pre-emption. The point is that China has a basic concern about the US using overwhelming military might to strike at other sovereign states before being attacked. To some degree, one might argue that the US stretched the concept of pre-emption well beyond its normal usage and actually declared a policy of preventive war.[20] Certainly, Washington recognises that

> under the most dangerous or compelling circumstances, prevention might require the use of force to disable or destroy weapons of mass destruction in the possession of terrorists or others or to strike targets (e.g. terrorists) that directly threaten the US or US friends or other interests.[21]

At a wider level, the US concept of pre-emption calls into question the basis for a just war and how a war should be fought in the current international system.[22] This is relevant to China as it raises the question of US military intervention in the international arena with or without formal authorisation by international organisations such as the United Nations. In other words, the use of force in international relations is intricately linked to the issue of intervention in other sovereign states. The US's posture on both these two issues has elicited concerns for China at the strategic as well as the operational levels.

In addition to how the US actually employs military force in the international system, China is well aware it lags behind the US in terms of conventional military power. This explains why China is spending heavily in defence to close this gap, in addition to the fact that it has to defend itself and ensure national survival in an anarchic international system. In this regard, China has stated that it plans to increase its national defence spending by 7.5 per cent to about US$76.3 billion in 2010.[23] Despite these indications, Beijing explicitly rejects suggestions that it will enter into an arms race with the US. In this vein, the Chinese People's Liberation Army (PLA) has focused on deterring or preventing w   the basic tenet is that "strategic deterrence is a major means for attaining the objective of military strategy as well as political objectives and [that] its risks and costs are less than strategic operations."[24] From the perspective of China's defence planners, the corollary is that "war-fighting is generally used only when deterrence fails and there is no alternative" and, more importantly, the crux of the matter is that "the more powerful the war-fighting capability, the more effective the deterrence."[25] In essence, this is a defensive strategy as China knows that it cannot match the US in military modernisation.

Moving from conventional capabilities to the nuclear realm, China also has clear concerns about US superiority in an age where the number of nuclear warheads worldwide has actually decreased. During the Cold War, China lagged behind the two superpowers and this is still the case today; compared to the US and Russia, China's nuclear arsenal remains much smaller. Hence, it is inevitable that China has consistently called on all nuclear-weapon states to reduce the role of nuclear weapons in their national security policies, to honour their commitment not to target its nuclear weapons against other states and not to develop easy-to-use low-yield nuclear weapons.[26] In particular, China urges countries with the biggest nuclear arsenals such as the US to bear special responsibility for nuclear disarmament and to take the lead in drastically reducing their arsenals. Such a posture indicates China's inability to match the US in the nuclear realm and therefore a more realistic option is to put pressure on the lone superpower to reduce its nuclear forces, possibly by mobilising world public opinion on this issue.

Currently, one specific Chinese concern is the US development of a theatre missile defence (TMD) system in East Asia. The conventional Chinese argument is that such TMD systems undermine strategic stability and therefore should not be developed. Again, the truth is that China lags far behind the US in terms of nuclear ability, hence it is calling for a reduction in the role of nuclear weapons in its backyard of Northeast Asia. It is important to note that the US has to offer extended deterrence to its allies Japan and South Korea in East Asia, given the threats by emerging nuclear-armed states such as North Korea. From then US perspective, it must protect its allies against nuclear threats or intimidation; continuing to do so will also reduce any incentives these allies might have to seek their own nuclear deterrents.

Essentially, China today maintains a policy of retaining a limited nuclear force and no-first-use (NFU) policy, which can be described as case of "minimum deterrence".[27] In general, states with this kind of nuclear strategy maintain only second-strike (nuclear retaliation) capabilities and do not pursue war-fighting capabilities. Accordingly, throughout the development of China's nuclear forces since the 1960s, great emphasis has been placed on survivability and reliability. The Chinese aim is to ensure deterrence remains effective in different circumstances and survival after an enemy's first strike by maintaining a basic retaliatory capability. Since the 1970s and 1980s, other countries have rapidly improved their precision strike capabilities and have made great progress with their missile defence systems. Correspondingly, China's nuclear force has also gradually modernised from the first generation using liquid fuel and fixed silos to the second generation using solid fuel and mobile launching pads with better penetrability. Nevertheless, China's nuclear strategy remains a defensive one with the aim of maintaining an effective deterrence in the new strategic environment.[28] Such a strategy remains a realistic one as long as the huge capability gap with the US remains.

Currently, China is undertaking long-term modernisation and expansion of its strategic nuclear forces, which some US strategic analysts perceive as a latent threat. At the same time, these forces will remain relatively small, and the US will retain a massive retaliation deterrent. Hence, even in the event of direct US–China military conflict, the prospects of China launching nuclear missiles against the US will remain slim. Nevertheless, China's nuclear capabilities are a meaningful coercive instrument politically – however remote the prospect. From this perspective, defence planners in the US are right in taking into account China's possible use of nuclear weapons directly against the US National Missile Defense (NMD) deployment and in devising strategies to mitigate the political utility of this threat. In general, the lack of transparency surrounding China's nuclear programmes – their pace and scope as well as the strategies and doctrines that guide them – raises questions about Beijing's future strategic intentions. For example, China's test of an anti-satellite weapon against a defunct weather satellite in January 2007 drew formal protests from the US as well as Australia, Canada, Japan and South Korea; the main issue, from the perspective of the international community, is whether the development of such an offensive weapon is incompatible with the China's declared principles of peaceful development. In addition, the 2007 incident raises questions about civilian control over the Chinese military, co-ordination in the Chinese bureaucracy and China's crisis management capability. It is clear that, at a wider level, the US and China's Asian neighbours remain concerned about Beijing's current military modernisation efforts, including the qualitative and quantitative modernisation of its nuclear arsenal.

At the same time, it is important to note that China had only destroyed its own satellite in 2007 and that the two superpowers had already conducted such tests about two decades earlier. From China's perspective, it has consistently voiced opposition to the weaponisation of space and an arms race in space. An important point is that, having witnessed the demise of the Soviet Union, Chinese leaders do not want to sacrifice the country's economic modernisation in a costly arms race with the US. Matching the lone superpower missile for missile or developing a Chinese national missile system (NMD) system would require diverting huge resources and many of China's technical personnel away from the task of economic modernisation. This re-allocation of resources will only delay China's emergence as a truly global power and ultimately hinder China's overall military modernisation. Hence, a key challenge facing the current generation of Chinese leaders today is how to allocate resources between military modernisation and economic infrastructure enhancement in an optimal manner.

From the US's perspective, it is important to maintain a dialogue on strategic stability with China as this provides a venue and mechanism for each side to communicate its views about the other's strategies, policies, and programmes on nuclear weapons and other strategic capabilities.[29] Such a dialogue will enhance confidence, improve transparency and reduce mistrust. As stated in the US's 2010 Ballistic Missile Defense Review Report, "maintaining strategic stability in the US–China relationship is as important ... as maintaining strategic stability with other major powers." In other words, the US aims to facilitate a more stable strategic relationship with major states such as China and with a view to achieving a greater restraint on their nuclear programmes and postures simultaneously. The reasoning is that, in the longer term, such a stance will also have a reassuring and stabilising effect in China's as well as Russia's spheres of influence. From the US's perspective, it wants to facilitate trilateral co-operation with China and Russia in order to counter nuclear proliferation and nuclear terrorism: hence, America repeatedly stresses that the missile defence systems under development are designed to thwart limited attacks by rogue states or terrorists, not to defeat a large conventional threat posed by established nuclear states such as China and Russia.

Co-operation with the US

The above analysis does not suggest that strategic competition between China and the US cannot be paralleled by some form of co-operation between these great powers in the current international system. A case in point is the US war against terrorism and on this particular issue, it is important to note that that China is basically on the American side. Notwithstanding the general negative perceptions of the US use of force, as discussed earlier, China was actually given a chance to highlight its role as a responsible great power through a common undertaking to denounce and combat terrorism, at least in the short term.[30] Immediately after the events in New York and Washington in September 2001, China was aware of strident global opinion against terrorism and shrewdly distanced itself from the Taliban regime.[31] In general, China supports the US in the war against terrorism to show the international community that it can shoulder the responsibilities that comes with being a great power. Inadvertently, this leads to some notion of great power convergence on a critical international security issue although one might argue that the Bush doctrine actually forced China to make a clear-cut decision to support or oppose the war against terrorists. From the US's perspective, the main question in the aftermath of September 2001 was how China would fit into the framework of the war on terrorism; China could emerge as a key ally in this war or it could scupper the US's efforts. For China, a key decision was whether total support should be offered to the US on international security issues in general and in the fight against terrorists in particular.

The important issue for great power co-operation, at least on a tactical level, relates to the fact that China did not actively seek to oppose US-led efforts on the initial war on the Taliban regime.[32] At a wider level, Beijing knows that this tacit backing will serve useful as a bargaining chip in encounters with Washington over a host of important issues such as Taiwan, human rights and trade concessions. By not vetoing a proposed anti-terrorism action in the United Nations (UN), China hoped to see reduced US arm sales to Taiwan; basically, it earned some goodwill by backing the UN Resolution 1373 endorsing the use of force by an 18-nation International Security Assistance Force (ISAF) against the Taliban regime. However, this does not mask the fact that China was worried about growing US unilateralist tendencies, hence Beijing consistently stressed the need to fight the terrorists through a proper international framework.

At a wider level, more active participation in global anti-terrorism efforts would steer China towards the path of multilateral engagement in international security issues, contrasting with the US's unilateral ethos. Traditionally, China has never been keen on multilateral security dialogues, preferring to resolve specific problems on a bilateral basis instead. However, waging a successful war on transnational terrorism today requires a degree of co-operation among the major powers; this gives China a chance to move cautiously towards some form of security arrangements with other countries in order to defeat transnational terrorism. Apart from boosting the confidence of China in its role as a leading global actor, enhanced co-operation with other states also serves as a means to prevent any multilateral security regimes from exclusively targeting China in future. Moreover, joining regional efforts in the war on terror gives China a chance to assuage the concerns of smaller states in Asia as well as the international community about its growing military strength. In other words, China does accrue some benefits from co-operating with the US on the war against terrorism.

Hence, it is in China's interest to further anti-terrorist co-operation with other states in the international system as well because this serves to demonstrate one of the positive aspects of Beijing's increasing clout in international relations. In the formulation of military security, China has already stressed that a country's military forces should have a wider role, including cracking down on terrorism. Like the US, China realises that terrorism poses a serious threat to international security and also to its northwestern flank in Central Asia (see Chapter 8). To a certain degree, the war on terrorism has played right into the hands of China because, through combating terrorism, China can demonstrate its role as a responsible great power to the international community. Working more closely with other states to eliminate terrorism also serves to assure the world of its cooperative credentials and by extension, peaceful rise.[33] On its part, the US recognises the value of having a strategic dialogue with China, which was first driven by the war against terrorism in 2001 and reinforced recently by the need to maintain global financial stability (see Chapter 3). Viewed from this perspective, it can be argued that China accommodated to the US taking the lead in eliminating the threat of transnational terrorism because it did not obstruct the US explicitly. The real challenge is how far China and US national interests can converge once the major bases of transnational terrorism have been destroyed.

Quest for international stability

Moving beyond the task of eliminating global terrorism, a more enduring common interest that China shares with the US is the desire for a stable international environment. Such an environment fosters quick modernisation for China and facilitates the continued accumulation of national power. Hence, largely out of self-interest, China has inadvertently come to share with the US the need to maintain international security. Today, there are suggestions of a Group of Two (G2), that is, some form of great power management between the US and China on international issues, although the concept has not been accepted by China. In general, China prefers to deal with most security issues on a case-by-case basis rather than take on a bigger role in the international arena, as noted earlier.

Currently, China holds a permanent seat in the United Nations (UN) Security Council and has indicated its willingness to play a constructive role in international affairs, on issues such as the Middle East peace process and the nuclear impasse in Iran.[34] Today, China is gradually moving towards multilateralism but it must be stressed that this is a slow process rather than a quick one. Essentially, China's contribution to regional and international security will arise from its great power management – with the US for example – rather than through international institutions. The historic case of the League of Nations is instructive: collective security institutions had failed because not all the great powers were involved, given that the US had chosen to adopt an isolationist policy then.[35]

In the near future, China's involvement in global affairs will become more apparent as it drives closer to truly global power status. For instance, China is important to the bigger goal of nuclear non-proliferation. China became a signatory to the Non-Proliferation Treaty (NPT) in March 1992 and it has reached a tacit agreement to abide by the Missiles Technology Control Regime (MTCR). On the Comprehensive Test Ban Treaty (CTBT), China was among the first signatories in September 1996. China is currently working on its domestic legal procedures for the ratification of the CTBT and has established a national agency to prepare for its implementation.[36] In the post-September 11 era, China supports efforts to ban biological and chemical weapons, acceding to the Biological Weapons Convention (BWC) and the Chemical Weapons Convention (CWC). However, in the eyes of the international community, China still does not go far enough in its commitment to non-proliferation; from their perspective, although

China no longer openly opposes these non-proliferation regimes, it has not taken effective steps to prevent the export of missile and nuclear technology to countries such as Pakistan.

At a regional level, China has a role in maintaining stability, which can be traced back to ancient times. Currently, China participates in the ASEAN Regional Forum (ARF) and the non-governmental Council on Security Co-operation in the Asia-Pacific (CSCAP). At a wider level, Chinese scholars have acknowledged that the ARF started some form of security co-operation in Asia and could in the long run resolve the security dilemma facing states, as the European Union (EU) has already set a good example of how to build up mutual trust among countries.[37] It is fair to say that for any attempts at setting up confidence-building measures or forming security regimes in Asia to have any chance of success, great powers such as China as well as the US must be involved. It is therefore plausible to argue that for any enhancement of Asia-Pacific security, China needs to be actively involved in any regional schemes, alongside some form of concrete US input. As stated in the Introduction, some form of great power management between China and the US in Asia may emerge in the longer term. One might argue that the critical issue is socialisation, a process whereby states internalise norms, originating elsewhere in the international system. This may be normative internalisation, not behavourial compliance, as in the case of China. Such a socialisation process would incorporate ideational factors, including rudimentary forms of identity. A historical comparison is Wilsonian liberalism, premised on human rights and the promotion of democracy free trade and development of international institutions for constraining interstate conflicts. In the current era, the advocates of US unilateralism marginalise international institutions and this is also to some extent the case with China. However, given the need to undermine US hegemony, it must be pointed out that China has at times used international institutions such as the United Nations (UN) or Association of Southeast Asian Nations (ASEAN) to check overwhelming US power.

Specifically, in the long run, the notion of achieving international or regional security is linked to whether China and the US can act in a great power concert. For example, the US had envisioned a concert of powers involving the Soviet Union, Britain and China to maintain a liberal international order in the post-Second War World era although this eventually fell apart as the Cold War ensued.[38] In general, the historical record of great power concert is not particularly encouraging, even in cases where participants share similar worldviews and political systems. Given that China and the US have quite fundamentally different conceptions of world order, it might be difficult for them to work effectively on security issues such as the North Korean nuclear stalemate (see Chapter 6). From the US perspective, a more sensible foreign policy might actually be one that seeks to identify more closely with fellow democracies such as Japan.[39] This could mean continuing to engage China simultaneously or simply neglecting China. The former option is arguably better for the enhancement of Asia-Pacific security as well as international security, as the latter would be unwise given China's ascendancy.

Conclusion

The objective of this chapter was to explore in what ways the US dominance in the international system presents challenges to China's national security interests. Firstly, China has struggled to cope with unipolarity and it has not come up with a full solution to counter this. In reality, the power structure in the international system cannot be easily changed and hence a more realistic option is to operate within the given structure in the most effective manner. On the more specific issue of US hegemony, how China perceived the lone superpower's war on terrorism was important. The US is justified in its merciless pursuit of groups such as Al-Qaeda because it was a victim of terrorism on September 11, 2001 but from China's perspective, America has also used this global war on terrorism as a pretext to maintain hegemony. In the meantime, a sound strategy for China is to assail American leadership in international affairs indirectly; one of the ways that this can be achieved is to constantly highlight the US's hegemonic ambitions to the international community.

Taking a longer chronological perspective, it is inevitable that Sino-American relations will go through periods of friction and clashes but this does not necessarily mean war will break out between these two great powers. From the perspective of the international community, it is important that they must not be overly pessimistic or optimistic; the critical thing is recognising the existence of certain ambivalences in Sino–US relations. In the current era, there are cases where China and the US share common interests; the two main ones discussed in this chapter are eliminating transnational terrorism and promoting international stability. We now move on to look at the case of ideological competition between China and the US.

2 The US and liberal values

In examining China's strategic competition with the US, one must also take into account the contestation of political values espoused by both sides at the international level. Officially, China still clings onto the banner of socialism and retains an authoritarian political system, despite the introduction of market reforms and the concomitant policy of opening up to the outside world since December 1978. In contrast, the US is the champion of liberal democracy and has on occasions employed the use of military force to spread this value to other parts of the world.

In this chapter, we will examine the US export of liberal democracy and how this affects China. China's rejection of the universality of Western values in general and US ones in particular will be critically examined. The US advocacy of human rights is also relevant to the contours of Sino-US strategic competition and its impacts on China will be analysed. Finally, we examine the continuing relevance of the US strategy of peaceful evolution, which has the ultimate goal of undermining the Communist regime in Beijing. We begin by exploring the US strategy to promote liberal democracy worldwide, which is deeply embedded in the history of American foreign policy.

US export of liberal democracy

First and foremost, the US's intention to spread liberal democracy to the rest of the world has implications for China in the twenty-first century. Basically, the lone superpower believes that the transmission of liberal values is the basis for a stable international order in the long run.[1] The philosophical rationale for efforts to promote peace in the international system through the spread of democracy – under the auspices of international institutions such as the League of Nations – is well documented.[2] Intellectually, the foundation for democracy promotion lies in the theory of democratic peace. Essentially, this theory points to two well-established empirical relationships: democratic states seldom fight against each other; and perhaps more controversially, democracies have a greater propensity to avoid serious disputes with other countries that could boil over to war.[3] The latter is more relevant for the purpose of our analysis here, as it potentially pits the US, a liberal regime, against an authoritarian state, China.

In general, the theory of democratic peace posits that democracies are peace-loving and non-threatening to other states in the international system. The implication of this second-level type of analysis is that the elimination of dictatorships must be an effective way to reduce potential conflicts among nation-states. In the post-Cold War era, this reasoning has provided the underlying rationale for the US forward strategy of freedom and democracy promotion. Moreover, from the US perspective, there is a widespread conviction among policymakers that American economic and security interests are often best advanced by the spread of liberal values and democratic institutions abroad.[4] It has been asserted that American values are universal, with the corollary that other states should recognise that American interests and global interests are indivisible.[5] Importantly, from China's viewpoint, this assertion is clearly not fully accepted, although the US does contribute international stability while spreading liberal values worldwide.

Perhaps the neoconservatives embody the strategy of democracy promotion most clearly. Hence, they provide the strongest support for the notion that American foreign policy should actively, and at times forcefully, work to spread democracy. For example, according to Charles Krauthammer, "with the decline of communism, the advancement of democracy should become the touchstone of a new ideological American foreign policy."[6] By embracing democracy as the universally best form of government, and by committing themselves to spreading democracy across the globe, neoconservatives are in many aspects the heirs of Wilsonian liberalism. In this sense, there is a degree of continuity in US foreign policy from the League of Nations era to the current one: ideology does constitute a key factor in the US's actions abroad. In a similar vein, John Mearsheimer has characterised the neoconservative Bush Doctrine as "Wilsonianism with teeth"; he explains that "the theory has an idealist strand and a power strand: Wilsonianism provides the idealism, an emphasis on military power provides the teeth."[34] From China's perspective, this is significant as the end of the Cold War saw the collapse of authoritarian regimes in regions such as Eastern Europe while China has retained its political system. Added to this is the US employment of military force, as discussed in the previous chapter, to spread liberal democracy in states such as Iraq.

In general, it must be noted that moralism has been a central component of American political culture at least since the Jacksonian era. In this sense, one might argue that Americans are evangelist, exceptionalist, pragmatist and populist – often all at the same time. A careful examination of the rhetoric of Manifest Destiny, for example, through which American adventurism in Mexico, the Great Plains and Cuba was legitimated, suggests that a sense of unbounded power shackled to moral principle has been a motivating force in US political life from a time well before the end of the Cold War.[7] Today, it is plausible to argue that neoliberal scholars and activists have masterminded and championed the two principal theoretical breakthroughs that provided the intellectual case for democracy promotion and humanitarian intervention: democratic peace theory and democratic transition theory. Those lines of thought, those logics, when put into practice, have provided the intellectual rationale for interventions such as in Kosovo and Iraq. At the same time, viewed from a liberal perspective, it can be argued that the contemporary intellectual triumphalism is not profoundly different than earlier formulations in US foreign policy history. Hence, while there is no need to overstate the historical uniqueness of Bush Doctrine, the important point is that the synthesis of liberal and conservative foreign policy thought in US foreign policy has important implications for China's relations with the lone superpower today.

Today, US politicians regularly assert that the development of a free market economy, brought about by greater international trade and investment, creates the foundations for democracy and individual freedom in totalitarian states such as China. From the US's perspective, "democracies that respect the rights of their people remain successful states" and they are Washington's "most steadfast allies".[8] Moreover, the US insists that other great powers share common interests and values with itself, noting that China "will in time find that social and political freedom is the only source of national greatness".[9] Naturally, China is concerned about such assertions and often makes the point that its political values are different from those of Western powers in general and those of the US in particular. It is important to note that the contestation of political values between China and the West must be traced back to an earlier time, when the European nations first projected their power into Asia during the nineteenth century.

At the wider level, the US advocacy of liberal democracy can be regarded as an element of soft power, which is part of a given state's comprehensive national strength.[10] Chinese scholars have made comparisons between the soft power of their country and the US, acknowledging that their country is lagging behind the US.[11] We have already noted China's status as a great power in material terms but here the focus is on China's identity. In the realm of strategic competition, it is fair to argue that no great power in the international system operates without some sort of ideological base and identity. For instance, in a previous era, the Soviet Union led the Communist bloc, although China did make attempts to challenge this leadership. Given China's current and historical great power status, it is inevitable that claims to exceptionalism in political culture will be made, especially at a time when Beijing increases its profile on the international stage. The point is that China is now engaged in a contest with the West in general over identity. From a theoretical perspective, a Constructivist account would be that state identities of the US and Western Europe balance against China's identity, which could take the form of Communist or totalitarian. In such an account, each identity is rooted in domestic socio-cultural milieus and each produced understandings of one another based on differences in practice. Although opposing identities may co-exist peacefully, the Sino-US case is essentially a conflictual one. Specifically, the US advocacy of liberal democracy represents a direct challenge to China's identity most clearly.

Given the US advocacy of liberal democracy, the key point is that China is drawn into ideological competition with the lone superpower. In this sense, China is now America's biggest ideological competitor after the collapse of the

Soviet Union in 1991. Importantly, it is clear that a Leninist strand persists in the Chinese political system, as articulated in the Four Cardinal Principles, whereby the overriding role of the Chinese Communist Party (CCP) and its ideology are emphasised.[12] The CCP also learned a free lesson in political control from the collapse of the Communist political system in the Soviet Union. Specifically, Chinese leaders consider attempts to restructure the Communist Party of the Soviet Union (CPSU) as a bad example of inducing political change; Mikhail Gorbachev's resignation as the general secretary of the CPSU and dissolution of the CPSU was described as "the greatest betrayal in the international history of communism".[13] Specifically, from 1989 to 1991, it was evident that Chinese leaders were extremely concerned about their grip on power as the ideological underpinnings of their own regime had come under direct threat. To a large extent, this underlying concern remains today because the Chinese leaders know that the Leninist system in China will never be fully accepted by the Western powers, in particular the US.

During the critical period from 1989 to 1991, the Communist regime in Beijing realised an urgent need to guard against the further dissemination of Western values in China. To avoid being further isolated in the international community, it sought to cultivate the hard-line East European states with high-level visits, which produced joint statements warning of the need to stem the spread of Western liberal values. The few governments that supported China at that time included hardline communist states such as North Korea, Romania, East Germany and Bulgaria, but most of these states later disintegrated.[14] Today, the key fact is that the number of ideological allies for China has decreased: with the demise of Communism in Eastern Europe, China is primarily limited to seeking allies among authoritarian states in the Third World, in its ideological contest with the US-led capitalist democracies.

Basically, the general Chinese concern is that once the Soviet Union has been defeated in ideological terms, China will become the next key target for the US. Effectively, China has now become the sole significant socialist power, alongside countries such as North Korea, Cuba and Vietnam, in a world where capitalist nations are preponderant. One can argue that this leaves China in a precarious position, for the socialist ideology that has sustained the Chinese Communist Party (CCP) since 1949 is on the verge of extinction in the international system. This ideology – notwithstanding doubts about its practical relevance – still to a large extent underpins the CCP's internal legitimacy and the CCP's security is still primarily equated with national security. Despite embracing economic reforms since 1978, Chinese leaders are not willing to abandon Communism totally as this forms the basis on which they had come to power and at least part of the basis on which they have manage to remain in power till this day. In this sense, the advocacy of liberal democracy by the US is viewed by Beijing as a national security threat, or more specifically, a threat to regime security.

In bilateral terms, the 1989 Tiananmen incident was the apex where China and the US confronted each other on the issue of political values. At a time when the totalitarian regimes were in decline, it is important to note that the US was seen as encouraging the export of liberal democracy into China. Specifically, on the causes of the Tiananmen incident, China held the US partially responsible for fomenting the demonstrations and contributing to their sustenance; at that time, Beijing pointed out that "leading political figures of the US monopoly capitalist class" trained "some so-called fighters for democracy" and gave them economic aid so that they could undermine the regime in Beijing.[15] The late Deng Xiaoping himself had identified the Chinese "counterrevolutionaries" as "agents of Western subversion"; it was reported that at that time, Chinese students in Tiananmen Square quoted American revolutionaries.[16] In 1989, at a time when the survival of Communism in other parts of the world was at stake, the Western call for political liberalisation in China to accompany the country's economic opening up since 1979 was therefore seen as a plot to undermine China's political security. In short, the threat of liberal values spreading further in China was undoubtedly magnified in the period from 1989 to 1991. Above all, the Tiananmen event emphasised the Chinese leaders' concern for political security or more specifically regime security and how the US had an indirect role in the causes of this event.

Universality of US values

At a wider level, there is definitely a clash of Chinese and US political values and this is important in explaining the ideological competition between these two great powers. It is important to note that China does not reject the Western concept of democracy totally but it rejects the notion of the universality of this concept, as championed by America today. In fact, during the age of the monarchy, China's leaders had probed in the darkness of the feudal system; they had looked to the West as their teacher and tried to borrow the parliamentary democratic politics of the West to help China's survival and rejuvenation. To a large extent, both the constitutional monarchy model advocated by the reformist faction of the Qing dynasty and the democratic republic supported by the revolutionary faction were all products of the influence of democratic politics of the Western powers. However, China's imitation and replication of the multi-party democratic politics of the West have all without exception ended in failure, as the country descended into warlordism in the 1920s.

A closer examination of the causes of implementing Western-style political models leads to the conclusion that such systems are not suitable for China, certainly not during the interwar period. The fact is that it took more than half a century of exploration before China found a path for the development of democratic politics that is suitable for itself, and this, as the Beijing regime argues, is the system of National People's Congress and political consultation that is implemented by the Communist Party after 1949. From Beijing's perspective, the aim is therefore to continue proving that Western liberal democracy is unsuitable to the realities of China in relation to issues such as social stability, economic development and improvement of the people's living standards.

Importantly, it is evident that China clearly rejects the notion of the universality of a Western style of democracy and its universal applicability – including to the Chinese people. From China's perspective, the Western powers have always considered their democratic systems to be the universal truth that holds the key to the solution of all the problems of the world – including corruption, political chaos, human rights violations, lagging development – and therefore it has "marketed and publicised it by force around the world."[17] Several examples have been used to argue the Chinese case: After the end of the Cold War in the 1990s, the Western powers promoted Western-style democracy separately in the Soviet Union, the former socialist states of Eastern Europe and the impoverished African countries. The immediate result was the implementation of the multi-party systems, with all types of political parties, but these systems disintegrated just as rapidly. In other words, in a succession of elections of leaders and parliaments, the leading figures took their turns on the political stage while power changed hands incessantly in certain developing states.

From the perspective of the Western powers, it appears that the promotion of their democratic models in these developing nations have been successful. However, the Chinese view is that those developing states that have adopted the Western style of democratic political systems very quickly either plunged into political chaos, underwent military coups or experienced ethnic violence; more critically, in the aftermath, there was a decline in economic production, which China particular wants to avoid as it is fully focused on accumulating national power. The overall argument made by China is that those developing states which have carried out the experiment on the Western style of democracy have in the end achieved very little: essentially, Beijing emphasises that the Western style of democracy is unsuitable to the political realities of the developing world. In rejecting the notion of the universality of Western values, China is also trying to strengthen its ideological position regarding the Western powers, including the US. Overall, China does acknowledge the need for lessons from the developed nations of the West but more critically noted that attempts to adapt Western institutions and values in the developing world have failed in general.

Moreover, an examination of the implementation of Western-style political systems in the Soviet Union and Eastern Europe has revealed a similar conclusion. There is added relevance in these cases because China was once in the Communist bloc with the Soviet Union and Eastern European states, in opposition to the capitalist bloc. In the 1990s, following the dissolution of the Soviet Union and the dramatic changes in Eastern Europe, the Western style of democratic system was introduced widely, but the Chinese conclusion is that the process of Western democratisation not only failed to promote economic growth but has instead led to serious economic decline and social crisis.[18] Effectively, in just a few short years, the gross domestic product of those former communist countries fell dramatically, the people's living standards dropped and their economies went into recession. In China's eyes, the crux of the matter is that the link between Western-style democracy and economic progress remains tenuous. More importantly, the experience of these former Communist allies reinforces

China's argument that it must adhere to its current political structure while carrying out economic reforms suited to its own national conditions, which is essential for achieving truly global power status.

Basically, one can discern that China has a different interpretation of democracy from the US. China does not reject democracy per se, but argues that democracy is always relative and specific; therefore, it must conform to and be compatible with the national conditions of a particular country. In short, China does not accept the universality of American values. Essentially, Beijing stresses that it will undertake political reforms only in accordance with the goal to develop a "socialist democracy suited to its national conditions".[19] On the whole, Chinese leaders are often confounded by the American commitment to pluralism in domestic politics. To them, the coexistence of various channels of political participation in the US is often interpreted as a sign of the disintegration of the state control rather than an expression of the competitive dynamics of the domestic system. Compared to Western countries, the notion of liberal governance, which provides a space for societal autonomy, is generally less accepted by China.[20] For centuries, China has taken the stance that the state should be privileged over society and America's frequent efforts to stress the latter's legitimacy are seen as unnecessary and often deemed as political interference. Fundamentally, it must be pointed out that the US political model runs against the traditional Chinese desire for social order, which has throughout the centuries been mostly achieved by the institution of an authoritarian system interspersed with Confucian principles. Essentially, the Confucian system places an emphasis on hierarchy and order in social as well as political life. For the purpose of our analysis, the point is that there is a basic incompatibility between China and the US in relation to the organisation of political life. In practical terms, China cannot afford to lose the ideological competition to the US as this will have serious implications for regime security.

Furthermore, for a developing nation like China, social order is arguably more important as it attempts to cope with the ramifications of fast-paced economic growth such as uneven development. In this vein, Chinese scholars argue that Confucianism has helped "countries and regions in East Asia modernise at a much quicker pace" and "steer clear of defects that the West encountered in achieving modernisation", suggesting that it might replace the modern and contemporary Western culture in the twenty-first century.[21] To a certain extent, the Western notion of competitive domestic politics with its relative lack of coherence in social and political agendas is regarded as undesirable for a country that wants to modernise rapidly. This proposition is also linked to the notion of "Asian values", with various Asian leaders arguing that such values are more suitable for their countries' developmental needs.[22] The key point is that political liberalisation is often regarded as an impediment to quick economic development by Beijing's leaders. In other words, China focuses heavily on the relationship between liberal political systems and economic development. Overall, it rejects the notion of a Western-style democracy, exemplified by the US, as unsuitable to its economic development goals and concomitant quest to become a truly global power.

The above analysis leads to the current debate on the Beijing Consensus and the Washington Consensus. Adherents of the Washington Consensus have reached their conclusions on the basis of actual acceptance of neoliberalism in the international system while the Beijing Consensus has been brought forward spontaneously by certain international opinions against the background of China's fast economic development since the introduction of reform and opening up, with a considerable rise in people's living standards. Although the Beijing Consensus does not have universally recognised documents and its content is still under debate, one of its strength lies in its real-life applicability. In practical terms, the Beijing Consensus may be deemed as superior to the Washington Consensus because of its growing influence in the world, particularly among developing countries. In this sense, China will, to a certain extent, pose a challenge to US values and political thought, especially in the long run. In this sense, challenging the US mode of development comes into the scheme of Sino-US strategic competition and this will become more evident in the next chapter.

US and human rights

Alongside the promotion of democratic values, the US champions human rights and this must be seen as part of the Sino-American ideological contest. Since the end of the end of the Cold War, human rights have increasingly taken centre stage in international politics. The main reason is the ending of the East–West conflict. When the superpowers and their respective allies were engaged in the Cold War confrontation, less emphasis was given to the notion of human rights in international affairs. For the US, many of the Third World countries that it had close relations with were right-wing dictatorships, so human rights issues were largely not raised by mutual tacit agreements; essentially, America's main objective was to present a united challenge to the Soviet bloc. From China's viewpoint, during its strategic alignment with the US to counter the Soviet threat in the 1970s and the 1980s, moral issues such as human rights generally received less attention in the grand scheme of Sino-US relations. The Sino-US strategic alignment meant that, on the whole, China did not face severe criticisms on its human rights record from the US, compared to other communist states in the Soviet bloc, for instance. At that time, it was clear that for the US, the more pressing concern was tapping into China's national strength to counter the Soviet threat.

With end of the Cold War, the international environment became more conducive for the US advocacy of human rights. In general, in the twenty-first century, China finds that most of the countries that it wants to deal with are democracies and human rights issues are mostly on the agenda in bilateral relations, albeit to varying degrees of importance. Furthermore, non-governmental organisations have emerged as an important international lobby, obliging various Western governments to take up the issue of human rights with China more forcefully. For example, enjoying greater access to US Congress and the media, non-governmental groups such as Asia Watch and Amnesty International have succeeded in placing political repression, imprisonment for political activities, torture and prison labour exports on the agenda of Sino-American relations at various points in time. The implication is that China therefore needs to concoct an effective strategy to deal with such issues, which were deemed as low politics in the Cold War era but have now become important in Beijing's relations with the world in general and the US in particular.

Hence, China has taken steps to engage with the international human rights regimes in order to portray a benign global image. For instance, in February 2009, China received the Universal Periodic Review from the United Nations Human Rights Council for the first time.[23] Domestically, China implemented the National Human Rights Action Plan for the first time in 2009, which focused on the development of human rights in various fields including politics, culture and economics. In general, China now has to pay more attention to the international human rights regime. To date, it has joined the International Covenant on Economic, Social and Cultural Rights and is working on the approval of the International Covenant on Civil and Political Rights. Nonetheless, in the eyes of the US, China has not fully complied with the international human rights regime so the issue of human rights will remain on the agenda of Sino-US relations in the foreseeable future.

More specifically, the notion of humanitarian intervention became increasingly important in particular in the post-Cold War era; the classic case was US humanitarian intervention in Somalia in the 1990s.[24] While the promotion of human rights may be carried through non-military means such as aid, medicine, food, expertise, diplomacy and sanctions, the general connotation is that humanitarian intervention usually refers to the use of force. Specifically, humanitarian intervention in modern usage refers to

> the threat or use of force across state borders by a state (or group of states) aimed at preventing or ending widespread and grave violations of the fundamental human rights of individuals other than its own citizens, without the permission of the state within whose territory force is applied.[25]

In the most recent development of this notion, the concept of the Responsibility to Protect (R2P) entails that states must protect their populations from "genocide, war crimes, ethnic cleansing and crimes against humanity". Furthermore, more pertinent to our analysis here are the arguments that the international community must assist a particular state to fulfil its "responsibility to protect" and that in cases where a particular state has manifestly failed to do so, the international community must take action – including military means – to fulfil those agreed humanitarian obligations.[26] It is clear that the US practice of humanitarian intervention raises concerns for China as protecting human rights have now become a reason for the lone superpower to use force in relevant cases.

Clearly, the consideration of military options to enforce humanitarian norms is controversial in the international system and especially so for China, given that Beijing has embraced the Westphalian concepts of sovereignty and non-intervention entirely. In general, the case for humanitarian intervention rests on three key points: the international community has a moral obligation to promote and protect human rights worldwide, internal instability due to human rights abuses could spill over to regional conflict, and interventions based on an interpretation of the human rights provisions in the United Nations (UN) Charter would significantly contribute to international peace and stability. On the other hand, the case against humanitarian intervention is built on the following arguments: states should not intervene for primarily humanitarian reasons as this violates the Westphalian principle of non-intervention, states will generally be unwilling to risk their soldiers' lives on humanitarian crusades, states will not intervene for primarily humanitarian reasons but will abuse it to promote national interests, states will apply principles of humanitarian intervention selectively and in the absence of a consensus on what principles should govern the right of individual or collective humanitarian intervention, such a right will undermine international order. In other words, there are arguments on both sides of the issue of humanitarian intervention in international relations. The main objective in this chapter is not to debate the pros and cons of humanitarian intervention but to note that China and the US have divergent views on this increasingly important issue. Specifically, China disagrees with US intervention into the domestic affairs of other sovereign states.

From the viewpoint of China's political security, it must be noted that the issue of human rights relates to the rights of minorities in China. Specifically, this issue is linked to China's concern that the US may use human rights as an excuse to interfere in its non-Han region such as Xinjiang and Tibet. In these regions, the US has at times viewed the Chinese government's treatment of Uighurs and Tibetans through the lens of human rights. Fortunately, from China's perspective, the US war against terrorists in Central Asia has in general temporarily diverted attention away from Uighurs' plight (see Chapter 8). In comparison, the Dalai Lama has made more inroads with Western liberals on issue of Tibetan autonomy. For instance, China had face challenges from a handful of US Congressmen who pressed for protecting human rights in Tibet.[27] The real danger, from China's perspective, is that human rights issues could snowball into a bigger threat of separatism, as secessionist forces on China's western regions of Xinjiang and Tibet could tap into the US's humanitarian concerns in the longer term.

From the perspective of economic security, China is concerned about the general Western strategy to link the human rights issues with access to the international capitalist system. Given the need for rapid modernisation, China wants access to Western capital and investment so any linkage between economics and human rights is deemed as unnecessary. A specific problem is that China needs ready access to US-dominated international economic institutions, such as the World Bank and International Monetary Fund (IMF), for affordable loans to facilitate its ongoing modernisation. This was especially the case in the 1980s when China first implemented market reforms. Importantly, US dominance in the international economics (see Chapter 3) gives it the ability to link economic issues to political ones such as democratisation and human rights in its dealings with authoritarian states. Specifically, certain US laws instruct American representatives in intergovernmental lending organisations, such as the World Bank, to oppose loans to countries that are guilty of human rights abuses. From China's perspective, affordable credit is needed to facilitate modernisation and the US can hinder its search for funds, albeit less effectively, today. Overall, China resents the US linking economic issues to political ones such as human rights because Beijing wants to use the international capitalist system without being curtailed by Western liberal demands. To a certain extent, the human rights issue can then be regarded as weapon used by foreign governments to impede the economic progress of China, which in turn delays China's rise to truly global power status.

In China's eyes, the linkage between economic security issues and human rights was best represented by the Tiananmen event of 1989. In the aftermath of that event, the US led a group of Western countries and Japan in imposing sanctions on China. Among other measures, Washington cancelled all high-level exchanges with China, cut off arms transfers and military-related sales, suspended financial credits and economic assistance, and conditioned their restoration on substantial evidence of Chinese progress toward political reforms. Fortunately for China, as a direct consequence of its co-operation in the 1991 Gulf War, economic sanctions imposed by the industrialised nations were rescinded within a relatively short span of time; hence, a major obstacle to China's plans for rapid economic development was removed. The point is that in return for China's tacit co-operation in the Gulf War, the US eventually worked to end the moratorium on further World Bank loans to China that were put in place after the Tiananmen incident. The linkage in both events of the Gulf War and Tiananmen means that the nexus between political and economic aspects of security needs to be more thoroughly worked out by China henceforth: in other words, for China, learning how to deal with such types of complicated interconnections in international relations is critical for coping successfully with the lone superpower today.

In addition, what is important to our analysis here is that the US generally adopts a tougher stance against China compared to other Western nations on the human rights issue. In this sense, the US is at times at variance with its allies over human rights policy towards China. For instance, as the case of the European Union (EU) arms embargo on China demonstrates, some European countries were more willing than the US to lift the ban that was imposed in the aftermath of the 1989 Tiananmen event. At a theoretical level, one can note that a less punitive form of leverage used by the US and other Western powers on target countries is to impose international trade restrictions until those countries make democratic concessions. While there is much debate in academic and foreign policy circles on the efficacy of economic sanctions, especially on an autocracy where the leadership can shift the cost from itself to the larger society, the point is that China is today reliant on international trade for its accumulation of power so this issue is critical for Beijing.[28] In essence, the major short-term challenge facing

Chinese foreign policymakers is how to accommodate to American political power without totally submitting to it while attempting to maximise Beijing's economic security in the international capitalist system.

From a broader perspective, given that China and the US have different social systems, values, levels of development and historical traditions, it is inevitable that both countries will adopt different approaches to human rights. This is an extension of the debate delineated earlier about the universality of Western values. In general, China's rulers and their supporting intellectuals claim that China's historic, demographic and economic situation is unique. For instance, the preface to the Chinese government's first white paper on human rights states that "the situation pertaining to human rights is circumscribed by the economic, historic, social and cultural conditions of various nations, and involves a process of historical development."[29] Furthermore, the case be made that contemporary human rights concepts and practice is anchored in Western liberal thought and as an ancient civilisation, China has its own traditions and ways of protecting the welfare of its citizens. This is China's claim to exceptionalism, which is also often found in the strategic fabric of great powers.

In China's case, it has been argued that Confucianism has been an influence for about two millennia (221 BC to AD 1911) and that today's conceptions of Chinese human rights have been moulded by pre-existing Confucian thought.[30] In many respects, one might argue that Confucianism was inhospitable to the concept of human rights, and that the emphasis on duties and collective rights overwhelmed any idea of individual rights that were championed by Western liberals. In other words, the Confucian social order was based on a moral hierarchy in which people occupying some statuses, such as officials, husbands, fathers, were regarded as morally and socially superior to their complements: non-officials, wives and children. The above illustrates how China views the relationship between individual and collective rights, which is different from Western thinking.

Conceptually, China counters the Western criticism of its human rights record by distinguishing between civil and political rights, and "positive rights" (economic, social and cultural rights), and then prioritising the latter over the former. Whereas civil and political rights require governments to refrain from taking actions that violate them, "positive rights" require government to make provisions for citizens; China is definitely more comfortable doing the latter. Moreover, it is generally acknowledged by Western human rights experts that "positive rights" are less subject to theoretical controversy. Overall, the Chinese argue that human rights encompass not only civil and political rights but also economic, cultural and social rights; this broader view of human rights is in general extremely suitable for authoritarian states that are experiencing high growth rates because it serves as a way to emphasise a particular regime's achievement, primarily in terms of raising living standards, while de-emphasising its defects such as a lack of political liberties. Overall, the US advocacy of human rights – as part of the strategy of spreading liberal values across the globe – is seen as a direct challenge to the Chinese Communist Party's (CCP) political security as it calls into question the regime's legitimacy.

Basically, China views human rights as a "Western package" that has been thrust upon itself as well as a means for the Western powers to intervene in its internal affairs in the name of international standards. This resonates with the notion that China was forced to open up to the West during the nineteenth century and it had to absorb certain European norms and values. When viewed from China's recent experience as a victim of Western and Japanese imperialism, it is hardly surprising that Beijing is today adamant that no foreign power should intervene in its affairs again, let alone undermine Chinese Communist Party (CCP) rule, under the pretext of protecting human rights.

The relevance of peaceful evolution

As argued in this chapter, the strategic competition between China and the US includes the ideological realm but this is given further significance because China, more specifically the Communist regime in Beijing, feels threatened by spread of liberal values across the globe. Here, the argument is that the concept of peaceful evolution (*heping yanbian*) remains relevant to capture the perceptions of Chinese leaders towards the US values. Broadly speaking, the strategy of peaceful evolution seeks to undermine the values of socialism through the political, economic, cultural penetration of Communist states. This penetration, especially in the later era, often derives from Western economic assistance and commerce. In this vein, the provision of such assistance is regarded as a bait to induce socialist countries such as China to abandon Marxism-Leninism as well as its authoritarian political system. Former Chinese leader Deng Xiaoping had described this as the West "waging World War Three", noting that this is a war "without the smoke of gunpowder".[31] According to the peaceful evolution strategy, the levers the US used against the former Soviet Union, which would also apply to China, were trade, economic co-operation, technology transfer, diplomacy, cultural and educational exchanges and religious freedom.

At the same time, the concept of peaceful evolution employed by the Chinese tends to be vague and all-embracing; its meaning ranges from dark conspiracies involving the alleged plotters of the counter-revolutionary rebellion, the official term for the 1989 Tiananmen event, to the broad spectrum of cultural, social and economic exchanges with the outside world. It is important to note that this vagueness has often allowed Chinese leaders to denounce security threats to their regime as manifestations of the negative aspects of political liberalisation. Notwithstanding the doubts on the coherence of the concept of peaceful evolution, there is no mistaking its resonance for the Chinese leadership. The concept was in part magnified by the demise of communist regimes in Eastern Europe and the Soviet Union from 1989 to 1991.[32] Earlier, it had become an acute concern in the 1950s when the Communist regime had just come to power in China after decades of internal strife and war against foreign invaders. The aim to undermine the monopoly of the Chinese Communist Party (CCP) is worrying from the Chinese perspective as they witnessed how the former Communist giant the Soviet Union disintegrated. After all, the Soviet collapse was attributed to the West's efforts in issuing "propaganda about the inferiority of socialism"; in particular, the US had highlighted economic difficulties arising from "the implementation of socialism by the Soviet leadership".[33] A general conclusion for the CCP is that it needs to be responsive to societal demands in order to ensure its own legitimacy.

The crux of the matter is that as a post-revolutionary society, the US is often seen as exporting its democratic ideas and institutions abroad, with China now being a prime target after the demise of the Soviet Union. There is a perceived attempt by the US "to remake China in its own image", this time by exporting a secular philosophy rather than by spreading religious teachings as it had done during the age of imperialism.[34] In fact, it has been argued that America's agenda is to change China, as evident in the century-long American "missionary complex" underlying policy towards Beijing, and this agenda indicates a strong "American paternalism towards China" that has been present since at least the 1920s.[35] It is this type of paternalism that irks China's leaders because they wish to enforce an authoritarian political system on their subjects. This is even more evident when the concept of sovereignty enters the equation, as China adheres to this Westphalian notion vehemently, primarily due to the impact of the "century of humiliation".

One important point is that peaceful evolution comes across primarily as a political security threat to China's leaders rather than a military one. Here the aim of the West is to undermine the organisation and process of government in China as well as the ideology that gives the rulers of that country legitimacy. The authoritarian political structure in China is being questioned today, with calls for liberalisation not only coming from the outside world but also from within the country. Moreover, as Beijing becomes increasingly drawn to the capitalist orbit in the search for resources for its economic development, contacts with Western ideas and values will increase. In the long run, this will undermine the ruling ideology – Communist or authoritarian. The strategy of peaceful evolution aims to transform the Chinese political system by encouraging the introduction of private ownership, free markets, human rights and liberal democracy, all of which would eventually lead to the erosion of Marxism-Leninism as an official ideology in China as well as the end of the Chinese Communist Party's (CCP) political monopoly. This is precisely why the US espousal of liberal values is seen as threatening, leaving the CCP with no alternative but to confront and challenge this directly for its own survival.

Among the various forms that the strategy of peaceful evolution might take, the US's advocacy of liberal democracy and human rights is perceived to be particularly dangerous, as far as Beijing's political security is concerned. Given that China regards human rights issues as a matter of national sovereignty, it is hardly surprising that such issues are perceived as constituting a political security threat as well as a key obstacle for better relations with the US. Hence, there are several scenarios that China aims to avoid: the adoption of a multiparty system, which abandoned the leading role of the Communist Party; a pluralist ideology, in which Marxist-Leninism no longer formed the only ideological foundation;

and rejection of central control of the Communist Party and its transformation into a loose political organisation tolerating overt factions.[36] Despite the triumph of Capitalism over Socialism in the period leading up to 1991, the contest between China and the West over values remains open till this day the Communists in China cling onto power.

One of the main features of the US strategy of peaceful evolution is that it does not target the Chinese state directly. To a certain extent, this represents a departure from the traditional state-to-state type of analysis in international relations. The strategy of peaceful evolution works best through the dissemination of bourgeois ideas and ways of life to the Chinese masses via educational, cultural and intellectual exchanges. Basically, the purveyors of this strategy hope that having absorbed some liberal values, via mass media such as the Internet, the Chinese masses would press for further political liberalisation or call for an end to the political monopoly of the CCP. Therefore, Western media are seen as a threat to socialist ideology at various levels in non-capitalist countries such as China. For example, Western radio, television, newspapers and magazines are seen as capable of influencing social psychology, social opinion and social thinking as well as propagating capitalist ideologies and theories in China. The Voice of America, the British Broadcasting Corporation and other Western media are alleged to have contributed to the "corruption" of the Chinese people with "bourgeois spiritual pollution"; this reflects China's fears of Western attempts to subvert the Chinese socialist system through "media propaganda", by confusing the Chinese people's minds and weakening their "ideological commitment to communism".[37] With the advancement of communication technologies, it appears that Western capitalist nations, led by the US, are now in a better position to subvert the Beijing regime through the strategy of peaceful evolution. In fact, the West is seen as enjoying superiority in the "weapons" of electronic media for infiltrating socialist countries and disintegrate them; by the mid-1980s, the estimated advantage that the Western countries enjoyed over the socialist countries in material terms was calculated was 3:1 but in terms of mass media, the advantage was calculated to exceed 20:1.[38]

Basically, the strategy of peaceful evolution assumes that opening up to the West will gradually imbue the Chinese population with notions of civil liberties, political pluralism and the like. Today, being the lone superpower that espouses a different set of political values, the US represents this threat most clearly in the eyes of Chinese leaders. Moreover, with the use of military force becoming less cost-effective in international relations, it appears to China that peaceful evolution might be a more viable foreign policy instrument that the US could use against itself. According to the reasoning of the peaceful evolution strategy, Western powers such as the US should then step up their efforts to spread bourgeois ideas in China through educational, cultural and intellectual exchanges. Given that China engages in strategic competition with the US in the international system over a range of issues, the strategy of peaceful evolution does constitute a key weapon for the US. To a large extent, the drive to truly global power status could be stalled or ended by the strategy of peaceful evolution.

Conceptually, it is important to note that the US's desire to change China and hence affect China's political security are based on two basic sources of international influence: leverage and linkage.[39] The first is leverage, that is, the target government's exposure to external pressure. As China is a major state in its own right, it is less susceptible to US demands than a smaller developing state. The second source of international influence is linkage, that is, the density of external economic and political ties. Here, the engagement school in the US has aims to tie China into a thicker web of economic relationship in the hope that this will eventually undermine China's authoritarian system. It is clear that both leverage and linkage raise the cost of authoritarianism but in China's case, it may be argued that linkage is likely to contribute more consistently to democratisation in the long run. The above analysis vindicates Levitsky and Way's speculation that external democratising pressure is probably going to be less effective, including on China. Expanding linkage, however, seems likely to act slowly and incrementally in producing regime transitions. More aggressive efforts to accelerate the process through leverage, it may be argued, seem to be counterproductive in the absence of favourable internal conditions. As far as the concept of linkage is concerned, the fact is that China has been committed to economic opening-up to the outside world since 1979 because pursuing autarky is no longer a realistic option today.

Overall, the debate on external versus internal sources of regime change and democratisation in a country like China remains unresolved. On one hand, scholars of international relations often emphasise external elements such as membership of international organisations and highly integrated trading relationships among states in inducing domestic change. On the other hand, scholars working in the field of comparative politics stress indigenous social and economic preconditions and domestic political bargaining and coalitions.[40] Despite their differences, the truth is that it is hard to deny that regime change is multi-causal; in other words, the international and national factors interrelate in complex and varied patterns. Such analysis is definitely applicable to the case of China, which is still a one-party state. From Beijing's perspective, it aims to counter the US policy to spread liberal values in the international system because it knows that its domestic political situation may change in the near future, partly as a result of American efforts.

Conclusion

Unlike the Soviet Union and the US, Chinese strategists after the 1980s do not believe that they are advancing any higher international ideological interests such as world communism or freedom, and are on the whole more pragmatic. At the same time, the US export of liberal democracy is seen in a negative light by China as it tries to formulate an effective strategy to counter this strategy. From the US's perspective, spreading liberal democracy to the wider world is deemed to have a positive impact on international security but China does not accept this argument totally. At the theoretical level, it must be emphasised that China rejects the universality of Western political values, questioning its applicability the developing world in particular. Furthermore, China challenges the US advocacy of human rights as this is regarded as the imposition of Western values on the rest of the world. At the same time, human rights and humanitarian issues have become too important in international relations for China to ignore totally, so it has no alternative but to increase its engagement with these issues.

Finally, this chapter has explored the enduring impact of the US strategy of peaceful evolution (*heping yanbian*) on China's national security. This non-military strategy has retained its significance in an era of the lone superpower. Specifically, the strategy of peaceful evolution still constitutes a specific challenge to the political security of the Chinese Communist Party (CCP), because the leaders in Beijing know that China has to continue opening up to the Western world for the sake of economic modernisation. This challenge has become tougher since the post-1978 reforms, with China increasingly being drawn to the global capitalist orbit in its search for financial resources to spur development. Overall, through increasing interactions with the outside world, in particular with the most advanced industrial capitalist nations, mean that human rights and liberal democracy can filter through to the Chinese masses more easily and this will in turn challenge the CCP's legitimacy. From this perspective, one might argue that the gradual undermining of the Chinese communist state system is inevitable. We now shift our focus towards the notion of Sino-US competition in the economic realm, which the subject of the next chapter.

3 The US and the international economic system

In this chapter, the aim is to examine how China perceives and attempts to counter US dominance in the international economic system. The point is that this dominance has enabled the US to maintain its pre-eminence in international politics. We begin with a discussion of China's initial experience of joining the US-led capitalist system. Then we look at how China could challenge the US's economic hegemony, analysing some of the elements of neoliberalism espoused by the US. We then turn to examine the lone superpower's role in the two specific aspects of this system – international trade and international finance. Finally, we examine the possibility of co-operation between China and the US in the name of international economic stability.

Joining the capitalist system

In the previous chapter, we saw how the US defeated the Soviet Union in the ideological realm. Here, the focus is on the triumph of the capitalist system over the communist one, in terms of strategic economic thought. Specifically, there is a need to take a historical perspective on this issue. From China's perspective, a key lesson is how the US defeated the Soviet Union in economic terms. Overall, it can be argued that decades of overly centralised planning and excessive military expenditures were the root causes of the Soviet collapse. It is estimated that the Soviet defence budget was 20 to 25 per cent of the gross national product (GNP) at the time of its collapse, and almost all the research efforts of the Soviet industrial base served the military.[1] In comparative terms, the Soviet GNP was one-third that of the US GNP: it is evident that maintaining parity with the US in strategic weapons and surpassing the US in conventional forces had put an unbearable burden on the Soviet economy in the long run.

From China's perspective, the lesson gained from the Soviet economic collapse is how to fully understand the strengths and weaknesses of the command economy. If China were to reject the notions of value, profit, and competition, and it overemphasised state-owned enterprises, which had no autonomy and had their production geared to an arbitrary state plan rather than market commands, the likely result is damaging the vitality of the private sector as well as hampering the quantity and quality of production. In that case, technological progress and competition with Western powers such as the US were to become an unrealisable goal. After all, stagnation and isolation had caused the Soviet economic system to fall behind that of the US, along with its highly centralised planning and an excessive military budget. The implication of this diagnosis is that if China could avoid highly centralised planning, excess defence spending and isolation, then it could also avoid the fate of the Soviet Union. This is a vital economic lesson to be learned for China's strategic competition with the US.

Hence, with hindsight, one could argue that China was correct in opting for reforms and opening up to the capitalist world from December 1978 onwards. The conclusion drawn by China is that peaceful evolution should not be cut off by seclusion and isolation from Western cultural influences; rather, while retaining the Communist political system, it will engage with the capitalist bloc economically. In the reform era, the main challenges are the successful management of the economy to maintain ever higher living standards, further devolution of planning toward a market economy and efforts to continue technological progress. Meeting all these challenges will drive China towards more effective competition with the US and truly global power status.

Taking a wider historical perspective, it is worth noting that China today no longer challenges capitalism directly but does so in a much subtler way, as discussion on the battle between the Beijing Consensus and the Washington Consensus in the previous chapter indicated. Basically, Beijing had to abandon its more confrontational approach to the global capitalism of the Cold War era. Initially, during the 1970s, China's delegates to the United Nations strongly supported the Third World calls for in New International Economic Order (NIEO), backing the view that the industrialised and richer countries should provide more aid and better terms of trade and finance to the poorer ones. However, by the 1980s, Beijing had shifted its policy from challenging the US-dominated international economic system outright to seeking to become part of it while still criticising certain aspects of this system. The late Deng Xiaoping's policies since 1978 mean that, instead of totally rejecting or seeking to reform international economic institutions such as the World Bank, International Monetary Fund (IMF) or World Trade Organisation (WTO) wholly, China should in the short term join these organisations to extract resources from them in order to fulfil its own development needs. It must be emphasised that this represented an important change in Chinese strategic economic thought.

More importantly, China came to terms with the fact that, as the leading Western trading nation, the US is the key to a wider acceptance of China into international economic organisations. Today, China is a member of the WTO and it is in the G20 forum for co-operation and consultation on matters pertaining to the international financial system.[2] On the whole, China has so far been rather successful in using foreign actors to serve its own needs. The World Bank's and Japanese government's assistance in building China's infrastructure are examples of this. The use of international capital markets, sale of shares abroad and other sources of international finance will increase as a means to enhance China's overall economic security. For the foreseeable future, China will continue to seek concessionary loans from financial institutions dominated by the West, in particular, the US. It will also continue seeking Western venture capital and technology transfers.

The point is that China realises that it is more cost-effective to absorb foreign investment to hasten its modernisation rather than try to pursue an autarkic development programme, as was the case during Mao Zedong's reign. Basically, The Great Leap Forward (1958–1960) showed that self-reliance may not be the most effective way to catch up with the advanced industrial nations in the shortest possible span of time. In this vein, foreign capital utilisation is now an important part of China's policy of opening up to the outside world. In the tenth Five-Year Plan period (2001–2005), China used about US$383 billion of foreign funds, 34 per cent more than in the ninth Five-Year Plan period. This total includes US$286 billion of direct overseas investment, US$38 billion of funds raised by Chinese enterprises listing abroad and US$46 billion of overseas credit.[3] Importantly, the accumulated total of the actual input of US direct investment has already exceeded US$60 billion.[4] In other words, using capital from states such as the US to facilitate modernisation is now part of China's economic strategy.

It must be stressed that foreign capital utilisation is tied to the healthy development of foreign trade, which provides the base for enhancing comprehensive national strength. Since 1978, economic reforms have transformed China from a typical state socialist economy with minimal foreign trade to a mixed economy in which foreign trade is growing in importance. Currently some half of China's exports are contributed by foreign-funded enterprises. China has become a leading economic and trading nation in the world, with its foreign exchange reserves having topped $1.9 trillion. In 2010, China's foreign trade has jumped 34.7 per cent to US$2.97 trillion, with surplus falling 6.4 per cent to US$183.1 billion.[5] It also portends foreign trade in general heading towards a more balanced structure. In addition, China's population of 1.3 billion constitutes a huge domestic market for the global economy. At the same time, China still needs outside assistance, particularly in the areas of technology and management skills. The advanced technology and management experience brought by Western trade partners is needed to achieve rapid modernisation.

Challenging US hegemony

Although China is now part of the international capitalist system, the fact remains that it aims to challenge US economic hegemony in the long run. In theoretical terms, US dominance in the international economic system can be explained by proponents of the hegemonic stability theory. This theory postulates that, for an international system of trade and finance to function smoothly, there must be a hegemon taking the lead in regulation and institutionalisation of trade and finance, which is a public good.[6] The important point is that the hegemon takes the lead in providing this public good partly because of the benefit it gains. Like Britain in the past, the US relies upon its politico-military dominance to ensure that the world markets are adequately accessible for the flow of its capital and products.[7] Since 1945, the US has led a hegemonic liberal international order based on a special kind of liberal welfare state; the main elements comprised the Bretton Woods system, Marshall Aid and Cold War spending. At the same time, it is rather difficult for a single nation-state to take on this role today so one might argue that "a new ideology of the market (and of market access) is being embedded in and reproduced by a group of liberal states – the US and its allies, international institutions and even circuits of capital."[8] In other words, the US can sustain its dominant position largely because it has the backing of the liberal states on the premise of neoliberalism.

Although the Cold War has ended, the US's economic hegemony may last many decades partly because of its success in providing the links between Europe and Asia. For instance, no matter how the European economy is reorganised or integrated, Europe will be unable to control the Japanese and the Asia-Pacific economies unless the US participates in this process. Similarly, no matter how the Asia-Pacific economic co-operation zone develops, Europe will be unable to play a significant role in the Asia-Pacific economy unless the US takes part in this process. In sum, the US links the Asian and European economies, helping the lone superpower retain its dominance in the international economic system. For the purpose of analysis here, the point is that the US is able to continue to shape and at times manipulate the organisational structure of the world capitalist system to its own advantage. This has implications for China's leaders, who want to use the economic base as a springboard for power projection in the longer term.

Above all, the important point is that economic prowess underpins a nation's rise. When individual states moved from one rank to the next, their foreign policies eventually followed suit. As Paul Kennedy argues, the historical record suggests that over the longer term, there is a very clear connection between a great power's economic rise and fall, and its growth and decline as an important military power.[9] This argument applies to China as well as the US. America's economic strength buttresses its pre-eminence in the international system. Conversely, it is fair to argue that military prowess helps the lone superpower maintain its dominance in the international economic system. The linkage between economic strength and military power is important and both elements reinforce each other in the pursuit of the national interest.

Given that the US model of international economic activities is based largely on neoliberal principles, the 2008 financial crisis has given China an opportunity to challenge neoliberalism. At a theoretical level, the 2008 crisis can be attributed to the failure of the neoliberal economic thinking. Essentially, neoliberalism is a revival of traditional liberal ideas: its main economic policy goal is to minimise a government's economic intervention with the attendant argument that over-regulation often obstructs market development and innovation. In the 2008 case, although the excessively free financial model of the US has very strong innovative capacity and higher efficiency, its great potential for moral risks has been cruelly exposed. To a large extent, the 2008 crisis can be attributed to the

US regulatory agencies' supervision that lagged far behind financial innovation. Effectively, these agencies dismantled the protective elements, causing, in just a few years' time, the erosion of the financial regulatory system set up after the Great Depression. The point is that the US has, to a certain degree, caused the controls to lag behind. For example, in the development of asset securitisation and the process of the development of financial derivative tools, what kind of information disclosure should be required and what kind of control should be exercised were inadequately dealt with.

From China's viewpoint, there is a reason to argue that the international financial development and the supervision system rooted in the Anglo-Saxon model can no longer keep up with the pace of financial globalisation and innovation, and therefore the original financial order must be reformed to design the proper and effective financial development and supervision models. In general, the 2008 crisis offers valuable lessons on issues of correct management and supervision of global financial innovation as well as the development of the financial derivative tools. It also points to excessive US consumption and over-reliance on debt as the main causes. In this vein, China has urged the US to raise its savings rate and reduce its budget and trade deficits.[10] From China's perspective, it is naturally concerned that neoliberal practices must not be pursued uncritically in its economic development plans. At a wider level, the lessons stemming from the 2008 crisis relate to the *laissez-faire* system and how far China should move towards this model, if it has to continue being part of the global capitalist economic structure. At the domestic level, attributing the financial crisis of 2008 to the failure of neoliberal economic thinking serves to mirrors China's internal policies, which is one strong of government intervention in the economy.

Hence, in comparison to the US, China was less exposed to this crisis. One reason is that China's financial system has not been fully liberalised and because the bubble on China's real estate market has in part been diffused due to earlier rounds of macro regulation and control, therefore, the impact of the financial crisis on the Chinese economy has been more limited. With its ample foreign exchange reserves, China has the ability to weather the shock delivered by the turmoil on the international financial market since 2008. In contrast, the US had to cope with recession with the three traditional mainstay industries – finance, real estate and car – being hit particularly hard. In comparative terms, the financial crisis of 2008 has weakened the US's comprehensive national strength while China has in general maintained the steady and fast growth of its national economy.[11]

Importantly, China is able to gain insights from how the 2008 crisis weakened the US, its strategic competitor. For the increasingly open China, an important lesson of the 2008 financial crisis is how to perfect supervision in the course of opening up the financial sector. In this sense, China can learn from the mistakes made by its strategic competitor. Basically, China insists that a country's regulatory system must be compatible with the stage of its economic and financial development and opening up; it must cover all risks; hence, there must be continuity along the entire chain of production and innovation of financial products and services. At the same time, China acknowledges that innovation is essential to economic undertakings and cannot be denied totally therefore innovation and financial supervision should be like of "a chess game where one move prompts another".[12] The point is that China will now be more confident in the international economic arena while the US's influence there has decreased.

Critically, increasing economic links with the US-dominated global capitalist economy has inadvertently give rise to new problems for China. For example, China is bound to be more vulnerable to economic sanctions as its economy becomes increasingly interdependent with the US economy and the world economy in general. Essentially, the notion of economic security is fundamentally a tricky one. At present, one can discern that China will tolerate interdependence with America for the sake of its own economic goals. China is interested in international trade but only as a means to build up its economic power. In short, in an era of economic interdependence, growth is seen not as an end in itself but as a necessary means for China to achieve truly global power status in the long run. As China develops economically, it will be able to exercise greater leverage in international investment, finance and trade.

From a wider perspective, it is evident that China's economic rise has implications for the US in the twenty-first century. China has already leapfrogged Japan to become the largest holder of American Treasury securities, holding US$585 billion compared with Japan's US$573.2 billion. For instance, the buying up of significant portion of US debt means that if Chinese investors redeem a sizeable amount of their bond holdings, the American financial system may malfunction.[13] One might argue that the balance of power in economic terms will slowly shift towards China as time goes by. At the same time, the notion of a financial nuclear weapon is not without its problems. The holding of some US$2,400 billion of foreign reserves held by China constitute US bonds and other types of US securities and shares. The proportion of asset denominated in US dollars is high. If China sells them, the US dollar will depreciate, which in turn leads to the depreciation of China's assets denominated in US dollars: The move could harm the US but China will also have to bear huge losses in the process.

The US and international trade

In this section, we shift to focus on how the US's dominant position in international trade can pose a challenge to China. The US economy accounts for 30 per cent of the whole world and its import accounts for 15 per cent of the world trade. In an earlier period, the US was regarded as an obstacle to China joining the international trading system, especially in relation to the World Trade Organisation (WTO). The issue of linking trade to political issues first surfaced during the 1990s: at that time, the annual debate in the US on whether to confer the most-favoured nation (MFN) status on China became a key component in bilateral relations in the aftermath of the 1989 Tiananmen event. As discussed in the previous chapter, human rights issues surfaced and were for a time linked with trade in the course of Sino-US engagement. Under an MFN clause, a country that grants trade concessions to one party of the agreement must grant the same concessions to all signatories of the agreement; the impetus for such a trade agreement is the reduction of tariffs and import taxes. The MFN was subsequently renamed to Permanent Normal Trade Relations (PNTR) in 1998, and this status was eventually conferred upon China by the US in 2000. This conferment was important as it paved the way for China's entry to the WTO, the premier international trade institution.

The point is that the MFN case indicated that henceforth, China needs to accept the norms of global trade, which are heavily influenced by American ideals. With US dominance of the international trading system, a corollary is that in order to engage with this system, China needs to accept some of these norms. This may at times impinge on China's sovereignty. At the same time, it may be argued that the US eventually realised that the delinking human rights to trade – under the rubric of engagement – was a better way to deal with a key trading partner which has the biggest consumer market. To a certain degree, it can be argued that the US can ill afford to use economic sanctions against China today as most of its companies have invested in China and because the US could actually lose more. As for China's leaders, they become more certain that other countries need Beijing as a trading partner. For instance, although countries generally remain displeased with much of the Chinese government's domestic and international behaviour, companies throughout the Asia-Pacific region in particular are rushing to trade with China and invest in China. Part of the reason why states do not restrict their investors is the fear of losing out in profiting from China's economic growth. Given that foreign companies benefit from doing business with China, the incentive is for more investment.

Moreover, the fact that one government refuses to do business with China does not stop other countries from grabbing their share of the huge Chinese market. This, of course, serves China's long-term economic security objectives. China's leaders are aware that foreign investors prefer investing in countries that offer political stability because their main objective is to get a good return on their investment. In addition, China offers cheap labour and a large consumer market for Western goods. Ironically, it is thus the trade and investment of Western capitalist countries that constitutes one of the main reasons why China could sustain high growth, enhancing Beijing's economic security in the process. This is a trend that benefits China as it drives to truly global power status.

At the same time, since becoming a member of the WTO, China has faced new problems in relation to the international economic system. One issue is the debate over market economy status. Under agreements signed in 2001 when China entered the WTO, Beijing will automatically attain market economy status in 2016. Among WTO members, about 97 have agreed to grant China market economy status but China's top trading partners, such as the US and the European Union (EU), have refrained from doing so. On this issue, China's argument is that without market economy status, its firms are often at a disadvantage; for example, when facing anti-dumping investigations by the US or Europe, as the production cost information they provide are regarded with scepticism.

Overall, it is evident that the Western industrialised powers, led by the US, have pressurised China to conform to global economic norms in an age of increasing integration. For instance, although China's average tariff dropped to 9.9 per cent in 2005 from 15.6 per cent in 2000, and almost all pledged cuts have been made by the end of 2005, this is deemed as inadequate in the eyes of the Western powers.[14] In its 2005 scorecard on China's World Trade Organisation (WTO) commitments, the US–China Business Council concluded that, despite certain progress, Chinese trade policies still violate WTO rules.[15] Basically, the Western trading nations want China to fulfil its pledge to complete the transition to a full market economy and, in particular, reform certain trading practices that currently failed to fully meet WTO membership rules. In general, there is a variance between Chinese and Western trading practices. For the purpose of our analysis, it must be noted that a key difference is that Chinese state-owned companies appear to have an advantage over their US counterparts. Due to the nature of the Chinese political system, Chinese firms have more subsidies from the state, which often gave them an unfair advantage in the international trading system. The relationship between states and firms is a complex one in the study of International Political Economy; the important point for our analysis here is that China is able to steer its companies towards certain national objectives more easily than Western states.

One of the major issues with regards to China's engagement with the US-dominated international trading system is protectionism. This tradition of mercantilist thought can be traced back to Friedrich List, who had argued for protective measures to allow German infant industries to become competitive with British production in an earlier era. In general, China has come under Western pressure to open up its industries to global competition in the spirit of free trade. Overall, the US is seen by China as interested in opening up the Asian markets further as this will also increase the vitality of America's Asia policy in general. After all, the US had facilitated the East Asia economic boom during the Cold War era through its role as security guarantor, particularly for its allies Japan and South Korea, as well as formal ally Taiwan. Today, the relative decline of the US economy compared to the Asian economy implies that the US may take an increasingly hardline position on trade issues with China.

At the same time, China counters Western pressure by accusing the US of practising protectionism in particular. The Chinese view is that the US, which acts as a long-term promoter of free trade, lacks the sincerity to tide over the current economic crisis together with the rest of the world; for instance, the invocation of the "Buy American" Bill shows that in the process of the US government's long and active participation in the formulation of international trade rules, America's most important goal is still to gain maximum national interest from international trade.[16] While US Congressmen may wish to provide protection for the country's domestic manufacturing industry, they must take into account the possibility of retaliation by major trading partners such as China. The fact is that China has criticised the US for engaging in protectionism on the international stage. From China's perspective, the Doha Round's failure to achieve any breakthrough after nearly seven years of negotiations was largely attributable to the fact that developed countries such as the US refused to abolish agricultural subsidies and were unwilling to open their agricultural markets to developing country members.[17] The Doha Round was initiated in November 2001 with the main purpose of establishing a more rational global multilateral trading system by promoting liberalisation of global agricultural, manufacturing, and service trade. Although China no longer confronts the developed world directly, it still takes a stance of challenging the developed countries in the international trading to some extent. Basically China see itself representing the developing world against the interests of the developed countries in the tussle over international trade.

Currently, Chinese trade surplus with US constitutes one of the major issues in bilateral economic relations: it came about as a result the Chinese export surge, which turned a positive American trade balance with China into a negative one. Taking a longer chronological perspective, trade relations between China and the US have developed swiftly since 1978. Bilateral trade volume grew from US$80.5 billion in 2001 to US$298.3 billion in 2009, and China and the US are now each other's second largest trading partner.[18] In fact, since the late 1980s, the US has been the largest market for Chinese exports. Natural complementarities exist between the world's foremost economic power and the world's largest developing economy. From China's perspective, it wants access to the vast American market, advanced technology, financial investment and capital while the US acknowledges the importance of China's huge consumer market. At the same time, frictions between these two trading partners became apparent by the late 1980s. The growth of China's exports to the US, which had followed the earlier path taken by Japan, South Korea and Taiwan, began to elicit accusations of unfair trading practices similar to those that Americans regularly voice against its other Asian trading partners.

Currently, China's huge trade surplus with the US has led to charges that this resulted from unfair Chinese trade practices, such as bureaucratic practices, closed markets, dumping, evasion of quotas, violation of copyrights and currency manipulation. For instance, the US Congress' US–China Economic and Security Review on bilateral trade from 1989 to 2003 concluded that the US trade deficit with China during that period caused the displacement of production and some 1.5 million job losses in the US, with such losses doubling since China's entry into the WTO.[19] Another example would be the expiration of the quota-system governing global textiles trade at the end of 2004, which led to a surge of imports of Chinese clothing into America and the US textiles manufacturers urging Washington to take the necessary counter measures. More specifically, a US that suffers from an international balance of payments deficit will be less willing to tolerate an increase in Chinese imports, barriers to American exports and the growing. From China's perspective, keeping its trade surplus artificially high benefits its export-oriented state-industrial complex. This is one of the bases for China to achieve truly global power status. In bilateral terms, it must be pointed out that the US remains important to China's economic security.

After all, the economic rise of China can to some extent be attributed to the US economy's openness to Chinese exports.

In examining the causes of China's trade surplus with America, the Keynesian "paradox of thrift" argument is relevant. The argument, which has been mainstream thinking among the developed countries, posits that increased savings would reduce consumption and eventually reduce investment and social wealth. In practical terms, it is said to have produced deep and far-reaching effects on contemporary US economy and society: debt-financed consumption became the dominant trend. In contrast, the Chinese economy currently has a problem of excess savings in excess of 20 trillion yuan, and the Chinese people's consumption as a percentage of the gross domestic product (GDP) ranks below the world average. In this regard, the Chinese view is that the actual solution for the US's trade surplus with China is that consumption and savings must be co-ordinated.

Second, there is the question of to what extent an undervalued renminbi led to China's huge trade surplus with the US. From the US's perspective, the Chinese currency's dollar peg artificially lowers the cost of Chinese exports – making them more competitive, while increasing the cost of imported goods in China. China has a managed mechanism on foreign exchange, under which the renminbi is partially convertible, since it has yet to liberalise the capital account. Although the market already has built in considerable investor speculation, betting on a move sooner rather than later, the US continues to prod Beijing to switch to flexible exchange rates due to the trade deficit issue. More specifically, China has come under consistent US pressure to accelerate the renminbi revaluation as well as shift the main driving force of economic development from exports to domestic demand. From China's perspective, there is no basis for renminbi revaluation by a big margin: appreciation of the Chinese currency would only rebalance China's international trade to some extent because the real issue is China's high savings rate compared with the US, as discussed earlier. From the 1870s to the 1970s, it is noted that the US maintained a favourable trade balance for a period of over 90 years but this later changed into a deficit. The debate is whether this was caused by exchange rates and evidence tends to suggest that there is no necessary connection between trade balances and exchange rates. Here the case of Japan's trade surplus with the US is instructive: the Japanese yen, for example, has appreciated enormously against the US dollar over the past 40 years but Japan's trade surplus with the US has been continuously on the increase over the same period. To a certain extent, the case with the Japanese yen demonstrates that international payment is not necessarily entirely linked to currency exchange rates; one might argue that international trade balance is rather determined by international division of labour and product competitiveness. In this sense, China feels that the US been putting unnecessary pressure on itself to revalue the renminbi.

From the Chinese perspective, the politicisation of the trade surplus issue is therefore largely seen as an instrument by those US politicians who advocate keeping China in check economically: the demand that China appreciate its currency is linked to the desire to contain China's growth. At a conceptual level, a country's exchange rate policy is a matter of sovereignty but being enmeshed with the international economy means some of this has to be ceded. The Chinese view is that every state has the right to choose a foreign exchange system compatible with its own national conditions so what it has done is to comply largely with the rules of a market economy while not yielding totally to US-led pressures.

US and international finance

In addition to wielding influence in the international trading system, the US is also dominant in global financial affairs. Specifically, America has huge influence in international financial institutions such as the World Bank and the International Monetary Fund (IMF), which were set up under the Bretton Woods system in 1944. Basically, the Bretton Woods system enshrined the principle of national sovereignty in the production and transmission of paper monies but embodied national controls on exchange rates.[20] More specifically, states were obliged to adopt a monetary policy that maintained the exchange rate by tying its currency to the US dollar and the IMF would bridge any temporary imbalances of payments. Effectively, the US dollar became the reserve currency of the world and the US has reaped the resulting benefits.

Given the current system, during crises, the US can use its interest rate policy and other means to change the value of the dollar and in turn shift the risks abroad. In general, concerns over the stability of a US dollar-based international financial system were further raised in the 2008 crisis. On one hand, the current international monetary system has to some extent abetted the Americans' unrestrained borrowing and their habit of spending unearned income and has stimulated the irrational prosperity of the housing market. On the other hand, through financial innovations, the US has been able to shift the risks to other investors in the financial market and in turn spread the risks to the rest of the world. From China's perspective, the 2008 financial crisis arose largely because the US's reliance on its superior dollar position to "hijack" the world economy.[21]

In addition, since the collapse of the Bretton Woods system in the 1970s, the US dollar's monopolistic status has been diminishing although it still occupies a leading role in international finance and trade. From China's perspective, a new system promptly set up with a fair and effective global financial supervision system that does not contain any kind of monetary hegemony would be ideal.

Overall, China has used the 2008 financial crisis as a key impetus for driving reform in the international financial system, arguing that the crisis has fully exposed the defects of the US-led system and the setup designed to address these defects. The point is that China often blames the US for these crises and has generally criticised the American way of managing them. To a certain degree, this is unjustified as America cannot by itself control the international system.

More specifically, China has called for the international financial system to be subject to supervision and regulation, in particular stressing the need to strengthen supervision and regulation of countries with their currencies serving as major foreign exchange reserves as well as to set up a rational global financial relief mechanism.[22] The argument is that the goal of the global financial reform for the next 50 years should be to build a system that contains several major international currencies. In other words, China would like to see the dollar-dominated international financial system reformed as soon as possible. Given the importance of reform in the international financial system, G20 finance ministers met in October 2010 and agreed to move towards market-determined exchange rate systems and keep trade imbalances at sustainable levels but fell short of accepting Washington's proposal for limiting current account surpluses and deficits to less than 4 per cent of gross domestic product (GDP).

At a wider level, the debate on the dollar-dominated international financial system can be seen as part of the continuing chasm between the developed and developing worlds. The Chinese view is the rules of the international financial system were set by the developed countries so the system is regarded as less than fair, equitable and effective. Therefore, China is in favour of giving the developing countries a bigger voice in the international financial system. In this regard, international representation is a serious question, with China calling for an increase of the quota share of the emerging markets and developing countries, in the International Monetary Fund (IMF).[23] The overall Chinese argument is that the IMF, founded after the Second World War under US auspices and charged with the responsibility of handling financial crises, is clearly not up to the task of tackling crises in the current era. The corollary to the above argument is that there is a need for Asian states to create a new foreign exchange reserve fund to maintain monetary stability in the region. With the establishment of the Asian foreign exchange reserve fund, the argument that Asia should have a bigger voice in international financial affairs in future becomes more valid and China will aim to lead Asia on such matters. As the largest developing nation, China has been championing the call for developing countries to have a bigger say and more representation in the international financial organisations in general. This is one way to counter US dominance in the international economic system.

At a regional level, China has aims to lead a regional system and these first arose after the experience of the 1997 Asian financial crisis. At that time, China was concerned that the IMF's loans to South Korea, Thailand and Philippines and Indonesia included "stringent" conditions imposed on these countries to "obey" IMF guidelines to change, reform and open up their markets.[24] This clearly expresses China's fear that economic crises might lead to its sovereignty being violated by foreign powers. At a wider level, China continues to see itself as being engaged in the struggle against the dominance of the Western powers in the international economic system today.

Today, China is keen on regional currency swaps to prevent further crises in Asia. It played a major part the US$120 billion "ASEAN Plus Three" Fund that was launched in March 2010.[25] This Fund builds on the Chiang Mai Initiative that came into being in the aftermath of the 1997 Asian Financial Crisis to facilitate bilateral currency swaps. It is worth noting that during the Asian financial crisis of 1997, China had already gained a reputation for keeping a stable exchange rate for the renminbi. It is evident that China as well as other the East Asian states aim to transform the Chiang Mai Initiative into a more multilateral reserve pooling mechanism. The argument is that such regional currency swaps will help cushion shocks in the event of external currency speculation. The argument is that each state can swap its local currency with the US dollar for an amount up to its contribution multiplied by its purchasing multiplier as a means to provide short-term liquidity, which in turn contributes to regional economic stability. Importantly, European attempts to take concerted and co-ordinated action have been unsuccessful and reaching agreement on the terms of intervention or assistance in Asia when the stakes are so large will be just as difficult.

From China's perspective, it is now enmeshed into the Asian economic system so it must devise ways to cope with future financial crises as these would impede rapid modernisation and, accordingly, the drive to truly global power status.

In the longer term, China may challenge the position of the US dollar in the international financial system: it is possible that the renminbi could become an international reserve currency in tandem with its full convertibility, reflect a renewed interest in loosening control of the currency as the country deepens its involvement in the world financial system. However, the Chinese offensive is currently only operating at the regional level. In this regard, the renminbi has already been used as settlement currency in China's authorised border trade with Mongolia, North Korea, Myanmar and Vietnam. In December 2008, the Standing Committee of the State Council decided to allow the renminbi to be used in international transactions with some of its trade partners. As part of a pilot project, for instance, the renminbi will be used to settle trade payments between its Guangxi Zhuang autonomous region and Yunnan province, and the Association of Southeast Asian Nations (ASEAN) member countries. With the aforementioned decision, it is evident that China is aiming for a full-fledged pilot project that involves major trading areas in the longer term. In other words, this marks a first step on the road to making the renminbi an international currency.

At the same time, there are problems associated with the internationalisation of the renminbi. There are debates over the necessity of a regional monetary regime in East Asia, for example. From a standpoint of regional common interests, it may be argued that the renminbi should be pegged to a common currency basket and be Asianised by stabilising effective exchange rates. On the other hand, internationalisation of the renminbi may not constitute the most pressing concern because China is gaining a competitive edge in the region, which will lead to some form of renminbi currency area eventually. While there are pros and cons to the internationalisation of the renminbi, for the purpose of our analysis here, the crux of the matter is that against the backdrop of China's rapid economic growth, the renminbi will become one of the key currencies in Asia in the long run.

For now, the status of the US dollar as the main international reserve currency is still irreplaceable. Renminbi accounts for a very small proportion in international settlement. In this sense, it is more appropriate for China to first enhance the functions of the renminbi's settlement in the neighbouring nations before expanding its international influence. This will pave the way for the renminbi to become a major currency for settlements in international trade as well as encourage foreign investors to more yuan-denominated assets. In the long run, China would aim to challenge the US dollar as the international standard after securing monetary dominance in Asia.

Mutual interests in global economic stability

The above analysis does not imply that China cannot co-operate in international economic affairs. Although the US and China may have divergent economic interests, they share mutual interests in maintaining global economic stability. After all, China benefits from a stable international economic system, as much as the lone superpower. Whereas international trade involves the physical movement of one commodity from one state to another, the fungibility of money in a deregulated environment ensures that national identities as of little monetary significance. In this sense, both China and the US are together in the bid to counter the negative effects of international financial crises. This means that the US and China have to adapt their financial policies to take into account the contours of the global financial structure. In doing so, the intensity of their strategic competition would be attenuated.

At a wider level, the contention that increased economic interaction can trump military competition traces back to the theories of Immanuel Kant.[26] Although by no means universally accepted, commercial peace theory holds that, as countries trade with one another and become more economically interdependent, the probabilities that they will go to war against one another is sharply reduced. This is particularly true when countries share high expectations of future gains through co-operation.[27] In addition, various studies have found that wars have a significant negative impact on trade that may persist for years following the war's conclusion.[28] Hence, there are implications for future Sino-US economic co-operation. China and the US are partners in the international economy and both great powers know the importance of their bilateral ties. To that effect, China embarked on a series of strategic economic tasks with the US. Initiated in 2006, the twice-yearly Strategic Economic Dialogues (SED) were the highest-level among the existing China–US dialogue and consultation mechanisms. In total, five meetings were held between 2006 and 2008. Since then, the SED mechanism has been broadened to the Strategic and Economic Dialogues (S&ED), which have a security track as well as an economic one. Given that competition is endemic in the global capitalist system, the truth is that the US is a major economic competitor to China and this is a prime concern to Chinese strategists. At the same time, China often points out that economic competition should proceed in accordance with international rules and regulations; noting that frictions and differences are normal but they should be resolved through dialogue on an equal footing, consultation and talks. In other words, there are elements of competition as well as co-operation in Sino-US economic relations.

Another key point is that while resenting US dominance in the international economic system, China has to cope with the costs of being enmeshed in it. Specifically, China has difficulty in coming to terms with the demise of economic sovereignty. This is particularly true of the field of international finance. In the money market, hard money put into circulation by states and central banks are expanded according to the activities of commercial banks who answer primarily to the international financial system. It is today the case that global economy markets can defeat even the most concerted efforts of governments or even groups of governments to defend particular national exchange rates and interest rates. The collapse of the European Community's Exchange Rate Mechanism (ERM) in 1992–1993 has already highlighted to European countries the poverty of national currency reserves when confronted by massive money movements on the open market. Essentially, financial crises are endemic in the global capitalist system and states cannot remain totally immune from them, the Great Depression in the 1930s and the 2008 financial crisis being cases in point. The fact is that in an age of globalisation, China can reap the benefits of an international economic system but it will also be subjected to global financial risks and crises; these risks and crises do threaten national security directly.

Therefore, China has work to together with the US as well as other major economic powers to maintain the stability of the current international economic system. In doing so, Beijing will have to accept US leadership in the international economic realm, at least in the short term, while increasing its influence there when opportunities arise. For instance, during the 1997 Asian Financial Crisis, China argues that it had helped to stabilise the regional economy by not devaluing the renminbi while implicitly recognising the importance of US leadership in preventing the crisis from spreading. Today, the 2008 crisis further illustrates the need for increased Sino-US co-operation in order maintain international financial stability in general.

However, it must be noted that China has rejected the notion of the "theory of economic responsibility" advocated by some countries such as the US.[29] Probably one major reason is that highlighting the responsibility of China – in terms of those of a country with a major trade surplus, a creditor, a major energy consumer and a country with huge savings – could create unfavourable public opinion to China in the long term. This is because the international community might get the wrong impression that China is the cause of the problems in the world economy. It could also lead to the wrong conclusion that whether the world economic situation can be return to better health depends largely on which measures China takes; this would then put unnecessary pressure on China, which is still a developing country. At the same time, China can contribute to the international economic system by giving a greater role to the market demand in renminbi exchange rate formation, make the exchange rate more flexible and maintain its stability on a reasonable and balanced level.

Essentially, financial crises are likely to occur again and China, the US and other great powers must learn to cope with those types of economic threats more adequately. Moreover, there are other major economic issues that need to be resolved. For instance, the fact that growth rates in the developed world have stagnated since the early 1990s and trade imbalances could create protectionist sentiments in the form of emerging trade blocs in Europe and North America. From China's perspective, a combination of recession and protection in world trade can paralyse its export growth while domestic demands for employment and expectations of higher living standards continue to rise; in that case, China's leaders might find it increasingly difficult to satisfy the demands of the masses as well as push towards truly global power status. The point is that China cannot remain immune from ruptures in the international economic system today so it undertake some form of co-operation with other great powers such as the US to uphold stability in the system.

Conclusion

In discussing China's economic security, one must explore its integration with the international economic system. This entails unfettered access to global markets and includes access to lending institutions as well as overseas export markets; such challenges arose when China first opened up to the capitalist world economically in 1979 and have been increasingly complicated in the age of global integration. To a certain extent, China has learnt the lessons of the Soviet collapse and is now a major part of the global capitalist system.

Given the importance of the US to world trade, any softening of the US economy, or even a recession, will cause the global commodity trade volume to decrease, which will in turn affect the global economy. The situation will be more serious to countries such as China that heavily depend on foreign trade. Essentially, China's current policy is to rely on bilateral trade arrangements, while seeking to participate in a global market system through membership in organisations such as the WTO. This represents a realistic way for Beijing to enhance its economic security.

In international finance, the US influence has decreased in the aftermath of the 2008 crisis. It is clear that China has been striving to wield its power in the financial world Accordingly, Beijing has capitalised on this by contributing to maintaining global economic stability while challenging the dominance of the US dollar in international financial affairs to some extent. The 2008 crisis presented a good opportunity for China to challenge US dominance in international economic thought, namely, neoliberalism. China has in general been able to assert itself more forcefully in global economic affairs since the 2008, which helps enhance the nation's overall status in the international community.

China's emergence as an economic power is set to continue in the coming decades. Today, it has the world's largest foreign reserves and it is the second largest trading partner of the US. China is now regarded as an important player in the international economic system and its role includes that of helping the US maintain global economic stability: In this sense, the national interests of China and the US converge as these two great powers aim to prevent instability. At the same time, China has to acknowledge that the US is still the key to the international economic system as well as to its economic security, albeit unwillingly.

The basic theme emanating from this chapter is that national security can only be fully grasped by abandoning the overconcentration of focus on military balance of power. In other words, economic strength is just as important and certainly in the case of China's strategic competition with the US. When Richard Nixon approached China in 1971–1972, trade was not a non-major consideration in the course of restoring bilateral ties but today the case is different. In the twenty-first century, understanding the contours of Sino-US economic relations is vital for understanding the wider strategic competition between these two great powers.

4 The US and the Taiwan issue

This chapter examines Taiwan as a case of strategic competition between China and the US. The key point is that the lone superpower is regarded by China as the key obstacle to its long-term goal of reunification with Taiwan. The chapter begins by analysing the importance of Taiwan in Chinese strategy as well as a component of US East Asian strategy. It then assesses the degree of US commitment to Taiwan, which constitutes a key factor in Chinese strategic thinking on cross-Taiwan Strait relations. In addition, the shared values of the US and Taiwan serves to strengthen their bilateral relations, presenting a challenge to China's political security interests. Finally, we examine the international status of Taiwan as this has implications for China's national interests. We begin by looking at the importance of Taiwan to China.

The importance of Taiwan

First and foremost, Taiwan is important to China because the leaders in Beijing regard reunification as a key long-term goal. China still regards Taiwan as a renegade province and has never renounced the use of force in reincorporating the island republic under its rule. In other words, China regards the Taiwan issue as part of its internal affairs and foreign powers cannot interfere in this issue under the Westphalian concept of sovereignty. In this regard, the US is seen as an obstacle through its continuing support for Taiwan. To the Chinese, American involvement in Taiwan, which began with support for Chiang Kai-shek's Nationalist Party in the 1930s, is regarded the latest episode in the long history of foreign interference in its domestic affairs. More specifically, Taiwan is regarded as the unfinished business of the Chinese Civil War by the more nationalist elements in Chinese policy circles. From Beijing's perspective, passing the Anti-secessionist Law in the National People's Congress (NPC) in March 2005 provides the legal basis for using military means in achieving reunification with Taiwan, both internally and externally.[1] In this sense, it may be argued that the modernisation of the China's submarine fleet is aimed at blockading Taiwan, if the island republic decides to opt for formal declaration of independence.

From Taiwan's perspective, the argument is that China's Anti-secessionist Law violates the United Nations (UN) Charter, which opposes the use of force or the threats to use force to resolve interstate disputes. In other words, Taiwan views its relationship with China as one between equal sovereign states. On its part, Taiwan has countered the Chinese move by soliciting support from its allies and these allies have actually brought the attention to the UN. However, it must be noted that the few allies that Taiwan has are small and weak states that have little weight in world affairs.[2] What really matters is that the great powers, the US in particular, have adhered to a one-China policy in principle since the 1970s. At the same time, there is a certain US strategic ambiguity in relation to the Taiwan issue; America wants to prop up and sustain Taiwan but is at the same time concerned about escalating tensions with China over the Taiwan issue. This strategic ambiguity will be further explored. It must be stressed that the purpose of our analysis in this chapter is to focus on Taiwan as an object of strategic competition between the two great powers rather than how Taiwan relates to China in bilateral terms.

Apart from the quest to reincorporate Taiwan under its rule, the island republic is important to China for strategic reasons. In military terms, the island republic constitutes a base for power projection. China has blue-water navy aspirations and these would include some sort of control over the seas surrounding Taiwan first before expansion into the Pacific Ocean in the long run. In this sense, Taiwan is in the "first island chain" with regards to China's gateway to the Pacific; controlling this "chain" will give China the platform to counter the naval superiority of potential adversaries such as Japan and the US in the longer term.[3] Taking a longer chronological perspective, China's strategic vulnerability from the sea is not a new issue: weakness along its long maritime frontier meant China resulted in defeat at the hands of naval power Britain in 1842, which ended the First Opium War. The lesson for China is that Taiwan could be used by potential adversaries, especially naval powers, to launch attacks on mainland China. The point is that Taiwan is strategically located and this is an enduring feature, notwithstanding the end of the Cold War. In other word, Taiwan relates directly to China's military security.

Moreover, from the economic security viewpoint, the Taiwan Strait is important for China's supply of energy; China relies on oil imports and wants to ensure the secure delivery of supplies from the Persian Gulf via the Straits of Malacca to its booming eastern coast. In the event of a conflict in the Taiwan Strait, the US could use its naval superiority to disrupt China's oil supplies. China's entire national strategy of reform and modernisation is largely dependent on maritime trade and commerce. The geostrategic reality is that China's economic centre of gravity is on its eastern seaboard, which is vulnerable to a US attack by sea and Taiwan could be the springboard. Obviously, such reasoning also has implications for defence planners in the US as they entertain the prospect of growing Chinese naval strength.

In economic terms, Taiwan is important to China as trade and investment helps fuel modernisation in China itself. The recent Economic Cooperation Framework Agreement (ECFA) is a case in point. The ECFA's "early harvest" lists detail Beijing's and Taipei's commitments to reduce tariffs over the first two years of the agreement: China will reduce tariffs on 539 Taiwanese goods while Taiwan drops the duties on 267 Chinese goods; within two years, the duties on those products will be reduced to zero.[4] It is worth noting that the imbalance of tariff reductions is in Taiwan's favour despite the fact that Taiwan enjoys a large trade surplus with China. As the content and principles of a ECFA and a Free Trade Agreement are quite similar, the signing of a ECFA with Taiwan will allow the free flow of merchandise, services, and capital between the two sides of the Taiwan Strait. To a certain extent, the outcome of the ECFA reflects Beijing's willingness to be more accommodating towards Taiwan in economic matters. More importantly, for the purpose of our analysis, closer economic integration with Taiwan can be used by China to put further pressure on Taiwan. In particular, this relates to China's ultimate objective of reunification. For China, the ECFA is a variation of the case of the former British colony of Hong Kong, which signed a Closer Economic Partnership Agreement (CEPA) in 2003, in line with Beijing's "one-country, two systems" formula. In democratic Taiwan, there are different views on closer economic integration with China. Although the ruling Kuomintang portrays ECFA as a purely economic agreement, the opposition both sees and portrays it in political terms as a move that would erode Taiwan's sovereignty and lay a basis for eventual reunification.[5] In this regard, the opposition Democratic Progressive Party (DPP)'s view is that China will eventually set a new agreement on Taiwan's acceptance of "one China." Hence, from Taipei's perspective, the key question is linking an ECFA to the issue of its sovereignty.

It is also important to note that the ECFA is technically an agreement between two authorised quasi-official associations – China's Association for Relations Across the Taiwan Straits (ARATS) and Taiwan's Straits Exchange Foundation (SEF) – in the absence of formal diplomatic relations. Hence, China has to constantly reassure Taiwan that the ECFA agreement, like other ARATS-SEF agreements, will not touch on politics. Essentially, SEF and ARATS are two intermediary bodies in charge of cross-strait negotiations in the absence of formal diplomatic ties and the general consensus is to deal with practical economic issues before complex political matters.

It must be noted that close economic integration with Taiwan is on the whole in line with China's national interest. From China's perspective, this represents another way of putting pressure on Taiwan politically. The crux of the matter is that a Taiwan that is overly dependent economically on China runs the danger of being absorbed by its larger neighbour in the long run. From Taiwan's perspective, the normalisation of economic and trade relations with China is at the core of its current cross-Taiwan Strait policy.[6] However, as China's economic power increases, the potential dangers of closer economic integration with China becomes more apparent. For instance, the overwhelming size of China's population, its geographic proximity and shared customs and language will magnify China's influence over Taiwan's economy, further hurting wages and raising unemployment.[7] In 2010, Taiwan's exports to China grew sharply, outpacing the growth of its exports to the rest of the world, rising 37.1 per cent to US$114.78

billion; China's share of Taiwan's exports was 41.8 per cent, a record high.[8] Such reliance may not be positive for Taiwan in the long run. From Taipei's perspective, there is, therefore, a need to avoid becoming overly dependent on China. The key issue is that China holds that further economic integration with Taiwan will advance its long-term reunification goal. At the same time, since the 1996 Taiwan Strait Missile Crisis, it must be noted that Beijing's declared policy of peaceful reunification has been buttressed by an increasing potent military component. We now turn to the importance of Taiwan in US East Asian strategy.

The US's East Asian strategy

In military terms, Taiwan constitutes a strategic asset to America, as much as to China. Taiwan is an island in the Pacific Ocean and it can serve as a base for the projection of US power in East Asia. During the period of the Cold War, Taiwan was regarded as an "unsinkable aircraft carrier" from the US perspective of strategic deployment and this feature is still relevant today.[9] As a superpower, the US must possess power projection capabilities in the important region of East Asia and Taiwan, which belongs to the US's group of friendly countries, continues to have a potential role in this regard. From the Chinese perspective, the Taiwan issue is used by the US to partly justify its ongoing military presence in Asia; the issue also creates the basis for US intervention in the Taiwan Straits, if and when needed, as well as arm sales to Taipei.[10] Hence, till this day, it is the combination of the threat of intervention by the US, primarily the navy and Taiwan's air defence that effectively keeps the Taiwan Strait a moat rather than a highway open to Chinese forces. As long as Taiwan remains in the US sphere of influence and remains informally protected by the US, then China's naval modernisation can be checked to a certain extent. This is of grave concern to China, given the lone superpower's unassailable military leadership, as discussed in Chapter 1. From the US's perspective, the informal obligation to protect Taiwan is linked in many ways to the notion of a China threat; in this sense, the US could then use the Taiwan issue to check China's ascendancy to a certain extent.

In economic terms, Taiwan is an important trading partner of the US. In 2009, the US–Taiwan trade amounted to US$46.8 million: American exports to Taiwan reached US$18.4 million while imports totalled US$28.4 million.[11] Taiwan was the US's tenth largest trading partner, its 15th largest export market and its ninth largest source of imports. US investment in Taiwan totalled US$261 million, while Taiwan's investment in the US amounted to US$1.1 billion in 2009. Moreover, several of Taiwan's industries are important to the global supply chain of high-tech products, including weapons systems. Specifically, the global computer manufacturing sector is to a certain extent dependent on Taiwanese components. Hence, in the event of disruption in the international information technology supply chain, it may be difficult for countries such as the US to find alternative suppliers with similar expertise levels as Taiwanese firms.[12] This economic importance of Taiwan is often underplayed and must be taken into full account by Western countries in formulating effective strategies towards Taiwan. Moreover, the US wants to preserve the existing liberal trading environment in East Asia, partly because it has economic interests there and partly because such an environment would foster further economic interdependence and promote peace in general. Taiwan is a critical part of the vibrant economic environment in East Asia and any disruptions to the regional environment will be not in the US's national interests.

As for Taiwan, which achieved economic success under US protection in the past, it relies heavily on foreign trade and this in turn made it especially vulnerable to any global economic upheaval. Comparatively speaking, in economic security terms, Taiwan has ample foreign exchange reserves, low household debt and business liabilities, highly resilient enterprises, and banks with a low proportion of bad assets: these are factors which allow it to bear external shocks and risks better than many other Asian countries in comparison. At that same time, Taiwan recognises that its economic development cannot solely depend on trade and investment with political rival China today.[13] In this regard, the US's role as an economic partner is vital to Taiwan. The overall implication is that while Taiwan expands its business opportunities in China as welcome as other overseas markets, it must also rely on its own strengths by boosting domestic demand and maintain American economic interest in itself.

At a wider level, Taiwan is important to the US in terms of the lone superpower's strategy in the Asia-Pacific region. This strategy stems from the Cold War and the US still has an important role in guaranteeing the military survival of Taiwan today. To be precise, American military involvement in Taiwan dates back to the 1930s and was prominent in the 1945–1949 Chinese Civil War; the Chinese communists were prevented from gaining control over Taiwan then due in part to American aid to Taiwan. The outbreak of the Korean War in 1950 served as the catalyst for American enhanced support to Taiwan under the Kuomintang (KMT), and this backing was later further extended when the US sustained Taiwan's existence by the 1954 Mutual Security Pact, placing "China's Taiwan province under US protection".[14] Subsequently, the 1954 Mutual Security Pact was abrogated following Sino-American rapprochement in 1972 and since then, the US has not challenged the one-China policy in principle. However, the US stated at that time that it has an interest in a peaceful settlement of the Taiwan question by both sides on the Taiwan Strait. With this prospect in mind, the US affirmed the ultimate objective of the withdrawal of all forces and military installations from Taiwan under the terms of normalising relations with China in 1979; essentially, there would be a progressive reduction of US forces and military installations on Taiwan as the tension in the area diminishes.[15]

Undoubtedly, the legal abandonment or, more precisely, the sacrifice of Taiwan by the US was a security gain for China. At the same time, it must be stressed that the 1954 US–Taiwan Mutual Security Pact was eventually replaced by the Taiwan Relations Act (TRA). Passed into law by the US Congress in 1979, the Act assured a continuing American interest in Taiwan's security and importantly, it includes a US commitment to sell "defensive arms" to Taiwan. The arms sales issue remains a point of contention between China and the US today. From the Chinese perspective, any strengthening of Taiwan's military capabilities, with some form of assistance by America, raises concern and can even be viewed as an indirect challenge to its military security. In general, China regards US arms sales to Taiwan as one of the most sensitive area of Sino-American relations today; it consistently argues that such sales contravened the 1972 Sino-American agreement limiting arms transfers to Taiwan. A key Chinese argument is that US arms sales to Taiwan amount to an interference in China's internal affairs that obstructs and undermines its long-term goal of peaceful reunification with Taiwan. This is, of course, premised on the assumption that Taiwan is part of China. From a wider perspective, the arms sales issue reflects partly the trend that defence contracts are shrinking in the Western countries and wealthy Taiwan represents a major potential market for Western defence industries. Overall, Beijing reiterates that the three Sino–US communiqués of 1972, 1979 and 1982 should form the proper basis of Sino–American relations and it insists that, in particular, they must be applied to the Taiwan issue as well.

From the US's viewpoint, in the twenty-first century, its East Asian strategy is still based on a string of bilateral alliances with important states there. The point is that Taiwan retains a role in this – implicitly – despite the cessation of formal security links with the lone superpower. In the Asia-Pacific region, Japan remains the US's most important security partner with South Korea, Australia, the Philippines and Thailand making up the quintet. Clearly, the US recognises that it can achieve its strategic goals in the region only by maintaining and adapting the enduring alliances, which are regarded as its "greatest sources of strength".[16] In this regard, for the US, continuing to protect Taiwan would indicate to traditional allies such as Japan and South Korea the credibility of its commitment to the region. To various degrees, countries in this region have concerns over the implications of a China that is increasingly more powerful. For the US, commitment to Taiwan will indirectly provide some form of reassurance to its formal allies in the Asia-Pacific region in an era when Chinese power is growing rapidly. In East Asia, it must be stressed that there are no multilateral alliance structure analogous to the North Atlantic Treaty Organisation (NATO); effectively, the US has maintained extended deterrence through bilateral alliances and security relationships and through its forward military presence and security guarantees. Taiwan is still informally part of this US strategy today.

At a wider level, in the post-Cold War era, the US needs to maintain the military security of its allies in Asia against challenges not only from China but also North Korea and other non-state actors, specifically terrorist groups. Specifically, US nuclear weapons have played a vital role in extending deterrence to US allies and partners against recalcitrant states such as North Korea. Although Taiwan is not formally part of this umbrella, US nuclear superiority over China would still give defence planners in Taipei a certain degree of assurance for instance. Indirectly, a certain degree of commitment to Taiwan signals the US's resolve in ensuring stability in the Asia-Pacific; this in turn helps the US perpetuate its bilateral alliances in the region and preserve its strategic interests there. From China's perspective, it must be stressed that by itself, Taiwan does not pose a direct military threat. However, with the involvement of the US – direct or indirect – in the Taiwan issue, this threat is unduly magnified from China's vantage point.

US commitment to Taiwan

In the course of Sino-US strategic competition, it is the degree of US commitment in the event of a crisis in the Taiwan Straits, possibly initiated by China, which commands most of the world's attention. Although the US no longer has a formal defence commitment to Taiwan, the protection of Taiwan in the event of Chinese hostilities remains likely given that vital US interests are at stake, as stated earlier. In the absence of a formal link to Washington, the US can only maintain ties with Taiwan on an unofficial basis. To date, the most viable way to provide support to Taipei is through the Taiwan Relations Act (TRA); providing "defensive" arms to Taiwan is vital for the island republic's military security in the face of China with increasing military capabilities. From Taiwan's perspective, China has increased the number of short-range missiles aimed at Taiwan to about 1,500 and this represents a sign of continued distrust between the two sides despite a recent warming of ties. For instance, the Dong Feng 11 and Dong Feng 15 short-range ballistic missiles are believed to be based in southeast China, about 160 km away from Taiwan.[17] From Taiwan's perspective, an effective deterrence with some form of US input is a basic national defence strategy.[18] This is even more pertinent in an era where the balance of forces continues to shift in China's favour regarding Taiwan.

From a wider perspective, in a world of interstate competition, Taiwan needs to boost its defence capabilities to keep pace with China's massive arms build-up. In other words, Taiwan needs to conduct "internal balancing" against a rising China. In this regard, building a credible deterrence would require an upgrade of weapon systems, most likely to be acquired from America. For instance, Washington is currently in the process of selling US$6.4 billion of advanced weaponry to its former military ally.[19] This recent sale is a symbolic representation of the continuation of US–Taiwan security co-operation as well as the US recognition of Taiwan's efforts in improving relations with China. In general, from Taiwan's perspective, arms deals with the US allow it to procure the necessary defensive weapons systems while simultaneously working to improve its relations with China. In this sense, the US's unequivocal adherence to the TRA is vital to Taiwan's strategic interests.

From China's perspective, it has consistently opposed US arms sales to Taiwan and this stance has always been clear-cut and unwavering. By agreeing to sell the aforementioned advanced weapons to Taiwan, China sees the US as seriously violating the principles of the three Sino-US joint communiqués, especially the 17 August 1982 communiqué, which contains the issue of defensive arms sales. It is also important to note that Washington communicated the "six assurances" to Taiwan in the summer of 1982 as it completed negotiations with the Beijing over the joint US–China communiqué on arms sales to Taiwan. The assurances included promises not to mediate between Taiwan and China and not to pressure Taiwan into negotiations with China.[20] Overall, it must be noted that the TRA's longevity attests to the strategic importance of Taiwan to the US.

From China's perspective, the TRA remains a thorn in its flesh. For example, during the 30th anniversary of the TRA in 2009, the aims of certain US politicians to emphasise its importance elicited strong dissatisfaction from China. From China's perspective, the Taiwan Relations Act was enacted unilaterally by the US; the Act had gravely violated the basic norms guiding international relations, violated the US's commitment to China and intervened in China's internal affairs, which includes Taiwan.[21] At the same time, China has yet to implement an effective strategy to cope with the ramifications of the enduring TRA. This is an issue which it protests against US interference because it regards Taiwan as its domestic affairs but where it would not wish to challenge the lone superpower directly, at least in the short term. From the US perspective, the TRA constitutes an avenue for continuing to link up with Taiwan, despite various challenges.

Overall, American dominance in world affairs has an impact on the Taiwan issue and this increases China's concern in the post-Cold War era. From the Chinese perspective, the US acts largely unilaterally in international politics today and there is a possibility that it is likely to become more accommodating to Taiwan's national security interests. This is especially true if the war to eliminate terrorism comes to an end; a common aim between China and the US to defeat terrorists would then disappear. From a wider perspective, the Taiwan issue is intricately linked and entwined with China's perception of US pre-eminence in the international system. From Taiwan's perspective, it is in its national interest to play up the China threat theory to garner more support from the US and its allies. Hence, stressing the ambitious modernisation of the Chinese military and the implications for a more assertive Chinese foreign policy in Asia is useful for Taipei. For instance, former Taiwanese leader Chen Shui-bian had suggested that China's medium- and long-range missiles and intercontinental missiles target not only Taiwan but also Japan and the US. In addition, it is worth noting that Taiwan has actively sought allies who share similar concerns about China's growing military strength from US allies, most notably, the former colonial power, Japan. In this regard, it has been suggested that that both Japan and Taiwan should further upgrade their substantive relationship into a quasi-military alliance, on the basis that China's military expansion is something that no country in the Asia-Pacific region desires because Beijing poses a threat to the region.[22] In sum, continued dialogue with US allies such as Japan can only enhance Taiwan's national security interests, although the results are more likely to be marginal.[23] The fact is that the US holds the key and hence more explicit commitment from the US can only boost Taiwan's position with regards to China.

On its part, Taiwan has also attempted to get international organisations to become more directly involved in its tussle with China. In the recent past, under the previous administration of Chen Shui-bian, Taiwan has called United Nations (UN)-level inspections of the cross-Taiwan Strait security situation whereby staff and inspectors dispatched by the UN will make regular reports on the situation. Essentially, from Taipei's perspective, the expansion of China's military muscle is aimed at achieving beyond its stated purpose of deterring Taiwanese independence.[24] On the whole, one can discern an endeavour by Taiwan to internationalise the cross-strait issue, which will certainly involve a higher degree of commitment from the lone superpower. Such a development will raise China's security concerns because in general, China still prefers a bilateral approach to security issues eschewing any advanced forms of multilateralism. Nowhere is this preference more obvious than in the Taiwan issue, which China has regarded as its own internal affairs since 1949.

Overall, the fact that Taiwan remains under the US sphere of influence and it has not been absorbed by China means that Chinese power in East Asia has been checked to a certain degree. A worse-case scenario would be the US dropping its interest in Taiwan totally, leaving Chinese power unchecked possibly to the detriment of the island republic's national interest. From the perspective of Asian security, the Taiwan issue remains a flashpoint that could spark a great power conflict. From Taiwan's perspective, by continuing to be at the centre of the strategic competition between the US and China, it can, ironically, enhance its own security. Situated in the middle between China and the US since the 1970s, Taiwan will aim to maximise its security by manoeuvring between these two great powers. From Taiwan's viewpoint, although no longer formally allied to the US, its main strategic option is to maintain the lone superpower's interest on the island republic by emphasising the threat posed by a rising China.

In the twenty-first century, Taiwan remains important to the US, despite major changes in the international system since the Cold War ended. Specifically, the Taiwan Strait represents a likely battleground between China and the US in the future. In the 1950s, when China bombarded the Kuomintang-held islands of Jinmen and Mazu off the coast of Fujian Province, the US reacted with a dispatch of its navy to the Taiwan Strait in an attempt to deter further adventurism from China. For the first time since the initial US commitment to defend Taiwan in 1950, it must be noted that China possesses the military means to threaten Taiwan directly. For instance, while China cannot match the US in naval power in the western Pacific, it can access the Taiwan Strait and target Taiwan's military and civilian centres. Of particular concern are China's land-based missiles and air capability in the Taiwan Strait, which represent a certain degree of potential damage to Taiwan in the event of a conflict. It has also been argued that neither the US missile defence systems nor rapid deployment of American forces could protect Taiwan from a punishing Chinese military strike in the current era.[25] Hence, the commitment of the US to Taiwan is even more critical today, especially from Taipei's viewpoint. In the three Taiwan Straits Crises of 1954–1955, 1958 and 1996, the US was a key player: its support for

Taiwan, whether for Chiang Kai-shek or Lee Teng-hui, was a major concern for China. In those cases, one might even argue that China perceived that American involvement in the Taiwan issue threatened its own military security, at least indirectly. At the same time, the three Taiwan Strait Crises enabled China to gauge the degree of US military commitment to Taiwan. Overall, it is important to note that such incidents have often acted catalysts for actual conflicts in the international system and this certainly applies to the current tussle between China and the US over on the Taiwan issue.

US values and Taiwan

In many ways, Taiwan also represents a battleground between Chinese and US political values. In terms of the US export of liberal democracy, Taiwan can be regarded as part of this grand strategy although this linkage may not readily evident. The economic success of Taiwan as a developmental state had paved the way for political liberalisation in an earlier era when it enjoyed formal US military protection from Communist China. The island republic has moved away from its Kuomintang (KMT)-dominated authoritarian political system, with the US playing an influential role in Taiwan's democratisation process. For example, the US Congress conducted hearings on the Kuomintang's human rights abuses in Taiwan and the continuance of martial law on the island republic in the 1980s. The Taiwanese president at that time, Chiang Ching-kuo, eventually lifted martial law in July 1987 and removed the ban on forming new political parties in Taiwan.[26] Having achieved democratisation, Taipei makes claims to legitimacy in the international community by stressing its identification with global trends towards democratisation and capitalism.

Today, Taiwan is governed by the rule of law while China is not; the contrast becomes even sharper when one compares Taiwan's democracy in the late 1980s and China's suppression of student protests in Tiananmen Square in 1989.[27] Moreover, Taiwan serves as model to achieve a free and democratic Chinese society, an anomaly in the historical Chinese political system. Essentially, Taiwan represents the first democracy in Chinese history. This aspect is critical as it refutes the argument that democracy, with its emphasis on individual choice, is antithetical to traditional Chinese values, which include the desire for status quo and social cohesion as advocated in Confucianism.[28] The key point is that, although Taiwan's experience of democracy is relatively short, it has proved that the traditional authoritarian Chinese political culture is not an obstacle to achieving democratisation. Hence, China is bound to be concerned that the international community might gradually accept Taiwan as an independent state, in an age where liberal values are generally dominant and a lone superpower aims to export liberal democracy to the rest of the world.

To a large extent, the US brand of political ideas triumphed with the collapse of Communist regimes in the Soviet bloc and a sense of victory and confidence boosting has been evident since the early 1990s. Essentially, it can be argued that the US is keener to promote democracy in an age when superpower nuclear confrontation no longer commands the bulk of its resources and attention. Moreover, the liberal argument on the indivisibility between spreading democracy and international security, exemplified by the democratic peace theory, has resonance for Taiwan's national security strategy.[29] On the basis that democracies do not go to war against each other, it would be in the US's interest to maintain Taiwanese democracy in an age when Taiwan's rival China is still ruled by an authoritarian regime.

In general, it may be argued that shared values with the US and the achievement of democratisation in Taiwan have added further reasons for America to sustain Taiwan, especially in the face of Chinese threats. Taiwan is not only as one of the few thriving democracies in East Asia but more critically, an important component of the US's East Asian strategy – political as well as military. More specifically, if the US hardens its commitment to Taiwan on ideological grounds, that will be seen as unfavourable to Beijing's objective of reincorporating Taiwan under its rule. Such a scenario will magnify the political security concerns of China's leaders. From Beijing's perspective, the question is how far the US is willing to support Taiwanese democratic credentials. In this regard, freedom and democracy, which are pivotal to Taiwan's existence and development, can serve as Taiwan's soft-power assets in its relationship with China. For Taiwan, an effective deterrence strategy must include the political aspect; that is, there is a need to "deepen Taiwan's democracy and manifest Taiwan's freedom – the two values vital to Taiwan's existence and development", in its relationship with China.[30] Basically, soft power relates to a country's ability to lead by example and influence the behaviour or interests of other political bodies through cultural or ideological means.[31] The implication is that, in addition to hard power, which includes military and economic capabilities, soft power can be employed by states to enhance their national interests. In the case of the Taiwan issue, the importance of soft power must be explicitly acknowledged.

On its part, the US itself recognises that soft power is important in winning hearts and minds, as recent cases in exporting liberal democracy in Iraq and Afghanistan have indicated; essentially, military power can be backed up by some sort of moral authority and this often derives in part from a state's protection of democratic values. For Taiwan, this means that its recently acquired status of being a democracy can persuade other states such as the US to support its cause in the international arena. Politically, the island republic is a democratic nation whose values and internal structure share similar features with the lone superpower. From the perspective of the US policymakers, comparing and contrasting the political systems in China and Taiwan can lead to certain policy preferences. In general, such a contrast will have an impact on the mindset of US statesmen who accord a certain degree of importance to the promotion of democracy and human rights in the formulation of foreign policy. From the US's perspective, it has probably not invested enough in projecting its soft power through Taiwan.

In general, for Taiwan and the US, a common agenda on democracy promotion can serve as the basis for the spread and consolidation of liberal values in Asia, which is China's sphere of influence. In other words, the US's battle with China over values in the current era is one where Taiwan does have a role to play. From this perspective, the US should therefore link up more explicitly with Taiwan to export liberal democracy in East Asia. In this vein, Taiwan has stated that it is willing to share its democratisation experience with other developing nations.[32] This ties in with the American objective to promote liberal values in East Asia as well as worldwide. Logically, the US can take its soft power strategy one step further by explicitly bringing Taiwan into its quest to export liberal values worldwide in a more formal way. In effect, the democratisation of Taiwan and the island republic's newly acquired political values is clearly linked to the importance of ideology in US foreign policy.

Overall, the US promotion of liberal democracy challenges China's political security, that is, the survival of the communist regime in Beijing in the post-Cold War era. As noted in Chapter 2, this confrontation in the realm of political values can be viewed as part of the US's overall strategic competition with China. To China, the strategy of peaceful evolution to undermine communist regimes through non-military means, primarily via commerce, cultural exchanges and infiltration of Western values such as human rights and liberal democracy, remains relevant. Importantly, Taiwan can be regarded as a part of this strategy. On its part, Taiwan has rightly recognised that China will continue to undergo peaceful evolution because of the spill-over effects of political liberalisation in the island republic; it is right to emphasise that what "communist China fears most is the democratisation of Taiwan".[33] In fact, Taipei has stated that democracy will "defeat" China's authoritarian regime.[34] This type of political legitimacy issue relates to the political security of the Chinese Communist Party, as argued earlier, and is part of China's national security.

In the long run, the US is committed to encouraging democratic reform, the promotion of human rights, the establishment of a firm rule of law, and a more open and transparent government in China itself. The US strategy to induce change in China can be sudden or gradual but what is certain is that in the attempt to change China's political system, Taiwan can serve as the US's model of a true Chinese democracy. In this regard, it would be in Taiwan's interest to embrace and promote Western-style liberal democracy more vigorously. In this vein, explicitly supporting the US promotion of democracy in China will enhance Taiwan's national interest in relation to China. In that case, Taiwan's democratic credentials can be employed by the US indirectly as an instrument of foreign policy against China, in particular to induce political liberalisation in the authoritarian state.

From Taiwan's perspective, having achieved democratisation, it can make democracy promotion its central goal and this can only enhance its national interest. A vigorous strategy would include further participation in international democracy forums and engaging in public diplomacy to highlight its democratic achievements to the international community. For instance, it has been suggested that through non-government as well as government representative offices worldwide, Taiwan should advertise itself as the "land of entrepreneurship, liberty and democracy".[35] Such an application of soft power represents an important way for Taiwan to secure US support against an authoritarian regime in China, in the face of evolving Sino-US relations. In terms of Western liberal values, human rights are a vital component and here Taiwan has a role as well. Domestically, it is worth noting that Taiwan is setting up an agency to report specifically on the human rights situation throughout the country.[36] This agency will come under a human rights committee under the Presidential Office and one of the key tasks of the committee is to devise a mechanism for reporting on human rights nationwide, in line with two international conventions – the International Covenant on Civil and Political Rights and the International Covenant on Economic, Social and Cultural Rights. The point is that this represents Taiwan's commitment to the global human rights regime, which is to a large extent associated Western powers such as the US.

It is evident that the onus is on China to counter the democratic credentials of Taiwan. More specifically, democratisation constitutes another basis that can be used by the advocates of an independent Taiwan to further their cause, a danger that has to be stopped as far as China's political security is concerned. China had already pushed forward the concept of "one country, two systems" in 1979 in an attempt to placate the Taiwanese, who fear that they will lose their autonomy in the event of a Chinese takeover. In this sense, the challenge for China is how to present itself as a tolerant and benign government to the Taiwanese masses today if it aims to incorporate Taiwan under its rule successfully. In other words, China must win the hearts and minds of the Taiwanese masses if it hopes to take over the country peacefully. History has showed that the Kuomintang regime of the 1930s and 1940s had failed to win over the Chinese masses, compared with the Chinese Communist Party (CCP), which ultimately led to Communist victory on mainland China in 1949. The importance of political security must be acknowledged; the CCP wants to enhance its legitimacy and this policy is also being applied to Chinese citizens across the Taiwan Strait as well. Conversely, it is possible that China's gradual political liberalisation might accelerate and China might become a much more open, pluralistic and democratic society in the future.[37] These changes might make reunification more likely, or potentially could make a democratic China more willing to let Taiwan go its own way. For now, what is unmistakable is that a democratic Taiwan serves to highlight the need to induce change in China's illiberal political system and increases the chance of Taipei gaining more recognition in the international arena.

The US and Taiwan's international status

The democratisation of Taiwanese politics leads to another issue, that of Taiwan's quest for diplomatic recognition in the international system. This has implications for China's national interests. The US had already stopped recognising Taiwan in the 1970s, in favour of China, but this has not dampened

Taiwan's quest for international status. Basically, Taiwan's push for recognition in the international system has complicated bilateral relations between China and the US. At a wider level, being a democracy enhances Taiwan chances for regaining formal international recognition in the long run although this will probably require a certain degree of US support. In democratic Taiwan, debates on whether the island republic should join the United Nations (UN) under the name of Taiwan or write a new constitution to secure the independence and sovereignty of the country continue.[38] On the issue of the position of Taiwan's national identity, some Taiwanese have even contended that Taiwan should abolish its official title of Republic of China and institute a new constitution that would further secure the identity of Taiwan as an independent country. At the same time, Taiwan's strategy has its limitations because essentially, Washington had advocated no unilateral change in this status quo by either Taipei or China due to the fear of escalating tensions. Hence, from China' perspective, Washington does have a role to play in checking any further radicalisation of Taipei's foreign policy. At the same time, the reliability of this role is questioned by China and will continue to be carefully scrutinised by the leaders in Beijing.

As noted earlier, Taiwan has not been a member of the United Nations (UN) since 1971 when China took over the seat in the international organisation. Over the past 15 years, Taiwan's efforts to persuade the UN General Assembly to list the issue of Taiwan's membership on the agenda have failed largely because of China's obstruction. Taiwan's current diplomatic strategy is one that entails asking the UN to consider Taiwan's participation in affiliated UN agencies rather than its admission as a full member of the international organisation.[39] This moderate and pragmatic approach has been generally well received in the international community, which surely must worry China. Importantly, the US has stated that it supports Taiwan's attempts to participate in UN specialised agencies, to be an observer in World Health Assembly, and to join other technical conventions.[40]

Overall, the fact that Taiwan is not accepted as a sovereign state has undermined its full potential in participating in world affairs. Taiwan's predicament is that it belongs to a category of its own. By extension, its strategy to regain formal international recognition is also unique, defying the norms of the usual politics studied in international relations. In this regard, one might argue that Taiwan's democratic credentials serve to increase the chances of achieving success, although the main factor would be how much support it can garner from the lone superpower as well as the future development of Sino-US relations. For our purpose here, the crux of the matter is that Taiwan's desire to become a fully fledged member of the international community is intricately linked with the notion of Taiwan's independence. Although China's military security is not directly challenged by Taiwan, its political security can be undermined by Taiwan insofar as it seeks formal independence. In this respect, continuing arms supplies from the West, in particular the US, can provide the basis for further bolder political actions by those forces in Taiwan that seek formal independence, which challenges China directly. Therefore, it would be useful to examine the Taiwan independence movement and how this affects China's wider relations with the US.

Chronologically, the Taiwan independence movement roughly coincided with the end of the Cold War; it partly resulted from the democratisation of Taiwan's domestic politics, associated with a new generation of political leaders such as Lee Teng-hui and Chen Shui-bian. For example, in Taiwan's Legislative Yuan elections in December 1989, independence for the first time became an issue. Another milestone was the October 1991, when the Democratic Progressive Party (DPP) came to prominence in Taiwanese politics and adopted a resolution calling for an independent Republic of Taiwan, running counter to China's goal of reunification. During the mid-1990s, it must be noted that Kuomintang leader Lee Teng-hui's use of "flexible diplomacy" and "dollar diplomacy" to gain diplomatic status for Taiwan in the international system was particularly dangerous in Chinese eyes. Notwithstanding its ambiguity, the Taiwanese independence movement represented by Lee during his reign was regarded as a problem for China's security policymakers. Lee Teng-hui's overtures to the US in the mid-1990s – epitomised by his unofficial visit to his *alma mater*, Cornell University, with US permission in 1995 – represented a clear danger to China. On the whole, Beijing perceived that the US had implicitly encouraged this move. Lee's visit to America was seen as an "inevitable move on the US strategic chessboard"; it was part of the US strategy to cope with a rising China in the post-Cold War era.[41] In short, even a private visit by the Taiwanese president to America was perceived by the Chinese as an acute security concern. The point is that Lee's visit appeared to signify a certain degree of acceptance and recognition of Taiwan by the US, and Beijing was worried that the rest of the world may eventually follow suit. In other words, the US is regarded by China as having a role in abetting the advocates of Taiwan independence in the 1990s.

Essentially, the legalisation of the advocacy of Taiwan independence has since been interpreted by Beijing as a political security threat. When Lee Teng-hui contested in the first-ever direct presidential elections in 1996, Beijing resorted to verbal attacks on him as well as a military show of force. The Third Taiwan Strait Crisis vindicated China's goals of undermining the Taiwan independence movement and achieving reunification with Taiwan and it was evident that China came quite close to confronting the US directly on this occasion. Overall, the US military show of force in the Taiwan Strait in 1996 indicated that China needs to gauge the level of support for Taiwan, which may include some of the advocates of Taiwan independence.

Another stiff challenge for China came when the US was asked to support Taiwan's right to national self-determination. The Taiwan Solidarity Union (TSU) – the most ardent advocates of Taiwan independence – had called upon the lone superpower to back then – DPP president Chen Shui-bian's policies.[42] Essentially, Chen announced that the National Unification Council (NUC) and the National Unification Guidelines had "ceased to function" and "cease to apply", respectively but argued that they symbolised Taipei's own concept of reunification, as opposed to outright independence. Nonetheless, from China's perspective, Chen's move was seen as an attempt to deceive Taiwan's public and international opinion; Beijing's view was that Taiwan actually wanted to pursue *de jure* independence under the framework of Chen's constitutional reform plans.[43] The point is that the US is often associated with the issue of Taiwan independence in some manner from China's perspective.

From a historical perspective, China is unlikely to relent in its incessant pressure on Taiwan as the theoretical ambiguity of Taiwan's independence can equally likely be manipulated by hardliners in Washington or the more radical elements within Taiwanese politics. In this vein, China has rejected any comparison between the reunification with Taiwan with German or Korean reunification, arguing that both the two Germanys and the two Koreas had existed or are still existing as independent and sovereign states. In Chinese eyes, Taiwan has never existed as an independent and sovereign state hence any form of US support for this is totally unnecessary and only serves to create tensions in Sino-US relations. In other words, from China's perspective, Taiwan must be denied sovereignty at all costs, even if this means further damaging its relations with the US.

Conclusion

The US engages in strategic competition with China at both the global and regional levels, and Taiwan is a part of this contest that is being played out. In East Asia, Sino-US strategic competition, covering the realms of military, politics and economics, is most evident in Taiwan. Here, both great powers continue to have different interests despite the US cessation of formal ties with the island republic.

One of China's national goals is to achieve reunification with Taiwan. China sees the lone superpower as a stumbling obstacle in its aim of achieving reunification with Taiwan.

For the US, sustaining Taiwan ties in with its goal of maintaining East Asian stability, ensuring a conducive trading environment in the region, countering the rise of China, and promoting liberal democracy. The key point is that Taiwan remains vital to US security interests in the post-Cold War era where China is regarded as a credible strategic competitor. To ensure pre-eminence in East Asia as well as in the world, the US must not allow Taiwan to fall under China's control. The fact that Taiwan remains under the US sphere of influence and has not been absorbed by China means that Chinese power in East Asia has been checked to a certain degree. The Taiwan issue is therefore relevant to academic and policy discussions on China's ascendancy. From Taiwan's perspective, a worse-case scenario would be the US dropping its interest in itself, leaving Chinese power unchecked, possibly to the detriment of the island republic's national interest.

Currently, the US's unofficial support for Taiwan continues to sustain the island republic. In particular, continuing military commitment to Taiwan is very important as this is seen as a way to deter any attempt by China to achieve reunification with Taiwan by coercion. Furthermore, Taiwan's democratic credentials fit in with the US's promotion of liberal values worldwide and constitute a political challenge to China. In this sense, Taiwan – a Chinese democracy – occupies a central place in the ideological battle between China and the US. Moreover, the democratisation of Taiwan will increase the island republic's chance of regaining formal status in the international system in the future, although the US has not been a major factor in this issue yet.

From the perspective of Asian security, the Taiwan issue remains a flashpoint that could spark a great power conflict. More specifically, a Chinese use of force against Taiwan is likely to cause a major international crisis and American military intervention may follow. Most critical of all, such an unstable political environment will have catastrophic consequences for China's economic modernisation drive, thereby hindering Beijing's drive to truly global power status in the twenty-first century. Therefore, it is fair to say that only a greater convergence of great power interests can resolve the Taiwan issue totally. From Taiwan's viewpoint, although no longer formally allied to the US, its first strategic option is to maintain the lone superpower's interest on the island republic. The second pertains to gaining more support from the US on the basis of the island republic's democratic credentials. By continuing to be at the centre of the strategic competition between the US and China, Taiwan can, ironically, enhance its own security. Importantly, these two great powers also confront each other in relation to Japan, which is the subject of the next chapter.

5 The US and Japan

This chapter analyses, primarily from China's perspective, the role of Japan in relation to Sino-US strategic competition. In essence, Japan is the cornerstone of US East Asian strategy. The US–Japanese alliance is also bolstered by shared values as both states espoused liberal norms which are largely incompatible with China's political system. On the economic front, Japanese–US economic clout poses a challenge to China. Finally, the US has a certain degree of influence over the issue of Japan's re-emergence and its desire to play a wider role in the international system. We begin by looking at the importance of Japan to US East Asian strategy.

US East Asian strategy and Japan

In the arena of China's strategic competition with the US, Japan plays an important role, in particular in East Asia. For the purpose of our analysis, the important fact is that Japan has been a vital component of the US East Asian strategy since the Second World War. Under this strategy, the US assumed responsibility in preserving stability in East Asia through a series of bilateral alliances with anti-communist states in the region. The 1952 Mutual Security Treaty that Japan signed with the US is still intact, despite changes resulting from the end of the Cold War. Up to now, Japan is the US's most important ally in the Asia-Pacific region with South Korea, Australia, the Philippines and Thailand making up the quintet. The general US thinking is that its alliances are "force multipliers": through multinational co-operation and co-ordination, the sum of collection action will always be greater than if the US acts alone.[1] Moreover, underpinning this thinking is the notion that both the US and its Asian partners will benefit from the collective security provided by strong alliances.[2] The general conclusion is that although the US and its our allies and partners may sometimes disagree on specific issues, they act based upon mutual respect and in a manner that continues to strengthen an international order that benefits all other international actors.

At a wider level, it must be acknowledged that the US's alliance with Japan is important to the lone superpower's task to ensure stability in East Asia. In other words, Japanese support for the US will have a certain degree of impact on the effectiveness of American strategy in the East Asia. During the Cold War, US strategy in East Asia had focused on the Soviet Union as the main antagonist while keeping a close eye on Communist China. In the post-Cold War era, the US maintains the military security of its traditional Asian allies such as Japan and South Korea against challenges from North Korea and a rising China. Furthermore, the US–Japanese alliance is bolstered by shared values. In comparison to other US allies such as South Korea, it must be noted that Japan made the transition to democracy relatively early. After defeat in the Second World War, the country's new Constitution was drafted largely by American lawyers, which eventually led to the institution of democracy in Japan. Given their shared values today, it is natural that Tokyo and Washington would work together – both consulting and co-operating – to maintain peace and prevent conflict in East Asia.

Essentially, Japanese support strengthens the military presence of the US in East Asia. From China's perspective, the general conclusion is that the US–Japanese alliance has a goal of ensuring US preponderance in East Asia. In general, US–Japanese military collaboration is viewed in a negative light by China. A key worry for China is the possibility of enhanced US–Japanese military collaboration in the current era. This is to a certain extent represented by the Theatre Missile Defence (TMD) system that the US is developing with Japan in East Asia. The TMD is designed to protect Japanese targets from the threat of regional missile attacks, more specifically from North Korea. Arguably, North Korea's possession of missiles that can reach Japan has persuaded some Japanese that their country should rely less on the US – and more on itself – for security. To a certain extent, the threat of missile attacks from North Korea has provided the rationale for Japan to step up its military collaboration with the US.[3] For instance, Japan has come to the conclusion that a traditional ban on arms exports will no longer apply in areas like anti-missile defence.[4] From China's perspective, the North Korean threat is viewed differently (see Chapter 6) so US–Japan TMD collaboration is deemed unnecessary. In this vein, China has even argued that the transfer of US missile technology to Japan is a clear violation of the Non-Proliferation Treaty (NPT), which it is generally regarded as crucial to strategic stability in East Asia. At the same time, it must be noted that the Chinese People's Liberation Army's (PLA) crash programme to develop land-attack cruise missiles is of some concern to Japan and the US, as no TMD system is effective against such missiles. In this sense, it can be argued that Japan should consider acquiring a pre-emptive strike capability against missile bases in an enemy country although this would remind China of the current US emphasis on pre-emption in the use of force in international relations. Tied in with these Chinese concerns is Japan's participation in the US-instigated Proliferation Security Initiative (PSI), which is aimed at stemming the flow of weapons of mass destruction and support for further missile defence co-operation with the US in general. In reality, any increased US–Japan military collaboration increases China's fears that both countries would be able to strengthen their positions against itself.

Specifically, on the North Korean issue, Japan is closely aligned with the US to contain the nuclear threat posed by the Communist state. For instance, Japan – along with the US and South Korea – was concerned about North Korea's satellite launch in April 2009: the consternation was because the rocket was a Taepodong-2 and that the launch could be a trial run of technology that could be used to launch an intercontinental ballistic missile in future. Importantly, Japan also argues that the satellite launch constitutes a violation of UN Security Council resolution 1718 passed in the aftermath of North Korea's first nuclear test in October 2006. In contrast, China as well as Russia had a slightly different interpretation of the actions undertaken by North Korea. The point is that Japan takes a tougher stance on the North Korean issue, which is generally in line with US policies on this issue. After North Korea conducted its second nuclear test in May 2009, Japan played a role in pushing for UN Security Council Resolution 1874 as well as imposing tougher unilateral sanctions against North Korea. Under these measures, North Korea was placed under even harsher financial restrictions than had been imposed by the UN earlier, most notably the monitoring and potential inspection of its ships and aircraft suspected of carrying illicit weapons related to its missile nuclear weapons development programme.

Overall, from Japan's perspective, the US still provides a military commitment to deter the threat posed by a North Korea with nuclear ambition as well as a rising China in the post-Cold War era. For example, The *Defence of Japan 2010* noted China's increasing presence in the international system and the lack of transparency in China's strategic intentions in relation to "disclosing specific information pertaining to its defence policies and military capabilities."[5] Basically, Japan shares with the US the view that increasing military power will extend China's influence in regional affairs and will have an impact on its own security in the long run. From the US's perspective, the role of its marines in the Japanese territory of Okinawa remains indispensable in view of China's increasing military power. The continuation of this policy attests to the importance of deterrence provided by the US military forces in Japan. From Japan's viewpoint, it could exploit the benefits of US protection while limiting itself from risks over US unilateralism and adventurism simultaneously; the US is required to counter the rise of China and other regional threats such as North Korea but Japan also acknowledges the need to seize the opportunities, especially economic ones, offered by China's rise simultaneously.[6] In other words, Japan will continue to enjoy the benefits of US protection but it will also explore ways to engage effectively with a rising China.

From China's perspective, it's main goal is to undermine the US East Asian strategy and therefore it will exploit any cracks within the US–Japanese alliance when they arise. For the purpose of our analysis, it is helpful to compare the different perceptions of the US–Japanese alliance by the two allies, which can be exploited by China. During the Cold War, there were generally fewer differences between the US and Japan because there was a clear-cut distinction between the protector and the protected. In the post-Cold War era, questions on how long the US can prop up an old alliance with Japan without a common Soviet threat that created the alliance in the first instance have been repeatedly asked. The general point is that the US can no longer anticipate the degree of diplomatic compliance that Japan exhibited during the Cold War as the international system underwent a major change after the Soviet collapse.[7] In the current era, whereas the American approach to the US–Japanese alliance is more global and highlights the importance of the use of force to achieve certain national objectives, the Japanese stance focuses much more on the Asian region and stresses the non-military instruments of policy. From the US perspective, it wants to work with Japan to continue forging a leading role in regional and global affairs based on common interests, common values, as well as close defence and diplomatic co-operation; the idea is that the US–Japanese alliance would make contributions to the broader stability of the region over the longer term.[8]

Currently, several issues have been raised on the US–Japan alliance. It is a well-known fact that Americans resent Japan as an economic threat and unfair trader; at the same time, Japan's leaders have also faced increasing domestic pressures to stand up to the US on trade matters, given that the Soviet military threat has disappeared and the need for a strong alliance with Washington has diminished accordingly. Another point of contention between the US and Japan is the cost sharing of the defence burden. Basically, the US has been urging Japan to take on a bigger share of the costs, given that Japan had directly benefited from the military protection offered by the US over the years. Recently, the planned move of Futenma Air Station out of Okinawa was an issue between the two allies; the move was subsequently aborted as operational needs dictate any relocation of the military base should be within Okinawa. In reality, Okinawa is a better geographic location for the US forces to respond to emergencies in East Asia, compared with Hawaii or Guam, so this arguably led the eventual decision. For the purpose of our analysis, the point is that China would aim to exploit any tensions between the two partners, the US and Japan. At the same time, in comparison with other US allies in Asia, Japan is more closely linked to the US. Therefore, it is much harder for China to make inroads on the US–Japanese front, compared with say the US–South Korea one (see Chapter 6).

Expansion of the US–Japanese alliance

Given that the US's alliance with Japan is important to the formulation of Chinese strategic thinking, the main concern for China is the possible expansion of the US–Japanese security pact. The expansion can be seen in operational and geographical terms. Basically, an expansion allows for the US to impose a more vigorous strategy in East Asia, which in turn strengthens the US's presence in this region. One important question is, to what extent does this expansion receives support from Japan, who is traditionally a regional rival to China. For over a decade, Japan's security thinking and posture have been changing, as discussed earlier. While Japan has moved incrementally toward a more realistic security strategy, this has largely been an *ad hoc* process in which Tokyo responds to external events. Eventually, though, intellectual debate in Japan caught up with realities of the strategic landscape in Asia: Tokyo came up with a clearer vision for the future and its national security strategy.[9] In particular, Japan began to acknowledge the need for an integrated security strategy that is more flexible and outward looking than the self-defence approach that prevailed throughout the Cold War, which entails bolstering the credibility of the Japan–US alliance and continuing to rely on extended deterrence provided by the US. The calls for Japan to acquire effective ballistic missile defence systems in co-operation with the US – mainly with North Korea in mind – has come under China's scrutiny, as noted earlier.

More generally, the consensus in democratic Japan is that Tokyo must continually upgrade arrangements for co-operation with the US to deal with new types of security situation in the post-Cold War era as well as to enhance the reliability of Japan–US co-operation at the operational levels. In practical terms, this means Japan must relax its ban on arms exports, at least to the US. Doing so will ensure that Japan can fully participate in the development and deployment of an anti-ballistic missile system, as noted earlier. A similar logic also guides Japanese strategic thinking with the notion of "preventing the emergence of threats by improving the international security environment": in practical terms, the Araki report calls for the "Multifunctional Flexible Defense Force concept" that would allow the Self-Defense Forces (SDF) to become more versatile and to take on a wider range of functions, adding that structural reforms in decision-making and information management are needed to bring the integrated security strategy into being.[10] Overall, the Araki Report can be seen as Japan's first step towards a national security strategy, which mirrors the manner in which its security guarantor, the US, systematically formulates its strategies.

It is also worth noting that the National Defense Programme Guidelines (NDGP) repeat the two security policy objectives identified by the Araki Commission, to some degree, confirming the shift toward a regional and international emphasis, and endorses the multifunctional, flexible approach explained in the Araki report.[11] The idea is that Japan will aim to decide on a case-by-case basis whether to further co-operate with the US on arms development and production as well as to export defensive equipment to countries in support of their efforts to fight emerging threats such as terrorism or piracy. It is evident that an analysis of Japan's defence strategy reveals these main points: increased efforts to co-operate with the US on a missile defence system, the specific identification of China and North Korea's as potential threats to Japanese security, and increased anti-terrorism efforts.[12] Over the years, it is clear that Japan's focus has gradually shifted from defending against a possible Russian invasion to guarding the country from possible North Korean or Chinese threats. As part of a new military doctrine, Tokyo has even defined its role in the event of a conflict on the Korean Peninsula, called Operational Plan 5055, whereby Japanese forces would undertake the evacuation of civilians and conduct search and rescue missions for downed US and South Korean pilots.[13] At the same time, Japan's Maritime Self-Defense Forces (MSDF) would safeguard a sea route from the Korean Peninsula to Japan to keep a supply line open; furthermore, the MSDF would also patrol coastal areas adjacent to nuclear facilities in anticipation of possible North Korean commando attacks. Such a plan is natural in the sense that North Korean commandos are expected to operate deeply behind enemy lines in order to disrupt supply lines and disable command structures; given that Japan serves as an important base for US forces, it is likely that North Korean special forces would strike Japan if needed, so the Operational Plan 5055 is actually a realistic countermeasure. The key point is that Japan remains a vital component of US military strategy in East Asia, and in particular if a crisis ensues on the Korean peninsula.

At the same time, one major problem is that any discussion of realignment of US forces and new missions or responsibilities for Japan requires a hard look at Article 6 of the US–Japan Security Treaty, which stipulates that the purpose of US forces stationed in Japan is to defend Japan as well as to maintain stability in East Asia. From China's viewpoint, it has consistently asked Japan not to expand or broaden the scope of the security treaty with the US on grounds that it might complicate the situation in East Asia. From the US perspective, more effective input from Japan on bilateral security co-operation will be welcomed. For instance, despite its effort to allow for greater intelligence sharing with Japan, it has been noted that the US is frustrated by "the looseness of Japan's secrecy laws and lack of a uniform classification of secrets and security clearances"; hence, it can be argued that a comprehensive overhaul of Japanese secrecy laws can only engender confidence in the US that Japan could be brought into the pipeline of information sharing, on a par with allies such as Great Britain and Australia.[14] From China's perspective, an US–Japanese alliance reaching the level of closeness of the US–UK "special relationship" is undesirable as this will strengthen the US's position in East Asia, which in turn helps ensure US pre-eminence at a global level. At the same time, Japan has in principle rejected the US–British "special relationship" as a model for its alliance with the US, which would include expanding its security responsibilities in Asia. The point is that an expanded role for Japan in East Asia will change the strategic contours of Sino-US relations to some degree. In reality, what China really fears is that Japan might join forces with the US to contain itself in a more explicit manner.

From the Japanese perspective, there are constitutional concerns on the scope of the alliance with the US. Military activity in a situation that does not involve an attack on Japan could technically violate Article 9 of its Constitution. In Article 9, Japan formally renounces war as a sovereign right and bans the settlement of international disputes through the use of force. In this vein, for instance, allowing the US to move I-Corps headquarters to Japan would entangle Japan in activities well beyond the scope of national defence – reaching perhaps as far as the Middle East – and violate the Japanese Constitution. Critics from the left in Japan would argue that it signalled the abandonment of the pacifist Constitution and would make it easier for the government to send the Self-Defence Forces (SDF) overseas. Such debates within Japan are of relevance to China because it will have an impact on the evolution of Japan's alliance with the US. Given that Japan is a democratic country, where foreign policy debates are evident, it must be pointed out that the NDPG guidelines reflect bureaucratic compromises to a large extent and do not effectively provide an overarching guiding philosophy.

Certainly, from the viewpoint of both partners in the US–Japan alliance, there are arguments that Japan must move to loosen its restrictions on collective self-defence in a bid to strengthen this alliance. Following this line of reasoning implies that the Japanese ban on collective self-defence represents an obstacle to the effective functioning of the US–Japanese alliance. In effect, this relates to the fundamental question for both Tokyo and Washington as they seek to expand combined operations in missile defence, the maintenance of air superiority, maritime security and strike operations. One might argue that the Japanese ban on collective self-defence effectively means that Japan is "largely incapable of providing assistance legally to the US and other security partners, even in the dire event of a missile attack against the American or Japanese homelands".[15] At the same time, recent developments on the scope of the US–Japanese alliance are generally in line with the US's interests. On the whole, Japan now seems more willing to take on a bigger role to counter new security threats. The bi-annual Security Consultative Committee (SCC) meeting between the two allies are vital as Washington and Tokyo continue efforts to seek ways to modernise their alliance. Critically, both the US and Japan agree that interdependence and the proliferation of weapons of mass destruction (WMD) have erased old distinctions among national, regional and global security; they have also jointly articulated a list of regional and global strategic concerns, including military modernisation efforts within the region.[16]

Taiwan and the East China Sea

One specific concern for China on the US–Japanese alliance is how it relates to the Taiwan issue. From China's perspective, the geographical scope of the US–Japanese alliance is important; in particular, the question is whether the term "Far East" stated in the Japan–US Mutual Security Treaty includes the Taiwan Strait. This represents a problem as China harbours the long-term goal of achieving reunification with Taiwan while the US maintains an unofficial commitment to Taiwan's security through the Taiwan Relations Act (TRA), as discussed in the previous chapter. The crux of the matter is that, for China, Japan is a factor in the Taiwan issue because of its alliance with the US. In other words, the scope of the US–Japanese alliance and its possible expansion do include discussions on the Taiwan Strait. It is important to note that that Japan–US Security Consultative Committee (SCC) statements do not specifically call for co-operation between America and the Japanese Self-Defence Force (SDF) in the case of a military conflict in Taiwan Strait but they do hint at the US's intention to lay the ground for such co-operation if tensions increased there. From China's perspective, the argument is that the US and Japan must not include Taiwan under the scope of their military alliance, on the basis that inclusion of the island would breach the terms of a bilateral framework. Such Chinese concerns over the link between the US–Japanese alliance and the Taiwan issue are not new. Earlier, the

Guidelines for Japan–US Defence Co-operation in 1997 had already enlarged the scope of their joint defence and at that time, China expressed concerns that Japan's definition of the "peripheral state of affairs" actually included the Taiwan Strait.[17]

However, it must be stressed that on the issue of Taiwan, Japan is officially recognised as a supporter of China. Like the US, Japan broke off diplomatic relations with Taiwan in 1972 in favour of China and has since formally committed itself to a one-China policy. Furthermore, compared with the US, Japan is generally less willing to offer direct support to Taiwan in the face of Chinese intimidation. For example, Japan's reactions to China conducting large-scale military exercises during the run-up to the Taiwanese presidential elections in March 1996 were muted, merely calling for self-restraint on the part of Beijing. To a certain extent, this stands in contrast to the US's forceful response where the Seventh Fleet was put on high alert in East Asia. In general, it must be said that Japan's policy on the Taiwan issue is still in line with China's attempt to isolate Taipei in the international system. Nonetheless, the fact is that Japan remains a key ally of the US and could play a role in helping its security guarantor in the event of a Taiwan Strait crisis. Overall, the key point is that any expansion of the geographical scope of the US–Japanese security treaty is deemed as negative in terms of China's national interest.

Furthermore, Japan is relevant to the Taiwan issue because of its historical links with Taiwan. Japan was the colonial power in Taiwan from 1895 to 1945 and was resulted from China losing the First Sino-Japanese War in 1894–1895. Accordingly, Japan has traditionally taken a keen interest in Taiwanese affairs. Recently, for instance, Japan's assessment of the Taiwan Strait situation included the acknowledgement that the military balance between China and Taiwan has changed to the advantage of China; specifically, it was noted that China outnumbered Taiwan in terms of advanced fighters in 2009.[18] In other words, like the US, Japan takes an interest in the balance of power between China and Taiwan. Moreover, Japan has pointed out in relation to China's military modernisation, particular priority is given to the Taiwan issue "as an issue of national sovereignty and territorial integrity" and a specific aim is to "acquire the capability to deter Taiwan from seeking independence."[19] At the same time, it must be stated that in general, Japanese security planners have up till now chosen to remain ambiguous on the Taiwan issue in the event of a crisis, largely with the aim of avoiding upsetting China.

From China's perspective, apart from the issue of Taiwan, the geographical scope of the US–Japanese alliance is also important in relation to the East China Sea. Basically, China is worried that the US may get involved in its bilateral disputes with Japan in the East China Sea. From China's perspective, the crux of the matter is the degree of US support to Japanese causes in general. For the purpose of our analysis, the prime case is China asking the US not to recognise sovereignty claims made by Japan over the Diaoyu Islands/Senkaku Islands. The Islands lie just 166 km northeast of Taiwan and are situated halfway between Taiwan and Japan's Okinawa. Basically, China sees the loss of the Diaoyu

Islands as a result of past Japanese aggression, for it was forced to cede the territory of Taiwan, which then included the Diaoyu Islands, to Japan under the terms of the Treaty of Shimoneseki in 1895.

After Japan was defeated in the Second World War, the Diaoyu Islands were under the trusteeship of the US during the signing of the 1951 San Francisco Treaty between Japan and the Allies; subsequently, the US handed those islands back to Japan via the 1971 Okinawa Treaty.[20] The Chinese argument is that in 1951, Japan and the US had illegally signed a treaty in San Francisco in its absence, despite the fact that China was one of the victorious countries in the Second World War; specifically, it was pointed out that Article Three of the San Francisco Treaty incorrectly assigned the Diaoyu Islands occupied by Japan to the Ryukyu Zone which was then under US control.[21] Hence, a key issue is whether the US–Japan Security Treaty covers the Diaoyu Islands/Senkaku Islands. The US's basic position is that, since the reversion of Okinawa to Japan in 1972, the Diaoyu/Senkaku Islands have been under the administrative control of Japan; accordingly, the US–Japan Security Treaty is applicable to all territories that fall under Japan's administrative control. From China's perspective, the contest with Japan over the sovereignty of the Diaoyu/Senkaku Islands continues and Japan's alliance with the US has complicated this bilateral dispute.

Furthermore, at stake in China's dispute with Japan over sovereignty of the Diaoyu/Senkaku Islands are the potential economic resources, including fishing rights and energy sources in the surrounding areas. It has been argued that the really important issue is the legal jurisdiction over about 21,645 square kilometres of continental shelf that is believed to hold up to 100 billion barrels of oil. China requires energy resources to pursue economic modernisation and is therefore seeking to discover its own offshore oil with the aim of replacing imports, primarily from the Middle East. This is also the case with energy-poor Japan, which has already granted exploring rights in the East China Sea to some of its companies. In other words, energy competition is endemic between China and Japan, two major economic nations in Asia with huge needs for energy resources. On a more optimistic note, these two Asian great powers have in principle reached an agreement to joint gas development in the East China Sea as both sides also realise that they need to manage their differences over economic competition issues in the long run.

As regional powers, it is quite natural that both China and Japan will engage in competition and the ideal situation for Beijing is one which bilateral territorial disputes issues can be resolved with Japan alone, without the involvement of other powers, especially a superpower. It is quite clear that in general, China prefers to deal with Japan on a bilateral basis on any given bilateral issue. From China's viewpoint, a situation whereby other great powers, especially the lone superpower, support Japan's position on certain Sino-Japanese issues represents a challenge to its national interest. In the final analysis, the fact is that the strengthening of the US–Japan Defense Guidelines in 1997 conspicuously fails to define the geographic boundaries within which events could lead to joint US–Japan military operations. At the same time, from China's perspective, such ambiguities offer both partners in the US–Japanese alliance certain geographical latitude in the event of a security crisis in East Asia and this could be damaging to China's national interests.

The US and Japan's wider role

One of the important consequences of the US–Japanese alliance is that it helps Japan gain a bigger role in the international system. The end of the Cold War unravelled the Yoshida doctrine of the 1950s, which was generally based on higher economic growth and passivity in international affairs. After the collapse of the Soviet Union, the first post-Cold War international crisis – the 1990–1991 Persian Gulf War – revealed the diplomatic risks and reputational costs of Japan's pacifism. In addition, the North Korean threat convinced Japan that it should pursue a more active foreign policy as its own security was directly at stake. The point is, certain challenges in the post-Cold War era resulted in Japan embracing greater bilateral defence collaboration with the US as well as participating in international peacekeeping operations.

To a certain extent, the assertiveness of Japan was in part assisted by the events of September 11, 2001 when transnational terrorism became a prominent issue in international security matters. As the self-proclaimed guarantor of international security, the US has naturally urged its allies in Western Europe as well as Japan to play an active role in the war on terrorism. Moreover, the threat of transnational terrorism also led to a shift on the part of Japan towards a wider conception of national security, which had hitherto been limited to homeland defence: Japan now wants to engage actively to improve the international security environment, with US encouragement. For instance, the Japanese's Maritime Self-Defense Forces' (MSDF) eight-year (1992–2010) refuelling mission in the Indian Ocean backed the US-led mission in Afghanistan. In many ways, the mission was emblematic of Japan's wider real influence in international affairs. Subsequently, Japan announced a five-year US$5 billion aid package for Afghanistan including funds for education, infrastructure and vocational training for former Taleban soldiers. This move was actively encouraged by the US as the lone superpower wants to share the burdens of international security with its allies. Overall, from China's viewpoint, Japan's general conformity with the US global strategy portends a wider role for Japan in the international system in the year ahead.

Furthermore, domestically, there is the refocus in Japanese national security agenda, as noted earlier. Essentially, the National Defence Programme Guidelines (NDPG) introduced major policy shifts, such as a more active role for the Self-Defence Force (SDF) in international peacekeeping activities. Legislative measures have been undertaken to refine the categorisation of such activities under SDF duties, implying that Japan is ready to upgrade such overseas operations to a principal duty of the SDF. Specifically, during the Koizumi administration, a seven-point programme on how to respond to the new international environment came up with new measures such as allowing the SDF to provide logistical support to the US military in emergencies, strengthening security checks at key facilities in Japan, dispatching Japanese troops to gather information, stepping up immigration controls, giving humanitarian and economic aid to affected states, assisting refugees fleeing areas that might be affected by US war on terror as well as working with other states to stabilise the international economic system.[22] Some of these measures were applied in the conflicts in Afghanistan and Iraq as well as in relation to the North Korean nuclear issue. The point is that the Koizumi administration has paved the way for Japan to become more assertive in the international arena, which must heighten China's concerns.

In essence, the tendency of a Japanese government moving towards a tighter relationship with the US is vital to Japan's national security interests. From this tendency, Japan may want to push its alliance with the US, primarily one with a regional focus, towards one that is more global in nature. Domestically, regional developments such as the first North Korean nuclear crisis in 1993–1994 had already moved the Japanese public to accepting a more expanded role for the SDF. Further actions undertaken by North Korea – the Taepodong missile launch in 1998 into the Sea of Japan as well as its two nuclear tests in 2006 and 2009 – strengthened the case for Japan to become more active in the international arena. At the same time, the Japanese conception of self-defence moving from a domestic focus to a more global one should not constitute a major surprise to China. The key question for China is to what extent the re-emergence of Japan can be assisted by its strategic competitor, the US. This question has implications for China, given the traditional animosity between the two great Asian powers.

Overall, a Chinese concern is that, in the long term, the US–Japanese alliance will assist Japan in playing a wider role in international affairs. Although Japan may be unacceptable as a political leader in Asia, primarily due to its actions during the Second World War, it must be pointed out that the burden of its imperialist past tends to weigh much less heavily at the global level. Nowadays, with the efficacy of the use of force in international relations gradually declining, it appears that an economically strong Japan will emerge as a country with more political clout in the international arena and this will adversely affect China's security interests. For example, responding to calls for greater international responsibilities, Japan had earlier tried taken a more proactive role in places such as Cambodia in the early 1990s, which triggered a largely negative response in China. In general, China remains sceptical and apprehensive about Japanese participation in these multilateral peacekeeping efforts because it fears the possibility of the Japanese military's growing role in the global arena. At a wider level, military involvement in global crises will help erode Japan's isolationism and induce Japan to become more involved in any multilateral security policymaking, thereby increasing the country's influence in the international arena.

Beyond Asia, the wider US–Japanese relationship also affects Japan's chances of becoming a permanent member of the United Nations (UN) Security Council and this has elicited concerns from China. After all, the UN has long been a pillar of Japan's national security strategy, along with self-defence and its alliance with the US. Today the question of UN reform, triggered to a certain extent by disagreement about the invasion of Iraq in 2003, has given Japan a chance to push further for a seat on the Security Council. A main justification for this push is based on the fact that Japan contributes to about 20 per cent of the UN budget. Along with Brazil, Germany and India, Japan had unveiled a proposal to expand the Security Council by six permanent member and four non-permanent member seats.[23] These four countries, the G4, want to claim four of the six permanent member seats, with the other two going to African nations. In addition, the G4 states have also promised to support each other's bid for a permanent seat. In fact, Japan is also prepared to drop its demand for a veto for 15 years, notwithstanding the fact that it had previously complained that a permanent seat without a veto will not be a satisfactory outcome. Apparently, Japan felt that forming an alliance with other G4 states would garner additional international support and perhaps fend off some of its critics. Although the entire plan was subsequently derailed when it encountered opposition from most states, including the US, the key point is that such developments have come under China's scrutiny. From Beijing's perspective, it will block Japan in every possible way over the Security Council membership issue.

The basic conclusion from this issue is that Japan has the support of the US in gaining a permanent membership in the Security Council – but without veto power. The lesson for Japan is that it needs to work more closely with the US on this issue. From China's perspective, is it fortunate that reforming the UN Security Council ranks rather low among the US's priorities. Nonetheless, there is still a degree of US backing for Japan, and some US officials have even called on China to reconsider opposing Japan's claim. Ultimately, the permanent five (P5) members of the Security Council have the final say over any changes to the current set-up, and China would not agree to any proposal that gives Japan a permanent seat. At a wider level, the fundamental obstacle to UN Security Council membership – the deep and bitter antagonism between P5 members and G4 aspirants – should remain for some time, none more obvious than in the case of Sino-Japanese antagonism. From the Chinese perspective, granting the seat to Japan will enhance Japan's standing in the world.

If Japan plays a greater role in international affairs, it is generally not in China's strategic interests. Accordingly, a common Chinese strategy is to emphasise Tokyo's historical record of territorial aggrandisement, often comparing this with Germany's Nazi past. From China's perspective, Japan must seriously examine itself over its wartime actions before it can gain the trust of Asia and the world. This is in spite of the fact that Japan is not surrounded by weak neighbours, as was the case in the 1930s. For instance, countries such as South Korea and Taiwan are militarily stronger than they were in the interwar years. More importantly, the US is much more directly involved in East Asian affairs, unlike in the 1930s when it pursued an isolationist policy. Nevertheless, given Japan's encroachment of China's sovereignty in the past, Beijing remains wary of Tokyo's long term ambitions and has therefore urged its Asian neighbours to stay vigilant against Japan.

US–Japanese economic dominance

Another component of the US–Japanese alliance relates to the economic realm, which has received less analysis in general in analysing China's security agenda. From the Chinese perception, the US–Japanese alliance partly provides the basis for both Washington and Tokyo to sustain their influence in the international economic system. Economic security is vital to China's long-term goals, as already noted earlier. Today, globalisation of the world economy has further highlighted the need for US economic leadership and this often happens alongside Japanese assistance. Japan is one of the major players in international economic, financial and monetary institutions. Although Japan may encounter continuing difficulties in playing a bigger political-military leadership role globally, it finds it easier to expand its role in international economic organisations. In this aspect, Japan can actually help China further its economic security because Tokyo has a certain level of influence in such organisations. Furthermore, Japan is a big contributor to aid programmes in international system, as exemplified by its official development assistance (ODA) programme.

To China's advantage, the most relevant point is that there are often differences between Japanese and US policies when it comes to economic matters. For example, China can often count more on Tokyo's support to protect or further its interests in organisations such as the International Monetary Fund (IMF), the World Bank and the World Trade Organisation (WTO). China's partial dependence on Japanese clout in international economic organisations is further reinforced by the relative position of the two countries in regional banking organisations. China is the main recipient of loans from the Asian Development Bank (ADB) where Japan dominates. While the US remains the dominant force in the World Bank and has on certain occasions tried to cut off cheap loans to China, Japan's presence is now, officially at least, on a par with America's. This means that at times, Japan might maintain a fairly high level of funding to China, regardless of any contrary US policy towards China. In this sense, Japan can serve as a sort of balance against US dominance in international financial institutions; this is also in line with China's economic diversification strategy.

An instructive case is the imposition of sanctions on China following the 1989 Tiananmen event. In the aftermath, the US led a group of Western countries and Japan in imposing economic sanctions on China. Eventually, in return for China's tacit co-operation in the first Gulf War, the US eventually worked to end the moratorium on further World Bank loans to China. It is worth noting that Japan was one of the first nations to restore normal economic ties with China. On the whole, it must be said that China has been rather successful in using foreign actors to serve its own development needs and Japanese government assistance to build China's infrastructure in the recent past is an example.

In terms of economic strategy, global trends towards regional trading blocs, with countries becoming more interested in the economic activities of their particular regions rather than the world as a whole, will affect Sino-Japanese relations to some extent. In the light of such trends, China might see mutual dependence and co-operation with Japan as increasingly important for its national interests if regional trade blocs such as North American Free Trade Area (NAFTA) and the European Union (EU) become more important in the international economic system. While regional trading blocs may or may not become the most important form of economic activity in the years to come, there is no doubt that Chinese economic security strategists still need to take this possibility seriously. The fact is that both the Chinese and Japanese economies rely on the Asian economy, and this regional economy in turn needs co-operation between China and Japan.

Nonetheless, over the longer term, China and Japan are likely to engage in economic competition. From Japan's perspective, the growing economic importance of Asia followed a surge in private-sector investment into the region, provoked by the rising yen since the 1980s. This emerging Asianism was also sparked off by Japan's lessening economic dependence on the US and its growing ties with East Asia in general. In this vein, China is concerned that a series of economic policies, including the careful deployment of foreign direct investment and official development assistance (ODA), has given shape to a strategy that seeks to lay the basis for a soft region-wide integration of economies under Japanese leadership.[24] For instance, Japanese firms have been successful at creating production and distribution networks linking Asian economies and the consolidation of Japanese corporations in other East Asian economies.

In general, Japanese economic dominance in East Asia is perceived by most Chinese leaders as an undesirable phenomenon because it bears some semblance of the East Asia Co-prosperity Sphere that the Japanese had tried to impose on Asia during the Second World War. In short, China does not wish to see Japan imposing its economic dominance in Asia alongside possible greater military and political control. In this sense, when taking a long-term perspective, Beijing seems to have mixed feelings about Japanese investment in China and other parts of Asia. The Chinese leaders want Japanese technology and capital but they are concerned about Japanese domination of the Chinese and other Asian economies. This point must be understood in the light of China's own aim to become an economic powerhouse, matching or even surpassing what Japan has already achieved. Essentially, China needs to prepare for stiffer economic competition with Japan in the longer term. At the same time, comparing Japan and the US, China is clearly more concerned about US dominance in the international economic system than Japanese influence.

Benefits of the US–Japanese alliance

The above analysis does not suggest that from China's perspective, there are no positive effects stemming from the US–Japanese alliance. First, China benefits from the alliance in the sense that is has the effect of containing Japan, a traditional regional rival. In other words, the US's alliance with Japan serves to keep in check an increasingly powerful regional rival that may want to pursue certain national objectives. Moreover, when China faced the hostility of the Soviet Union during the Cold War, Japan was pulled into its anti-Soviet orbit: the normalisation of relations between China and Japan in 1972 was accomplished in an atmosphere of growing Chinese concerns of a hegemonic threat from the Soviet Union at that time. The end of the Cold War has cast doubts on the long-term ambitions of Japan. Questions on whether Japan might adopt a "normal" strategy to rebuild its economy and military and then bring these to bear in the international system had become more apparent even before the Cold War ended. In other words, Japan may move from its traditional notion of comprehensive security (*sogo anzen hosho*) – emphasising a cautious balance of military and non-military elements – to a harder-edged military stance that seems more "normal" in international relations. The Realist conception is that, historically, "countries with great power economies have become great powers, whether or not reluctantly".[25] Japan's economic successes, combined with the ending of the Cold War, imply that Tokyo is bound to reassess its role in international affairs. As skilled exponents themselves in turning limited national power to maximum use, the Chinese leaders cannot imagine that Japan will abstain from translating its economic strength into at least political power in the international arena; there is a degree of concern that chequebook diplomacy and free rides on defence will be replaced by a posture that is more active, robust, military focused and more nationalistic.

Above all, the Chinese concern about Japan's increasing national strength is linked to the impact of history. The most important factor was the second Sino-Japanese War of 1937–1945, which forms part of the wider Second World War. The key point is that Japan had pursued an expansionist policy in Asia, which subsequently impinged on China's sovereignty. In essence, Japan modernised rapidly following the 1868 Meiji Restoration and became a direct military threat to China. The Qing dynasty was defeated by a modernising Japan in the first Sino-Japanese War of 1894–1895 and among other things China had to cede Taiwan to Japan, as discussed earlier. Subsequently, Japan encroached on a Chinese sphere of influence, Korea, by engaging in a conflict with czarist Russia.[26] The fact is that the natural resources of China's Manchuria region had attracted the attention of Japan and Russia and these two imperial powers fought a war there in 1904–1905 when China was too weak to resist foreign intrusion. Victory over Tsarist Russia confirmed Japan's status as one of the great powers in Asia and Korea was annexed by Japan in 1910. More importantly, Japan followed the example of Western imperial powers in imposing "unequal treaties" on China.

In the 1930s, Japan set up the puppet state of Manchukuo when China was weak and divided in the era of warlordism. During this period, Japan's expansionist aims became clear with the greater east Asia co-prosperity sphere; certainly, economic motives had an input in the concept as Japan was lacking in resources. Japan also introduced concepts such as pan-Asianism for its cause but this on a whole had little appeal in Asia as the country lacks the required morality or a high culture. In the second Sino-Japanese war of 1937–1945,

Japanese forces succeeded in occupying almost the whole eastern coast of China. Ironically, it was US entry into the war that turned the tide of battle, resulting in the Japanese surrender. The point is that the Second World War has left an indelible mark on the Chinese mindset. Therefore, any re-emergence of Japanese power will warrant Chinese scrutiny. With this historical evidence in mind, it is only natural that Chinese leaders continue to worry about Japan recovering to its position as a great power in Asia. In short, one of China's underlying strategic goals is to impede Japan's return to being a major military power in East Asia.

From the Chinese perspective, a viable strategic option is to remain ambiguous about the future development of the Japan–US Mutual Security Treaty. If Japan is seen as the main danger, then America's constraining role is essential to ensure that Japan does not become too powerful. In this sense, China's security can be enhanced by manoeuvring between the US and Japan, as Beijing did between Washington and Moscow during the Cold War. If China does tolerate a strong American presence in East Asia at all, then it is primarily with countering a rising Japan in mind. As long as Japan is tied to the US security umbrella, any potential Japanese assertiveness and militarism could be at least kept in check until China itself becomes stronger to meet the Japanese challenge.

At a wider level, China benefits from the US's alliance with Japan as this serves as the cornerstone for East Asian stability. For instance, the alliance gives countries in East Asia a degree of assurance in the face of the North Korea nuclear issue. In this sense, while China has in theory rejected bilateral alliances as outmoded relics from the Cold War, it seems that the US–Japanese alliance represents a unique arrangement. China has not directly raised the US–Japanese alliance with Japan; there were no discussions between both parties on the implications of a US withdrawal, let alone the ending of the alliance. Indeed, it is unthinkable to conceive of a structure of regional order without the US–Japanese alliance, from the perspective of Asian security. Precisely, it is the absence of a regional security architecture that underscored the continuing relevance of the US role in Asia, supported by military alliances with key states such as Japan. In this sense, the US–Japanese alliance provides a public good, namely, regional stability which facilitates economic development in East Asia in general and it is vital for China to carry out its rapid modernization plans in particular. Indirectly, the US–Japanese alliance helps China drive to truly global power status.

Conclusion

This chapter has analysed the US–Japanese alliance and how it relates to China's strategic competition with the US as well as China's security goals in East Asia. The alliance is the lynchpin of US strategy in East Asia. Its expansion – geographical or operational – will have implications for China national interests. It will raise the issues of US preponderance in East Asia, Japan's re-emergence and the Taiwan for China's strategists. Clearly, a key Chinese concern is the evolution of Japan's alliance with the US, which is linked to Japan's future as a global power. Through the alliance, Japan may find it easier to play a wider role in the international system, which may not be in China's interest. At the same time, as a global economic power, Japan helps the US in dominating world economic activities indirectly and China needs to counter this dominance. Having already extracted substantial aid from Japan to develop itself quickly, China's will aim to overtake Japan in economic terms

Despite the general Chinese notion that the US–Japanese alliance serves as a form of containment, China does benefit from it. In the short term, the US–Japanese alliance can constrain Japan: the US can still influence Japan's foreign policy in a number of ways through the 1952 US–Japan Mutual Security Treaty. Since the ending of the Second World War, Japan has on the whole been restrained from becoming a military power largely by this treaty as well as its own pacifist constitution, specifically Article 9. A key point is that historical events play a huge role in shaping Chinese security thinking, none more so than its struggle with imperial Japan during the Second World War.

Today, from the Chinese perspective, the US–Japan Mutual Security Treaty can shift from protecting Japan to controlling Japan. American forces in the region are then seen as pre-empting the need for Japan to become a formidable military power again – an outcome desired by no nation in East Asia. Moreover, a continued US presence, even if reduced in size, reassures states in East Asia that Japan will not be drawn into a power vacuum. At the same time, relying on the US to check Japan is only a short–term policy. China will not be willing to put its faith in the lone superpower. Although the scenario of Tokyo breaking away from Washington totally seems unrealistic now, the US–Japanese alliance may undergo more structural changes in the longer term. At a wider level, the alliance continues to act as the cornerstone for East Asian security, engendering a peaceful regional environment for China to carry out its modernisation goals. This in turn allows China to further accumulate comprehensive national strength and drive to truly global power status in the twenty-first century.

6 The US and North Korea

This chapter focuses on the interaction of China's and the US's strategic interests in relation to North Korea, exploring the similar as well as divergent policies of China and the US towards the Stalinist state. The chapter starts by examining China's strategic interests in relation to North Korea and how far these can be threatened by US policy towards its ally. It then explores the importance of North Korea in China's aim to wield influence over the Korean peninsula. The chapter goes on to examine the specific case of the North Korea's nuclear issue, evaluating both the divergence as well as convergence between Chinese and American interests on this issue. We begin by examining the importance of North Korea to China.

China's security and North Korea

In this section, we examine the enduring importance of North Korea to China's strategic interests. Given that North Korea is a key "chess piece" in China's grand strategy and, in particular, its strategic competition with the lone superpower, we need to devote sufficient attention to the Stalinist state's role in China's national security. First, North Korea remains indispensable as a strategic buffer state to China. North Korea shares a border with China and is therefore regarded as vital to Beijing's military security. From Beijing's perspective, an adversary force controlling the Korean peninsula, especially the northern half, could use it as a launching pad to invade China itself. This was evident in the past when China lost its influence over the strategic buffer state of Korea, which was undivided then. In particular, China's regional rival Japan was able to make use of Korea's strategic location to threaten China directly. After annexing Korea in 1910, imperial Japan used the Korean peninsula as a springboard for attacks on China territories in subsequent years.

Furthermore, during the Korean War of 1950–1953, American troops under the auspices of the United Nations (UN) advanced northwards to the Yalu River from the southern half of the Korean peninsula, too close for China's comfort.[1] China then responded militarily by sending in volunteer troops to aid the North Korean regime of Kim Il-Sung, as it perceived its own military security was directly at stake. At that time, China came to the conclusion that American presence in the northern part of the Korean peninsula would have to be balanced, by military means if necessary. The result was that a young Communist China fought one of the two superpowers to a standstill on the Korean peninsula in 1953 – a feat that greatly boosted nationalist pride after a "century of humiliation," as well as reminding the world of China's potential national strength. In essence, US involvement in the Korean War has left an indelible mark on strategic planners in China as they contemplate the possibility of American interference in the northern half of the Korean peninsula in the current era. At the same time, one might question the importance of North Korea as a strategic buffer state for China today but the reality is that, in psychological terms at least, the Stalinist state still features heavily in Chinese strategic thinking on countering the US's presence in East Asia. The important thing to note is that the Sino-North Korea Friendship and Mutual Assistance Treaty of 1961 is still via valid, despite changes brought about by the ending of the Cold War – this means that China is legally obliged to come to North Korea's assistance if it gets attacked by another country.[2]

Perhaps less frequently acknowledged but no less important to China's national security is the fact that North Korea forms part of the Chinese ideological challenge to the US, specifically the opposition to the liberal values espoused by the lone superpower. In terms of ideology, North Korea shares a common value system with China in that both states have Communism as their official ideology. Hence, it is only natural that China sustains its bond with totalitarian North Korea at a time which Beijing's own political system and values have been subject to stiff challenges from the West in general and the US in particular. However, rather than strict emphasis on any form of Asian communism movement of the global proletariat, both China and North Korea today focus on fighting against foreign subversive influence and outside interference in their internal affairs. The task for China and North Korea includes fending off outside interference in their internal affairs, as exemplified by the US advocacy of human rights and liberal democracy worldwide in the post-Cold War era.

Essentially, North Korea is one of China's most important ideological ally against the US, which is keen to spread liberal democracy to the entire Korean peninsula. The importance of ideology in international relations becomes more obvious when one considers the strong ideological elements in US foreign policy towards North Korea. Today, US politicians regularly assert that development of a free market economy, brought about by greater international trade and investment, can create the foundations for democracy and individual freedom in totalitarian states such as North Korea. In discussing the case of North Korea, the concept of a "rogue state" has been employed by US foreign policymakers frequently.[3] Typically, rogue states are defined as those countries that develop weapons of mass destruction (WMD), defy international norms and support terrorism. North Korea does have a history of supporting terrorist activities and the best evidence of its terrorism links today is probably the continued presence in the country of Japanese Red Army terrorists wanted by Japan. In terms of defying international norms, the US would argue that North Korea challenges the principle of nuclear non-proliferation. In addition, North Korea has a record of supplying missiles and missile technology to certain states in the international system. Inevitably, North Korea has become a more obvious rogue state target for the US after the September 11 attacks, notwithstanding a joint statement in 2002 by both sides renouncing terrorism in all forms, including acts involving chemical, biological or nuclear devices.

In short, ideological elements do exist in US foreign policy towards North Korea. The important point is that implicit in American thinking is that rogue states will never moderate their behaviour; the leaders of such states are demonised as evil dictators and regime change is often assumed to be the only permanent way forward. Having practised the policy of regime change in Iraq and perhaps contemplating a similar move in Iran, the US has definitely given the North Korean leaders cause for concern. Effectively, the US's policies towards rogue states have driven North Korea even closer to China as both these East Asian totalitarian regimes perceive US export of liberal values, which may entail the use of force, negatively. For China, one of the ways that the US can induce change in rogue states, besides employing military force, is through the strategy of peaceful evolution. In this regard, there is a long-term US goal to foster democracy in North Korea as part of its liberal offensive.

More specifically, America has launched a human rights offensive on North Korea with the North Korean Human Rights Act of 2004. The Act encourages the US administration to focus on the well-being of ordinary North Koreans; it authorises humanitarian aid to refugees and provides about US$24 million a year to non-profit organisations to support human rights, democracy, rule of law, and the development of a market economy in North Korea.[4] Furthermore, the Act allows modest funding for refugee assistance efforts and directs the US to accept North Korean refugees if they choose not to go to South Korea. To North Korea, this employment of soft power is viewed as part of the US policy to facilitate political change in enemy states such as itself. In other words, North Korea's paranoid leaders remain concerned over US plans to bring about the collapse of their Stalinist regime. From China's perspective, the US's ideological posture towards North Korea is therefore viewed seriously. The point is that when the US criticises the totalitarianism in North Korea, it is also implicitly lambasting the regime in Beijing.

Specifically, from the perspective of China's political security, North Korea's relevance must be recognised in an era when American military might backs up the strategy of democracy promotion. Essentially, political security relates to the organisation and process of government, and the ideology that gives the rulers of a particular country legitimacy. In discussing Chinese political security, one must look at the Chinese Communist Party's (CCP) "blood ties" with the Korean Workers' Party (KWP). The fact is that China and North Korea are currently among the few Communist regimes left in the world and Communism, in any variant or form, still constitutes the ruling ideology and more importantly, the basis on which those respective regimes came to power and had retained power for such a long time. The "blood ties" between the

CCP and KWP has historical roots: Both parties had shared a common enemy in imperial Japan during the 1930s and 1940s and their ties were subsequently strengthened by the Cold War rivalry that pitted Communist states against capitalist ones. Today, the Chinese leaders still remind themselves of the Korean War and stress the importance of comradeship with their North Korean counterparts. Conversely, North Korean leaders regularly acknowledge China's role in the Korean War, which in effect secure the KWP in northern half of the Korean peninsula.

Essentially, an ideological bond between China and North Korea exists against the US, which has a long-term goal of spreading liberal democracy to the northern half Korean peninsula. The current situation is one where China and North Korea both face a lone superpower keen on promoting liberal values worldwide and this provides a common ideological enemy for the two East Asian communist states. Furthermore, given the impact of the "century of humiliation," the China – alongside North Korea – has become one of the most defendants of the Westphalian concept of sovereignty and is adamant to prevent any foreign intervention in its domestic affairs. This Chinese posture is given greater prominence in the light of negative perception of US interference in Iraq and other parts of the world after the Cold War ended. In this regard, it is only expected that North Korea supports China in criticising the US's security policies, which are regarded as being incorrect in the interpretation of China rise as well as representing "interference in China's domestic affairs".[5]

In terms of ideology, it is only natural that China sustains its bond with North Korea, its last communist ally in East Asia. From a wider perspective, the collapse of communist regimes in the Soviet Union and the Eastern European states has implications for the future of Chinese and North Korean political systems. Both China and North Korea continue to stress the common need to preserve the current ruling parties' hold on power by defeating the US-led strategy of peaceful evolution. As discussed earlier, this strategy aims to undermine Communist regimes through non-military means, primarily via commerce, cultural exchanges and infiltration of foreign ideas, especially human rights and liberal democracy. In other words, both China and North Korea denounced the US attempt to spread liberal values worldwide, largely because their political systems and values faced serious challenges in the current era. At the same time, it is possible to argue that one of the most important sources of change in China–North Korea relations is an erosion of their ideological affinity. Both countries have long since departed from orthodox Marxist-Leninism but while China has moved forward past it, most analysts agree that North Korea has moved backward toward feudalism, becoming a "post-modern dictator[ship]" with "dynastic succession".[6] The important point for our analysis here is that strategic competition includes ideology, and China and the US have different political systems so it is only natural that they perceive totalitarian North Korea differently and their wider policies towards North Korea will differ.

Influence on the Korean peninsula

Importantly, China competes against the US in its goal to increase influence on the Korean Peninsula. From a wider perspective, the entire Korean peninsula is important in China's conduct of international relations, in addition to being a vital component in Beijing's comprehensive security. As discussed earlier, this was evident during the Korean War, when China intervened and later enhanced its international prestige by holding the US to a stalemate on the 38th parallel. Overall, a major point is that, in 1992, China's influence on the Korean peninsula increased with the normalisation of relations with South Korea. On the surface, the normalisation seems to indicate a shift in Beijing's emphasis from Pyongyang towards Seoul but the reality is that China has extended its influence to the southern half of the Korean peninsula in the post-Cold War era, a feat unachievable during the Cold War. The crux of the matter is that in the current international system, China is the only great power that has formal ties with both North Korea and South Korea. This has in turn given China a good opportunity to enhance its status in the international system, given the enduring division of the Korean peninsula. Therefore, China continues to prop up North Korea for the reasons outlined earlier, despite the nuclear danger that it poses, but it also tries to exploit opportunities to increase bilateral ties with South Korea, a US ally (see Chapter 7).

Above all, China's aim to wield influence on the entire Korean peninsula has historical roots: China actually controlled parts of Korea before the founding of a unified Korean state in the seventh century. Korea then became a key tributary state of China or a part of the Chinese world order; in this sense, Chinese control over Korea was often regarded as a "natural order", with Chinese script and Confucianism, for example, being readily absorbed by the Koreans. Subsequently, Chinese suzerainty over Korea was lost temporarily because the weak Manchu dynasty could not deter a rising Japan at the end of the nineteenth century. Following defeat in the 1894–1895 Sino-Japanese War, China had to concede to the independence of Korea. Korea, as well as resource-rich Manchuria, then became the subjects of competition between regional powers Japan and Russia; this competition culminated in the Russo-Japanese War of 1904–1905. To a large extent, the weak Manchu dynasty was largely a helpless bystander as Japan and Russia fought for the control of Korea, a former Chinese vassal state. Japan prevailed over Russia in 1905 and subsequently annexed Korea in 1910, ruling the country until the end of the Second World War. Hence it is logical that when China became stronger in 1949 after decades of disunity, it aimed to revive its interests on the Korean peninsula. However, this was soon challenged by another great power, the US, this time. The result was the Korean War which led to division of the Korean peninsula. To some extent, from China's perspective, the loss of traditional hegemony over the Korean Peninsula is regarded as an error to be rectified today. In other words, China today seeks an active two-Korea policy, aiming to maintain its influence not only on North Korea but also to extend its reach further to US ally South Korea whenever opportunities arise.

At the same time, it must be acknowledged that Korea has a long history of both resistance and subordination to the Chinese empire. The Three Kingdoms period (57 BC to AD 676) and especially the Koguryo Kingdom (AD 37 to AD 668) is often regarded as a symbol of resistance to Chinese overlordship. On the other hand, the Yi/Chosun dynasty (1392–1910) is usually interpreted as a symbol of submission to Chinese hegemony. During the Yi Dynasty, the China–Korea relationship was structured on the ritual of the Ming tributary system: "By acknowledging Korea's ritual subordination and accepting Chinese centrality in a universal world order, the [Yi] founder solved, for the most part, the problem of Chinese military threat while legitimating his own rule".[7] In other words, such a tributary relationship had served both foreign and domestic goals of the Korean ruling elite in an earlier era. The point is that China would like to increase its influence on the Korean peninsula today but it must recognise that the two Koreas are independent states which aim to maintain their autonomy in the international system.

In the post-Cold War era, the debate on the extent of Chinese influence on North Korea is ongoing. It is commonly acknowledged that there are limitations as to how much Beijing can actually accomplish in reshaping Pyongyang's national security thinking and behaviour. China is today the principal donor to North Korea and continues to supply the reclusive state with energy, food and other necessities. From this reasoning, North Korea's heightened economic dependence on China certainly constrains its strategic options. However, this economic dependence does not always make North Korea any more subject to Chinese pressures, if they are exercised, or become co-operative in international security issues in general.

At the same time, strategically for China, North Korea's value stems from its unpredictability. The fact is that North Korea is often regarded, especially by Western policymakers, as an irrational actor in the international system. In this vein, by claiming that it is able to exert influence over an "erratic" state, China hopes to enhance its influence in international affairs. Moreover, North Korea's policies in relation to the countries with high stakes on the Korean peninsula suits China's national interests. Essentially, North Korea wants to normalise relations with the US and Japan first before contemplating formal ties with South Korea. This means that China can then present itself as a middleman for facilitating negotiations between North Korea and the US as well as Japan. At times, China can even present itself as a negotiator representing North Korea on the issue of North Korea establishing formal relations with the US and Japan.

In this sense, North Korea represents a trump card for China in the scheme of its wider strategic competition with the US as China can then use its influence over North Korea to bargain with the lone superpower over other bilateral issues such as Taiwan. From the historical times till today, the point is that North Korea occupies a central place in China's conduct of international relations. In other words, North Korea is a key piece on China's grand strategic chessboard. By being North Korea's key ally following the collapse of the Soviet Union, China is able to use this status to its advantage. By presenting itself as the middleman for North Korea's tussle with the US in particular and the international community in general, China can enhances its status in the international system. As the next section discusses, to resolve the North Korean nuclear issue, the international community generally acknowledges that China's co-operation will be needed.

Sino-US divergence on the nuclear issue

In this section, we examine the interaction of Chinese and US interests in relation to the nuclear issue. In essence, the root of this problem lies in the nuclear brinkmanship practised by North Korea, which can be traced back to the first North Korean nuclear crisis of 1993–1994. In the early 1990s, Pyongyang had rebuffed demands by the International Atomic Energy Agency (IAEA) for inspections and threatened to withdraw from the Non-Proliferation Treaty (NPT). Subsequently, under the 1994 Agreed Framework, the US and its allies consented to provide Pyongyang with heavy fuel oil and two light nuclear reactors (LWRs) in return for freezing nuclear-related activities. Drawing conclusions from the first North Korean nuclear crisis, the main point is that by adopting an engagement type of policy, the US was able to halt North Korea's nuclear goals – at least temporarily. This is because in late 2002, North Korea restarted its nuclear reactor at Yongbyon and refused to co-operate with United Nations (UN) inspectors. In January 2003, North Korea took the ultimate step backwards – as far as the US is concerned, by withdrawing from the Non-proliferation Treaty (NPT). This led to the second North Korean nuclear crisis, which remains unresolved. In principle, North Korea has stated that it will seek a settlement on the nuclear issue on three conditions: if the US recognises its sovereignty, gives assurance of non-aggression and does not hinder its economic development.[8] North Korea has also argued that South Korea should stay out of the nuclear negotiations with the US: it claims that the US provision of extended nuclear deterrence capabilities to South Korea had forced it to develop nuclear weapons for self-defence.[9] As noted earlier, one of the main principles in North Korean strategic thinking is to aim for direct negotiations with the US.

The point is that today, North Korea has entered into the international spotlight again. From the perspective of international security, North Korea is deemed as an issue because it has nuclear aspirations. In October 2006, North Korea undertook its first nuclear test, which drew condemnation from all five veto-wielding permanent members of the United Nations (UN) Security Council, including China. The important thing to note from the 2006 test is that, for the first time, China publicly criticised North Korea with regards to the nuclear issue. Eventually, the Security Council unanimously approved limited military and economic sanctions against North Korea, as set out in Resolution 1718. However, North Korea did not yield to international pressure and undertook the second nuclear test in May 2009. In this most recent show of strength and defiance, North Korea incurred the wrath of the international community again. The Security Council unanimously adopted Resolution 1874 in response to the 2009 test, imposing further economic sanctions on the country as well as authorising UN member states to inspect North Korean cargoes and destroy any cargoes that may be involved in the nuclear weapons programmes. From North Korea's perspective, there are several motives for pursuing the nuclear option, including US hostility, regime survival issues, prestige and inter-Korean issues. From Washington's perspective, North Korea may have developed a sea-based missile system that could pose a significant threat to the US mainland: Pyongyang might have assembled medium and intermediate-range weapons based on Soviet R-27 submarine launched ballistic missile (SLBM) technology.[10] An updated version of North Korea's Taepodong-2 land-based missile, which is theoretically capable of striking the western part of the US. Furthermore, North Korea's development of a sea-based ballistic missile system could destabilise the US missile defence system. The point is that a North Korean sea-launched missile capability could complicate intelligence collection efforts as well as present further challenges for the US and its allies in East Asia, South Korea and Japan. More importantly, for the purpose of our analysis, China calculated that overall, it is in its national interest not to challenge international opinion on the two North Korean nuclear tests explicitly. This is in spite of its traditional alliance with North Korea. From China's perspective, the important thing is that it retains a key role in resolving the North Korean nuclear issue. In particular, China holds the key to the implementation of any resolution as it has a degree of leverage over North Korea. Such a resolution could come through the six-party talks. Established in 2003, the six-party talks involve China, the US, North Korea, South Korea, Japan and Russia, and they have the specific aim of resolving the nuclear issue.

For the purpose of our analysis, the key point is that there are divergences in China's and US national agendas and these are reflected in their ways of dealing with North Korea. Generally, the Chinese policy towards North Korea is based on persuasion, while the US one is, by comparison a more hardline stance. China aims to induce change in North Korea gradually, by encouraging its ally to embark on economic reforms, for example. China also tries to facilitate North Korea becoming more engaged with the international community, as opposed to being totally isolated from the rest of the world. Above all, China's policies on the nuclear issue are guided by its national interests, as argued earlier, and this generally means sustaining its North Korean ally.

In contrast, the US often treats North Korea as an ideological enemy and has labelled the reclusive state as an "outpost of tyranny". By listing North Korea as one of the state sponsors of terrorism, the US denies the impoverished country technical and material assistance from international financial institutions including the World Bank and the International Monetary Fund. The point is that North Korea needs foreign economic aid and access to cheap international loans, all of which can help to resolve some of its financial problems. More importantly, the US's implementation of regime change policies in rogue states such as Saddam Hussein's Iraq induces paranoid behaviour among North Korea's leaders.

In general, US policies have led to North Korea's belief that it is at risk from a nuclear attack by the US for its "roguish" behaviour. Even if one considers that the military option to induce change in North Korea is unrealistic, the fact is that the US's wider goals to induce change in rogue states through the strategy of peaceful evolution remains threatening to the Stalinist state. Hence, although the US has stated its commitment to the six-party talks over the nuclear issue, North Korean leaders remain concerned over US plans to modify their regime. In other words, the issue of regime security is very much entwined with the nuclear issue from the perspective of North Korean leaders when they analyse US policies in the post-Cold War era in general.

In comparison with China, the US is a global power and it has taken on the role of guarantor of international security. Accordingly, it focuses on the notion that North Korea poses a challenge to international security as well as to its own security. In other words, from the US perspective, the North Korean case is seen as part of the wider global challenges of weapons of mass destruction (WMD) and nuclear proliferation. Ostensibly, it must be noted that the justification for the US-led campaign to topple in Iraq in 2003 was achieved on the grounds that that the Saddam Hussein regime might use weapons of mass destruction against other states. Having achieved the Iraqi objective – at least in operational terms – the US could now shift its attention fully onto North Korea. Certainly, North Korea has not only exported Scud missiles to US enemies such as Iran and Syria but also to Egypt, Pakistan and Libya; in effect, its proliferation of missiles, missile parts and their technology has generally been regarded as a source of strategic instability in regions such as South Asia and the Middle East.[11]

Even before the September 11, 2001 attacks, the US had good reasons to be concerned about North Korea's nuclear programme. As North Korea and its clients are not members of the missile technology control regime (MTCR), which restricts the exports of missiles to limit the proliferation of weapons of mass destruction (nuclear, chemical and biological), the process of keeping Pyongyang in check becomes even harder. For instance, both the Pakistani Ghauri and Iranian Shabab missile projects are based on the North Korean No Dong programme. From the US perspective, if North Korea can be convinced to stop its missile exports, the Iranian programme will slow down significantly, for example. As noted earlier, Iran and North Korea belong to the "axis of evil" and the US would want to prevent increased linkages between these two states in general and further missile development exchanges between them in particular. However, this would be a difficult task as ballistic missiles are arguably the single most competitive product for export for North Korea, which is currently facing huge economic difficulties. From North Korea's perspective, the sale of such weapons is necessary for increasing export earnings and is a way to alleviate its economic burden.

In general, North Korea has been both a key recipient and supplier on the nuclear black market and the US takes a special interest in halting such activities internationally. The key point is that North Korea's nuclear stance has caused the US to reconsider testing the ballistic missile defence (BMD) as well as the efficacy of international non-proliferation agreements such as the Comprehensive Test Ban Treaty (CTBT), the Biological Weapons Convention (BWC),

MTCR and the Non-Proliferation Treaty (NPT) itself. If the US can end North Korean testing and export of missiles, this will dry up a major well feeding several key national missile programmes and might even eliminate a major justification for a national missile defence (NMD) system in America in the long run.

At the same time, within the US, there are important debates on how to resolve the North Korean nuclear issue. In broad terms, one can distinguish between a harder approach emphasising tough economic sanctions and coercion as options, and a softer one stressing engagement. With regards the first approach, the US has already imposed financial sanctions on North Korea for alleged US currency counterfeiting. As part of its campaign to eliminate transnational terrorism and to bolster international security, the US has also targeted illicit financial activities facilitated by the North Korean government: eight North Korean companies suspected of spreading weapons of mass destruction (WMD) were sanctioned. Above all, the hardline approach contains the principle that the military option exists in terms of resolving the nuclear issue with North Korea. This is in spite of general concerns over the feasibility of the military option and the associated operationally issues.

In comparative terms, one might therefore argue a softer US approach on the North Korean nuclear issue is more effective. In other words, the US logic of engagement has become more realistic given the current impasse and given the involvement of China in the North Korean nuclear issue. In general, the logic of US engagement has at least two distinct strands, both of which are relevant to the North Korea nuclear issue. The more modest variant argues that positive economic inducements are more effective than sanctions or other threats in eliciting co-operative behaviour from hostile states such as North Korea. It is posited that positive inducements can signal co-operation intentions because they could affect the internal decision-making process in North Korea, amongst other things. Given that North Korean economic reforms in areas such as currency revaluation have been unsuccessful, the Stalinist state may become more amenable to such trade-offs today.

Another more expansive art for engagement policies focuses on the long-run transformation of the target state. Regardless of the political leadership, the expansion of economic ties can only creating conditions that are conducive for co-operation, it can be argued. In other words, instead of focusing primarily on the North Korean leadership, the US would offer aid to impoverished North Korea as well as facilitate North Korea's integration with international economic. The reasoning is that over the long term, North Korea will become more co-operative on international security issues because it will be undergoing changes internally due to the positive effects of complex interdependence. For the US, adopting such a posture towards North Korea would be also more in line with ally South Korea's Sunshine Policy towards North Korea (see Chapter 7). At the same time, there are theoretical reasons to argue that increased economic interdependence, if that actually happens in the North Korean case, can create the wrong sort of incentives. For example, the literature on foreign aid has correctly noted the Samaritan's dilemma.[12] In this sense, the donor's humanitarian agenda to give created a moral hazard problem: knowing the donor will provide support, North Korea, the target state, may see little incentive to change. The unintended effect is that increased access to foreign resources may actually allow North Korea to remain intransigent in international negotiations and directly sustain the regime in Pyongyang.[13]

Moreover, the economic support that China gives to North Korea is a factor in the effectiveness of US engagement strategies towards Pyongyang in general. From China's perspective, it wants to maintain its influence over North Korea so as North Korea's biggest trading partner is important. However, the actual amount of Chinese economic leverage over North Korea has come under greater scrutiny since October 2009, when the Chinese Customs Administration apparently stopped publishing official trade statistics on North Korea. This move has also fuelled speculation that Beijing will attempt to obscure data about the bilateral economic relationship with North Korea while United Nations (UN) sanctions are in effect. The latest official Chinese data indicate that China–North Korean trade grew 40 per cent between 2007 and 2008, reaching US$2.8 billion in 2008. Nonetheless, the point is that China has an important role to play in the wider scheme of US strategies, including those of the engagement variety, towards North Korea. In that case, the general argument is that in order to resolve the North Korean nuclear issue comprehensively, the lone superpower will need to work hand-in-hand with its strategic competitor, China.

Shared interests: non-proliferation

While there are causes for strategic competition between China and the US at the wider level, it must be noted that both great powers share do have common interests in resolving the North Korean nuclear issue. More specifically, China and the US share two similar aims of anti-proliferation and maintaining stability on the Korean peninsula. Firstly, China has a similar with its strategic competitor, the US, to prevent North Korean nuclear proliferation. For China, a nuclear North Korea would not only undermine its own nuclear monopoly in East Asia but also give regional states such as Japan, South Korea and Taiwan further justification to develop their own nuclear weapons. In this sense, it is in China's national interest to halt North Korea's nuclear ambitions. However, compared with the US, it must be said that China's interest in preventing nuclear proliferation are narrower and largely relates to security in East Asia, primarily because Beijing has yet to emerge as a truly global power. Nevertheless, as China accumulates further national power, it will increasingly adopt a more global outlook on the issue of nuclear proliferation. Effectively, this issue is global in nature anyway as it has an impact on the international security as a whole; in other words, nuclear proliferation generally increases instability in a given region as well as in the international system. In this vein, it is worth noting that China generally takes a keen interest in global nuclear proliferation issues today, Iran being a prime example, although Beijing may not have a deciding impact on this case yet.

For the US, North Korea is regarded as threat to international security because of its nuclear intentions. How to deal with this threat is a key concern for defence planners in Washington today. In general, the engagement strategies appear to represent the best way forward, as noted earlier. However, it must be pointed out that engagement strategies with recalcitrant states such as North Korea are successful only if there is some sense on the part of the advocator that the target state's intentions are amenable to change. Engagement will not be appropriate if the target's actions are aggressive or revisionist. For the US, pursuing an engagement policy despite uncertainty surrounding the target's intentions, on the assumption that such intentions can be transformed, would therefore be costly and dangerous from Washington's perspective. If this is the case, it might be better for the US to work more closely with other great powers such as China or through international institutions to resolve the North Korean issue rather than pursue the case wholly by itself. As the case of combating terrorism illustrates, the US in general needs to work closely with other great powers such as China to resolve such thorny international security issues.

At the same time, in the event that North Korea's nuclear programmes are disabled, the country would be left with an excess supply of nuclear-related material, including chemicals for producing plutonium. Unless these materials are secured by the International Atomic Energy Agency (IAEA), then it is possible that North Korea might try to sell on the black market, possibly to clients such as Iran or Al-Qaeda. From the viewpoint of the international community, the danger is that in the event of a breakdown of centralised control in North Korea, the bombs for fissile materials could fall in the hands of transnational terrorist groups. Hence, co-ordinated interdiction actions at the international level become even more important. In this regard, the US has led the Proliferation Security Initiative (PSI) to make up for a possible failure in non-proliferation controls. Launched in 2003, the PSI has about 70 countries as signatories and it allows multilateral forces to intercept ships or aircraft suspected of carrying weapons of mass destruction from rogue states. The implication is that as a great power, China needs to lend a degree of support to the PSI for the programme to work effectively. Hence, there is a connection between North Korean nuclear issue and the challenge posed by proliferation of weapons of mass destruction (WMD); in this sense, the US is naturally concerned about but an increasing powerful China also needs to take a more active role in such international security matters.

Shared interests: regional stability

The second common interest between China and the US in relation to the North Korean case lies in the quest for stability on the Korean peninsula. Such stability provides, for China in particular, with a stable regional environment to carry out its modernisation goals. Moreover, in terms of China's economic security, it must be noted that North Korea is situated close to China's key industrial region of Manchuria. Therefore, on a bilateral level, China is keen to step up its economic co-operation with North Korea. Specifically, China has set special development zones along the border with North Korea as part of its strategy to boost bilateral and regional trade as well as to revive the economies of its northeastern provinces. One example is the Tonghua–Dandong Economic Zone, which is among the new development areas in northeast China that extend to North Korea border. Specifically, the scheme is a joint agreement between Dandong in Liaoning Province, which accounts for about 60 per cent of China's trade with North Korea, and Tonghua in Jilin Province.

Furthermore, China has launched the Changchun–Jilin–Tumen pilot zone in the Tumen River delta to promote cross-border economic co-operation in Northeast Asia.[14] This can be seen as an extension of the United Nations (UN) backed Tumen River Area Development Programme that envisaged converting a sparsely populated outpost into an international trading centre that could rival the world's busiest ports. The five members of the Programme – Russia, China, North Korea, Mongolia and South Korea – agreed in 2005 to extend the 1995 agreement on joint development for another ten years. In addition, the geographical coverage will be expanded to China's three northeastern provinces of Liaoning, Jilin and Heilongjiang as well as its Inner Mongolia Autonomous Region, the entire territory of North Korea, the eastern provinces of Mongolia, the eastern port cities of South Korea and the Russian Far East.[15] This Greater Tumen Initiative aims to focus on its main activities in the areas of transport, energy, investment, trade and tourism, which can only be beneficial to China's economic security. Furthermore, China is carrying out a three-year project to construct about 1,400 km of railways in its three northeastern provinces in order to boost infrastructure and facilitate trade with North Korea. Overall, China plans to turn Dandong, its largest town on the border with North Korea, into the transport hub of Northeast Asia as this will further economic modernisation in its northeastern region. Although North Korea withdrew from the Tumen Programme in 2009, this programme – now officially known as the Greater Tumen Initiative (GTI) – aims to focus on its main activities in the areas of transport, energy, investment, trade and tourism, which can only be beneficial to China's economic security.

From the above analysis, it is clear that the economic well-being of North Korea is essential to China. Should the North Korean regime collapse, China will have to face an exodus of refugees. The point is that in the event of domestic instability in North Korea, China will have to respond in some manner. Hence, it is quite evident that Chinese national interests require the gradual evolution of North Korea towards economic reform rather than a sudden transformation or collapse. China definitely cannot condone the wholesale change of the Pyongyang regime as this would have implications for the security of the Beijing regime. This is because the economic systems of Communist countries are intertwined with their political ideologies: both the Korean and Chinese Communist parties have come to power by adopting the same political ideology and will not be able to renounce Communism entirely. In the current era, what China hopes will happen is that North Korea will follow the path it has taken to ensure the survival of the Communist regime in Beijing: pursuing economic growth and ensuring the continuing material well-being of the masses, as the reformers in China argue, is the best way to stave off demands by the these masses for political change. On its part, North Korea has been impressed by China's development strategies since 1978, especially in the southern provinces of China.[16] In other words, there is potential for North Korea to follow China's path to economic reforms without accompanying political liberalisation although this will entail giving up some the cherished principles of self-reliance on Pyongyang's part.

In the quest to maintain stability in its northeastern region, China aims to induce the opening up of North Korea to the rest of the world. Overall, the need to prevent any radical actions by North Korea forms part of China's emphasis on peace and development (*heping yu fazhan*). This emphasis also ties in with China's desire to assure the world of its co-operative credentials and, by extension, its peaceful ascendancy. On its part, Pyongyang has shown interest in attracting foreign investment and joining international financial institutions. In this regard, South Korea is particularly willing to offer assistance. For instance, South Korea has continued to push for economic engagement with its northern neighbour, with the Kaesong Industrial Zone under construction in North Korea some 40 miles north of the demilitarised zone being a prime example.[17] In principle, South Korea is willing to provide its northern neighbour with massive economic assistance if North Korea abandons its nuclear ambitions. In fact, South Korea's Unification Ministry has actually drawn up seven specific projects to help rebuild North Korea's economy in the event that Pyongyang agrees to give up its nuclear programme; these include providing energy assistance, modernising railways and ports, establishing joint farming complexes and organising tours to North Korea's highest peak of Mount Paektu, afforestation projects, and joint utilisation of rivers across their border.[18] However, this plan will still be dependent on at least, the US and South Korea dropping their severe restrictions on trading with North Korea and supporting Pyongyang's membership in international economic institutions.

Certainly, Beijing encourages such positive responses from other states, if only to ensure that it does not have to bail its North Korean ally out financially. To be precise, China's strategy in prompting North Korea to engage in economic reforms is not primarily designed to bring about liberalisation of the North Korean economy but more to do with promoting stability in its buffer state. In other words, China has formulated such a strategy with the prime objective of enhancing security on its borders in mind; in general it is China's self-interest that primarily drives its foreign policy towards North Korea and other related issues. Nonetheless, China can play a key role in opening North Korea to the rest of the world. Basically, China is likely to gain economically if North Korea opens up to the international capitalist system. Increased trade activities in the Yellow Sea region – China, the two Koreas and Japan – may represent one way to bring this about. At present, it seems the economic and political climate is not ripe yet to formalise any form of Yellow Sea rim economic co-operation but in the longer term, some form of inter-governmental arrangements might create a strong enticement for Pyongyang to become involved. In such a situation, it would be plausible that China and North Korea initiate bilateral economic agreements first before extending such agreements to neighbouring Japan and South Korea. In short, North Korea is a factor in regional stability and China takes this into account in policies on the Korean peninsula.

For the US, stability on the Korean peninsula is important because it has interests in East Asia. Since the Second World War, America has assumed responsibility in preserving stability in Asia and this was achieved through a series of bilateral alliances stemming from the Cold War. Today, despite the cessation of the Soviet threat, the US still needs to underwrite stability in Asia for various reasons, including the North Korean threat. The lone superpower needs to maintain the military security of its traditional Asian allies such as Japan and South Korea. For South Korea in particular, the US still provides a military commitment to deter the threat posed by North Korea. Moreover, the US wants to preserve the existing liberal trading environment in Asia, partly because it has economic interests there and partly because such an environment would foster further economic interdependence and promote peace in general. In this sense, China's economic security coincides with the US's on the Korean peninsula so the intensity of strategic competition could be reduced. Another war on the peninsula today means that China would have to come to the aid of North Korea in some form, lest its inaction be regarded as a sign of Beijing's declining military and political standing in the world. In any case, conflicts on the Korean peninsula will be detrimental to China's quest for a stable regional environment, which is a necessity for its economic development in the race to catch up with the Western industrialised nations.

Theoretically, one might argue that there are some grounds for optimism if the two great powers, China and the US, can work together on the case of North Korea. The role of great power management in international relations and in particular how such management contributes to sustaining regional and international order – in relation to the North Korean issue – appears to have some applications here. If the notion of an international society does not exist or does not count much in Northeast Asia, especially as far as totalitarian North Korea is concerned, it is even more pressing for the great powers to set some norms and then maintain them. At the initial stage, those norms could come from shared interests and the two particular ones discussed were nuclear non-proliferation and regional stability. How far China and the US could maintain these norms would be important for a final resolution of the North Korean nuclear issue.

Notwithstanding the Sino-US strategic rivalry, the main argument is the aforementioned shared interests can provide some starting point for China and the US to co-ordinate their policies towards North Korea. After all, it was Beijing that encouraged Pyongyang to adopt a more conciliatory stance towards Washington even before the end of the Cold War. For example, when the US eased its restriction on diplomatic contacts with the North Korea in the 1980s, Beijing hosted a series of North Korea–US councillor-level meetings. Today,

China continues to encourage North Korea to increase efforts in repatriating the remains of US servicemen who were unaccounted for at the end of the Korean War. To some extent, China can be regarded as the key intermediary between Washington and Pyongyang and this is a role that it continues to play in the six-party talks. For the US, in particular, it would like to see China play a bigger role in persuading North Korea to freeze its nuclear programmes.

Eyeing the dangers of instability on the Korean peninsula, it is obvious that China and the US will not let the six-party talks fail totally. To Beijing and Washington, a return to dialogue – no matter how ineffective – is better than an escalation of hostilities that might result in a military conflict on the peninsula. Under such a scenario, China would have to make a hard decision on the level of support to North Korea under their security pact. For the US, given the enormous distraction and challenge of eliminating global terrorism as well continued nuclear proliferation pressure from Iran, keeping North Korea in the six-party talks rather than advancing confrontational tactics or expending huge resources to achieve an immediate result might be more realistic. Persuading North Korea to stay at the negotiating table is in fact one of the few strategic realms where Sino-US interests converge as both great powers are anxious to avoid a full-scale conflict on the Korean peninsula. For the US, another military undertaking after Iraq and Afghanistan would best be avoided as this might draw domestic protest or widen the rift with its European allies, as well as using considerable resources. For China, an unstable regional environment definitely makes it harder to carry out economic modernisation, which is essential for achieving truly global power status to rival the US in the long run.

Conclusion

In this chapter, we have examined the importance of North Korea to China's national interests. For Beijing, Pyongyang is needed as a strategic buffer state as well as an ideological ally against the lone superpower. North Korea's importance as a buffer state to China – at least in psychological terms today – is further reinforced by a historical relationship. In terms of ideology, in the twenty-first century, China shares with North Korea the emphasis of preserving their political systems rather than a strict emphasis on socialist ideology. From a wider perspective, the key point is that the case of North Korea must be seen as part of China's wider competition with the US in the ideological realm. Furthermore, given the impact of the "century of humiliation", the Chinese have become the most ardent defendants of the Westphalian concept of sovereignty and they criticise virtually any foreign intervention in a given state's domestic affairs. This is accorded greater prominence in the light of Chinese perception of US interference in Iraq and possibly later in North Korea. Furthermore, having a certain degree of influence over North Korea allows for Chinese power projection on the Korean peninsula. In this sense, China competes with the US for influence on the peninsula and North Korea plays a vital role in this regard.

On the nuclear issue, as the lone superpower and lynchpin of international security, the US wants to stop unpredictable North Korea from further developing its nuclear capabilities. In the long run, it is therefore in US interests to undermine the security rationale for North Korea's quest for nuclear capabilities. For China, it does not want to put too much pressure on its ally North Korea so the basic strategy is to play as constructive a role as possible in the nuclear impasse. This will enhance China's reputation in the eyes of the international community. In essence, it is clear that the interplay of Sino-US security interests will have a huge impact on the evolution of the North Korean nuclear issue.

The key point is that China and the US are the two most important great powers when it comes to seeking a complete resolution of the North Korean nuclear issue. The crux of the matter is whether the shared goals of both great powers in preventing nuclear proliferation as well as promoting stability on the Korean peninsula can overcome their wider divergent national interests. From a wider perspective, it must be stated that China and the US are ultimately competing for influence over the entire Korean peninsula. In this sense, as a middle power, North Korea can be seen as a subject of great power competition. From China's perspective, it is plausible to view North Korea as a key piece as it plays out its confrontation with the sole remaining superpower on the strategic chessboard; Beijing can use the North Korean trump card to establish a stronger bargaining position with Washington on a wide range of issues such as Taiwan, human rights, Northeast Asian security and trade. We now move on to examine the southern half of the Korean peninsula, where China is also engaged in strategic competition with the US.

7 The US and South Korea

This chapter explores how South Korea relates to China's strategic competition with the US. The US–South Korean alliance is one of the main components in US strategy in East Asia. Hence, we need to explore Chinese perceptions of the South Korea–US alliance, as this is arguably the US's most important strategic partnership in Asia after the Japanese one. It will be argued that having a degree of influence on South Korea enables China to manoeuvre against the lone superpower; specifically, the strategic value of South Korea lies in undermining the US's position in East Asia.

Moreover, South Korea's stance on the North Korean nuclear issue is closer to China's, compared with the US's. At a wider level, establishing good ties with South Korea enables China to wield a broader influence over the entire Korean peninsula. More specifically, it relates to the role of South Korea in countering the dominance of the US in the military and political arenas in the international system. Like North Korea, South Korea has traditionally been the subject of great power competition so one can argue that both the US and China compete for influence over Seoul today. We begin with an examination of the strategic value of South Korea to US East Asian strategy and how this gives rise to implications for China's national interests.

US East Asian strategy and South Korea

Firstly, South Korea figures in the scheme of China's strategic competition with the US in East Asia. The fact is that South Korea has been a vital component of the US East Asian strategy since the Second World War. Under this strategy, the US assumed responsibility in preserving stability in East Asia through a series of bilateral alliances with anti-communist states in the region. Up to now, Japan is still the US's most important ally in the Asia-Pacific region with South Korea, Australia, the Philippines and Thailand making up the quintet. During the Cold War, US strategy in East Asia had focused on the Soviet Union as the main antagonist while keeping Communist China as a secondary focus. South Korea was a very much a part of this strategy. Today, the US maintains the military security of its ally South Korea against regional challenges, including North Korea and a rising China. From South Korea's perspective, the US military commitment to neutralising the threat posed by its neighbour North Korea is perhaps more relevant than the potential threat posed by a stronger China.

From the Chinese perspective, the key point is that the US continues to rely on a string of bilateral alliances to maintain its forward presence in East Asia. The US presence enhances regional stability in the process but those bilateral alliance also form part of the US's plans to maintain its pre-eminence in East Asia. In order to counter the US's East Asia strategy, China will need to enhance its ties with America's allies with the ultimate aim of luring them away from the US orbit. Overall, the long-term Chinese goal is to encourage these US allies to break their formal military ties with the lone superpower. With reference to South Korea, the ideal outcome for China would be that Seoul is no longer a US client state. Interestingly, a similar goal was achieved with regards to Taiwan in the 1970s, as discussed in Chapter 4, although the US still maintains an informal commitment to Taipei's security.[1]

For the purpose of our analysis, the critical point is that the US–South Korea Mutual Defense Treaty of 1953 is still intact, despite changes resulting from the cessation of the Cold War. From China's perspective, the enduring nature of the Treaty is on the whole not a positive sign, as it does have an implicit aim of containing rising powers in East Asia. In the post-Cold War era, the US commitment to South Korea remains strong. Recently, the lone superpower promised South Korea the same level of access to its weapons as the North Atlantic Treaty Organisation (NATO) members, Japan, Australia and New Zealand. In practical terms, South Korea was granted the same status as members of NATO, Japan, Australia, and New Zealand when the US foreign military sales (FMS) restrictions on military sales to South Korea was eased under House Resolution 5916.[2] For South Korea, the US decision represented an upgrade from its designation of being a major non-North Atlantic Treaty Organisation (NATO) ally.

Importantly, the US has guaranteed South Korea's defence against nuclear armed North Korea in writing, stipulating an extended provision of its nuclear umbrella.[3] Essentially, extended deterrence involves conventional weapons deterrence as well as the nuclear umbrella; the concept is that one partner in the South Korea–US alliance will mobilise all means available to help the other if it is attacked. The nuclear umbrella concept had earlier emerged after the US withdrew the entirety of its nuclear arsenal from South Korea soon after Seoul signed an agreement with Pyongyang on a nuclear-free Korean Peninsula in 1992. Since then, the nuclear threat posed by North Korea has given rise to South Korea's need for the US's continued protection. Therefore, frequent joint military exercises by the US and South Korea may be aimed at deterring North Korea but from South Korea's perspective, these exercises also serve to maintain the strategic interest of the US on the Korean peninsula. From the US's perspective, as long the North Korean threat remains in East Asia, it is able to use this threat to maintain and strengthen its ties with ally South Korea as well as Japan.

Furthermore, the US's alliance with South Korea is reinforced by shared values, in particular, since the 1980s when the East Asian state moved towards democratisation. At a wider level, there are longer-term plans for South Korea to contribute more to US-led efforts to spread democracy and free market values.[4] It is worth noting that South Korea recently joined the NATO-led International Security Assistance Force (ISAF) in reconstruction efforts in Afghanistan. To the US, NATO and the bilateral alliances with Japan, South Korea and Australia and others make manifest the strategic solidarity of free democratic states, promote shared values and facilitate the sharing of military and security burdens around the world. The US promotion of liberal democracy, which may entail the use of military force, has raised concerns for China, as discussed in the earlier chapters.

At the same time, it must be pointed out that South Korea's experience of democracy is relatively short and its shares a Confucian tradition with China. In general, Confucianism advocates the status quo, order and social cohesion in general, and it can be applied to thinking in international relations as well. It is worth noting that up until the 1980s, South Korea had been under authoritarian rule, with its own Kwangju Incident in 1980 often being compared to China's Tiananmen Event in 1989.[5] Hence, one might argue that South Korea is unlikely to embrace Western-style liberal democracy totally, let alone actively promote it. At the same time, the similarity in South Korea's and the US's political systems and values today serves to reinforce their military alliance. The key point is that China needs to be aware of the soft power dimension of this alliance and adopt an effective strategy to counter this.

While democratisation in South Korean domestic politics has helped to strengthen the US's alliance with South Korea, it can also present opportunities for China. The basic argument is that democratisation in South Korea has indirectly translated into the call for a more independent foreign policy without overarching American influence. In other words, the political legitimacy of Seoul's new elites increasingly depend in part on greater independence in foreign policy and defence autonomy from the guarantors of the recent past. Although tensions still exist between a growing desire for political independence from the US and an ongoing concern of a possible attack from North Korea, it is possible to argue that decades of dependence on external protectors – China before 1910 and the US since the Second World War – have inadvertently contributed to the rise of nationalism in South Korea. This tide of South Korean nationalism, more specifically anti-American feeling, has been growing in South Korea since the 1980s.[6] From China's perspective, this is a positive development that it may be able to exploit more effectively in the coming years.

Generally, democratic forces in South Korea would point out that America had played a big role in propping up military dictatorships in their country in the past. For instance, it can even be argued that there was American complicity in 1980 Kwangju Incident that culminated in the deaths of hundreds of civilians in that city; the US had played a leading role in the South Korean army's operation because technically the head of this army was American.[7] The point is that this type of anti-US sentiment in South Korea can be exploited by China in order to undermine the US's alliance with South Korea and weaken America's overall strategic position in East Asia. Hence, a key question for China is how far structural changes in South Korean domestic politics, in the form of democratisation and increasing nationalism, will force some serious rethinking in South Korea on the level of security dependency on the US in the long run.

Apart from increasing anti-US sentiment, as South Korea advances to become one of Asia's most industrialised nations, its economic relations with the US will become more complex and competitive, bringing along a diverse array of trade disputes and problems. For instance, when the US accumulated an increasing trade deficit with South Korea in the 1980s, it brought up the issues of fair trade and market access to Seoul. In response, South Korea argued that its economy is still fragile with many infant industries and it has high defence expenditure; moreover, South Korea depends heavily on the import of raw materials and crude oil while coping with problems of large foreign debts as well as a chronic trade deficit with Japan.[8] Today, South Korea has emerged as an economic power and the US is bound to raise more trade disputes with South Korea. A case in point is the negotiation of a free trade agreement (FTA) between the US and South Korea: the agreement was signed by the US and South Korea but it has been subject to a long delayed Congressional approval. Currently, South Korea remains heavily linked to global, and particularly US markets but it is possible that in the long run, this will be overshadowed by economic interdependence with China.[9] In this vein, a South Korea that is less dependent economically on the US would suit Chinese interests more. The point is that China needs to seek out the cracks within the US–South Korean alliance – including those relating to economics – as the alliance forms part of the lone superpower's overall East Asian strategy.

Essentially, there is a growing equality in the US–South Korea alliance compared with the Cold War era. As the South Korean economy grows at an extraordinary pace, the Seoul government has often sought to transform itself more rigorously into a political actor, with increased discretion commensurate with its enhanced capabilities.[10] During the 1970s and 1980s the cost of dependency on the US was acceptable as far as the ultimate security objectives were concerned. Since the Cold War ended, South Korea has shown signs of moving away from being a loyal US client state and this represents an opportunity for China. South Korea has become more confident as an independent actor on the world stage. Perhaps the desire for independence is best expressed by former South Korean foreign minister Ban Ki-moon holding the position of United Nations Secretary-General since 2007. This has the overall effect of not only generating interest in South Korea towards international organisations but also deepening the Korean people's appreciation of their country's role in international affairs. In the longer term, this will have an impact on the issue of how close reliance on the US is needed in the twenty-first century or should South Korea strive to engage more with international institutions rather than the lone superpower for its security needs? This type of trend would generally be positive from China's perspective. At the same time, if South Korea becomes more independent, it could also mean that the country leans more towards international institutions and places less emphasis on its growing ties with China. In other words, the results of a more independent South Korea cannot be ascertained but what is undeniable is that some distancing from the lone superpower can benefit China in the short term.

At a regional level, as South Korea's national strength increases over time, it is likely to pursue aims more active role in East Asia.[11] South Korea's desire for independence in foreign policy is evident in the enunciations of new ideas for regional co-operation and institution building. Successive governments – Roh Tae-woo's *Nordpolitik*, Kim Young Sam's new diplomacy (*shinwoekyo*) and Kim Dae-jung's East Asian Community (EAC) all espoused a commitment to some form of regionalism in which South Korea has a role to play. In particular, the administration of Roh Moo-hyun (2003–2008) had expressed interest in a balancing role between China and the US as well as between Japan and China, with the wider goal of reducing regional tensions.[12] Importantly, South Korea has never been an expansionist state, unlike Japan, that sought to dominate others in East Asia. Therefore, this fact alone makes South Korea more acceptable as a neutral party in China's eyes.

At the same time, it must be noted that any regional balancing role that South Korea might play in the future does not necessarily negate the existing South Korea–US alliance. With hindsight, it must be said that South Korea's balancing role proved too difficult to be implemented because China continues to harbour deep suspicions over the US–South Korea alliance in general and over US hegemonic intentions in Asia in particular. In this sense, there is a need for South Korea to recognise the inherent limitations to its foreign policy options as the balancing role has proved to be an overly ambitious one. The first limitation is South Korea's continuing dependence on the US for national defence as it contends with a nuclear threat from North Korea. The second limitation relates to the size of the country; South Korea is at best a middle power and does not possess sufficient clout in the international system to induce major outcomes.

At the same time, South Korea is aware that the possibility of conflicts in US–China relations constitutes potential major challenges to its security environment. In this sense, South Korea should make strategic use of multilateral tools engaging not only with its neighbours but also other Asian countries such as India, Vietnam, and Mongolia, who are also wary of China's rise. From this perspective, current president Lee Myung-bak's ambitious "New Asia Initiative," launched in March 2009, seeks to maximise South Korean diplomatic and economic influence throughout the region. This seems conducive to Seoul's strategy of co-operating with China while countering China's rise in the long term. Obviously, the New Asia Initiative reminds one of the balancing policy proposed by Lee's predecessor, the late Roh Moo-hyun. The point is that South Korea is now a more independent actor in the international system and it wants to have a more proactive foreign policy. Both great powers China and the US need to fully appreciate this fact and formulate their policies towards South Korea accordingly.

From a wider perspective, South Korea is still constrained by its position in the middle between the two great powers China and the US. An important point is that "lesser states", reflecting their "vulnerability", will sometimes balance and sometimes accommodate, largely dependent on the strategic context.[13] This is a fitting description of South Korea, which had traditionally been the object of great power competition by China, Russia and Japan. Today, South Korea is constantly caught between how far it should balance or accommodate a rising China. On its part, China must also take South Korea's aims into account in thinking when it contemplates undermining the US's dominant position in East Asia.

Hence, the current Chinese objective is to elevate its relationship with South Korea. In this vein, during presidential summit talks in May 2008, China and South Korea agreed to elevate their "comprehensive cooperative partnership" to a "strategic co-operative partnership".[14] Under the agreement, both countries will widen mutual co-operation beyond bilateral diplomacy, politics, economics, culture and environmental issues to cover global and future-oriented issues. This is a vindication of increasing Chinese strategic interest in South Korea since 1992, when the two states normalised relations.[15] More specifically, it is in China's national interest to increase its efforts to reach out to South Korea with a view to undermining the US–South Korean alliance, which has been subject to certain challenges in the post-Cold War era.

Issues in the US–South Korea alliance

Having outlined the main contours of the US–South Korean relationship, we can now turn to examining specific issues in the US–South Korea Mutual Defense Treaty of 1953. Generally, through the annual Security Consultative Meetings (SCMs), the US continues to engage South Korea in discussions regarding the regional security environment. These discussions include possible expansion of their Mutual Defense Treaty of 1953 from the Korean Peninsula to elsewhere in the world, which is of relevance to China.[16] In this regard, perhaps the most sensitive issue today relates to the "strategic flexibility" of the 28,500 US forces stationed on the Korean Peninsula, as far as China is concerned. According to the 1953 Mutual Defense Treaty, the role of the US Forces in Korea (USFK) is restricted to the peninsula and they can be relocated only in the event of an enemy attack. In South Korea, some politicians have argued that authorising "strategic flexibility" of the US forces in their country would violate Articles 2 and 3 of the Mutual Defense Treaty.[17]

On this matter, China clearly does not wish to see the scope of this treaty being widened.[18] The point is that expanding the scope of the treaty would ensure more American leeway in troop deployments in East Asia, and this would be undesirable from China's security perspective.

In effect, the US has sought acknowledgement from South Korea that its forces on the Korean peninsula could be reshaped as "rapid deployment forces" and deployed elsewhere in the event of a crisis, particularly in a military contingency involving China in the Taiwan Straits.[19] On its part, South Korea acknowledged the rationale for the transformation of the US global military strategy and necessity for "strategic flexibility" of the US forces in stationed on the Korean

Peninsula. In other words, there is an attempt to balance the positions of both partners in the US–South Korea alliance, partly because they accord different degrees of importance to the China threat. At the same time, the reality is that the US could redeploy forces from the Korean Peninsula for a Taiwan contingency regardless of the views of Seoul. In the final analysis, in the implementation of the notion of "strategic flexibility", the US was careful to maintain the position that South Korea would not be involved in a regional conflict in Northeast Asia "against the will of the Korean people."[20] It is evident that the US is aware that unless South Korea is directly threatened, most likely by North Korea, Seoul would in generally not want to be embroiled in regional conflicts, especially one that might involve China. Moreover, the US is concerned about is much support it can garner in operational terms from South Korea in a regional crisis that would disrupt South Korea's relations with China.[21]

Overall, it can be discerned that South Korea increasingly takes Chinese reactions into account when discussing the evolution of its alliance with the US. In the long run, South Korea might eventually deny US troops on the Korean Peninsula leeway to expand their role and become involved in other Northeast Asian affairs without Seoul's consent. From the Chinese perspective, that would be the ideal outcome although this depends on the evolution of US–South Korea security ties more than any active Chinese inputs. In other words, there is a limitation to what China can do to affect the contours of the US–South Korean alliance except to get ready to exploit any new cracks in the alliance as they arise.

Besides the debate on "strategic flexibility" of the US forces in South Korea, another issue in the US–South Korean alliance is the sharing of defence costs. In many ways, this is also the one of the major issues in the US–Japanese alliance. Today, the US constantly presses an economically vibrant South Korea to increase its financial support for American forces stationed there, given that the American desire to make cuts in defence spending in East Asia. Hence, negotiators on both parties continue to debate on the amount of Seoul's contribution to the cost of keeping US troops on the Korean peninsula.[22] Under the 2007–2008 agreement, the overall emphasis was on the need for South Korea to increase its military role commensurate with its economic development. For instance, it was agreed that the 2007 contribution from South Korea would be 725.5 billion won, a 6.6 per cent increase from the previous year; the 2008 contribution would be determined by increasing the 2007 amount by the inflation rate. From a wider perspective, a longer-term aim for Washington and Seoul would be to improve the current burden-sharing system, as this inevitably has an impact on the overall structure of the US–South Korean alliance.

Furthermore, there is the issue of the wartime operational controls (OPCON) of South Korean troops in discussions on the US–South Korean alliance. In military terms, the OPCON transfer issue tests the level of co-ordination between South Korea and the US. Under an agreement reached with South Korea in the aftermath of the Korean War, South Korean troops would come under US control in the event of another war on the Korean peninsula. However, since 1994, Seoul has acquired the authority within the Combined US–South Korea

Forces Command to control its military – but only during peacetime. Subsequently, the issue of transferring wartime operational controls to South Korea was discussed and it has been agreed to complete the transition of wartime operational control to South Korea in December 2015.[23] In the meantime, the US continues to provide significant bridging capabilities including continuation of the extended deterrence offered by the US nuclear umbrella, which is consistent with their Mutual Defense Treaty – until South Korea obtains full self-defence capabilities. To a certain degree, the OPCON transfer has been more controversial in South Korea than in the US. While it is primarily a military issue to the lone superpower, there are political implications for a new democracy like South Korea, as it is related to the issues of national sovereignty and the degree of Seoul's dependence on external protectors. As argued earlier, South Korea is now a much stronger country than in 1950 and, on the whole, it wants to become a more independent actor on the international stage. For the purpose of our analysis, the point is that the more strains there are in the US–South Korean alliance, the more it would be in line with China's national interests.

In sum, one can discern that US–South Korean relations are now plagued with a host of disputes that in essence involve the difficult transition from the Cold War military collaboration to a new post-Cold War normal type of relationship between two sovereign states. Basically, there is a growing equality in the US–South Korea alliance in the current era: South Korea is now more confident as an independent actor in the international system. From China's perspective, the aim is exploit any major ruptures in US–South Korea ties that may arise from the aforementioned issues in the US–South Korea alliance. In the meantime, China has to be adept in manoeuvring between South Korea and the US in order to enhance its security interests. To this end, China has actively established various communication channels with South Korea to keep up with its strategic competitor, the US. These included the first two Security Dialogues between South Korea and China in October 2002 and June 2006, where both sides focused on security ties and regional co-operation in Northeast Asia. Recently, China decided to institutionalise its deepening ties with South Korea through the creation of a high-level strategic dialogue mechanism between the two nations' diplomatic departments.[24] The aim is to increase exchanges between the leaders, government departments, parliaments, and political parties, which are likely to reap benefits for China, albeit in the longer term.

In the longer run, in order to adapt to the changing security environment, both the US and South Korea must find new ways to further promote their alliance. To date, various mechanisms exist, including the Strategic Consultation for Allied Partnership (SCAP) and annual Security Consultative Meetings (SCM).[25] The overall aim of such mechanisms is to establish a long-term blueprint for the future direction of the US–South Korean alliance and this will have implications for China's security goals in East Asia. Essentially, China needs to react quickly to opportunities that may arise should the alliance be altered in a major way although in the near term, South Korea is unlikely to part ways with the US totally.[26]

Overall, the current Chinese objective is to encourage South Korea to lessen its dependence on the US. After all, China had been the security patron of a unified Korea before the arrival of Western powers in Northeast Asia. In the Chinese world order, Korea was arguably the most important vassal state: China would intervene in Korea when there is domestic instability as well as when other foreign powers attacked Korea. A case in point is China coming to the aid of Korea when Japanese forces under Hideyoshi Toyotomi invaded the Korean peninsula from the south in the 1590s.[27] More generally, China had taken on the task of guaranteeing the security of the Korean state when it enjoyed hegemony in Asia. Hence, over the longer term, China might even present itself as a guarantor of South Korea's security. For instance, a recent survey of South Korean politicians indicated that 63 per cent of the noted that foreign relations should centre on China first rather than the US; this implies that the US has to work harder to compete with China in order to maintain its grip on South Korea, compared to the Cold War era when South Korea was almost entirely dependent on America for national security.[28] For the moment, South Korea has not moved too far away from the lone superpower's security orbit yet. In other words, cracks have appeared in the US–South Korean alliance due to the ending of the Cold War as well as transformations in South Korean domestic politics and society. However, they have not developed into major ones yet. In this sense, China's security strategy towards South Korea still depends largely on the evolution of the US–South Korean alliance. Nonetheless, the overall Chinese aim is to counter US dominance in East Asia adequately and South Korea is a major of the lone superpower's strategy there.

South Korea and the nuclear issue

Furthermore, South Korea has a role in the North Korean nuclear issue, where Chinese and American national interests are at stake, as discussed in the previous chapter. In general, on the North Korean nuclear issue, the positions of China and South Korea are closer compared with those of the US and South Korea. The current North Korean nuclear issue has already given China a key role in the eyes of the international community, who on the whole look to Beijing to persuade Pyongyang to give up its nuclear ambitions. The purpose here is to analyse how far South Korea's aims on the nuclear issue are compatible with China's and how far they diverge from the US's.

Essentially, China's stance on the North Korean nuclear issue is one of peaceful resolution; Beijing does not want to take a firm stance towards a traditional ally and this is general in line with South Korea's strategy. Beijing continues to emphasise that it will play a constructive role on the North Korean nuclear issue as this serves as a means to portray itself as a responsible great power, assure the world of its co-operative credentials and emphasise peaceful development (*heping yu fazhan*). Overall, China aims to promote stability on the Korean peninsula as it needs a stable regional environment to carry out its modernisation goals. North Korea could disrupt this environment because of its hostility towards South Korea; for instance, Pyongyang may initiate a military conflict on the Korean peninsula. Therefore, it is in China's interests to prevent any further radicalisation of North Korea's foreign policy.

Furthermore, China wants to prevent nuclear proliferation in East Asia. Specifically, a nuclear North Korea would not only undermine its own nuclear monopoly in East Asia but also give regional states such as South Korea further justification to achieve develop their own nuclear weapons. The viability of South Korea going nuclear has appeared on the horizon at various points in times and this issue surfaced again after North Korea's second nuclear test in May 2009. From South Korea's perspective, its own history of pursuing nuclear weapons began in the 1970s under then President Park Chung-hee, who feared a power vacuum on the Korean peninsula after a decision by the administration under then US President Jimmy Carter to withdraw a greater portion of American troops stationed in South Korea. Seoul's hope of becoming a nuclear weapons state, however, was thwarted by US moves to prevent South Korea from building nuclear reactors with the help of France and Canada. In late November 2004, the International Atomic Energy Agency (IAEA) had strongly criticised South Korea's failure to report scientific experiments, in 1982 and 2000, with weapons-grade plutonium and uranium that could potentially be used in nuclear bombs. However, the Agency decided not to refer the matter to the UN Security Council, sparing Seoul the possible imposition of sanctions.[29] From this case, it is clear that China has a vested interest in halting North Korea's nuclear ambitions lest South Korea use the North Korean case as a reason to pursue the nuclear route in future.

For the US, it is not keen on a peace regime on the Korean peninsula without the nuclear issue being satisfactorily resolved. Compared to South Korea and China, the US has a wider interest in removing the North Korean nuclear threat because it assumes the role of guarantor of international security. As discussed in the previous chapter, the US sees North Korea as part of the threat of global proliferation of nuclear weapons and weapons of mass destruction (WMD). Hence, the lone superpower often takes a harder line against North Korea, by threatening economic sanctions or military action. Accordingly, the US has urged South Korea to participate in imposing financial sanctions on North Korea, but on the whole, South Korea prefers to employ its own methods to deal with North Korea. In addition, it must be noted that South Korea only made the decision to join the US-led Proliferation Security Initiative (PSI) after the 5 April 2009 rocket launch by North Korea; previously, it had rejected the US's request to participate and remained an observer to the offshore exercise, citing as the main reason its unique geographical position to North Korea.[30] The PSI allows multilateral forces to intercept ships or aircraft suspected of carrying weapons of mass destruction from rogue states such as North Korea. The point is that up until 2009, South Korea had been reluctant to join the PSI out of concerns that it may provoke North Korea, given the direct military threat it faces from its northern neighbour. At a wider level, this implies that South Korea's support for the US on international security issues such as the PSI is also not always guaranteed in the current era, which must be a positive point from China's viewpoint.

Furthermore, as noted earlier, US policies towards North Korea contain strong ideological elements. There is a long-term American goal to export democracy to the entire Korean peninsula. The point is that South Korea shares liberal values with the US but it is generally reluctant to place them at the core of its policies towards its northern neighbour. In other words, South Korea does not fully adhere to treating North Korea as an ideological enemy or a rogue state; this means that in general, Seoul does not assume that its northern rival will never moderate their behaviour and that regime change is assumed to be the only permanent way forward with regards to North Korea.

Therefore, from South Korea's perspective, the US appears unwilling to offer additional incentives for Pyongyang due to the fear of appeasing the North Korean regime. From the US's viewpoint, it appears that South Korea might be prepared to undercut the common goal of countering the nuclear threat because of a fundamental desire to keep inter-Korean reconciliation on track. The fact that South Korea puts its relations with North Korea on an equal status with obligations to the alliance with the US must surely raise a degree of concern in Washington. At the same time, the US realises the strategic importance of South Korea and accordingly the need for a more co-ordinated approach with its ally towards North Korea; essentially, this means the lone superpower actively seeking South Korea's support for its position in relation to the North Korean threat. In that sense, the South Korean argument for the need to balance the nuclear issue with inter-Korean reconciliation has been partially acknowledged by the lone superpower.

Overall, it must be stressed that a harder line from the US against North Korea, by threatening economic sanctions or military action, risks seriously alienating South Korea and weakening the US–South Korean alliance. If the North Korean nuclear issue can widen the rift between the US and South Korea, China would gain in strategic terms. The implication is that South Korea's frequent emphasis on policy differences with the US over North Korea runs the risk of making the US bypass South Korea and focus primarily on China as the main partner for resolving the nuclear issue. Overall, the key point is that South Korea's views on the nuclear issue are closer to China's rather than the US's.

Basically, South Korea felt that its own engagement policies towards North Korea and its alliance with the US would put itself in a strategic position to act as an effective intermediary between North Korea and the US, although this clearly relies on North Korea being able to trust South Korea as an honest broker. The crux of the matter is that South Korea aims for a non-nuclear North Korea, a peaceful resolution of the nuclear issue through dialogue and an active role in the resolution process.[31] In the first North Korea nuclear crisis of 1993–1994, South Korea's role was largely confined to providing financial support for the Korean Peninsula Energy Development Organization (KEDO) under the Agreed Framework.

In the second North Korean nuclear crisis from 2003 onwards, under the framework of the six-party talks, South Korea has led the working group on providing economic and energy assistance to North Korea. Under the three-stage deal concluded in 2007, North Korea is obliged to abandon its nuclear programmes in return for economic aid and diplomatic incentives. A timetable was formulated for economic and energy assistance to North Korea along with the disablement of the Yongbyon nuclear facilities, with the remaining heavy fuel oil (HFO) and non-HFO assistance to North Korea to be fully implemented by the end of October 2008.[32] The South Korean-led working group on providing economic and energy assistance to North Korea also aims to lay the groundwork for integrating the infrastructure on the Korean Peninsula. This is important because of the need to rebuild North Korea's economy in any initial stages of Korean reunification.

In general, South Korea, like China, has been unwilling to force North Korea to make hard decisions and has taken steps to avoid any kind of military tensions. Basically, South Korea shares with China the rejection of outright "regime change" as a policy towards North Korea. With the advent of a more proactive foreign policy, South Korea has taken its own initiative to resolve the nuclear issue with its northern neighbour. The Sunshine Policy that was first proposed by former South Korean president Kim Dae-jung in 1998 epitomises South Korea's posture. This policy entails a shift away from the rapid German-style reunification toward a gradual negotiated transition on the divided Korean peninsula as well as offering unconditional economic and humanitarian aid to North Korea.[33] Despite its limitations, it has resulted in the landmark summit in Pyongyang between South Korean President Kim Dae-jung and North Korean leader Kim Jong-il in June 2000.[34] Since then, South Korea has continued to push for economic engagement with its northern neighbour, with the Kaesong Industrial Zone under construction in North Korea some 40 miles north of the demilitarised zone being a prime example.[35] Although current South Korean leader Lee Myung-bak has taken a tougher position towards North Korea, especially in comparison with his two liberal predecessors, the South Korean position on North Korea today is still closer to China's rather than the US. From China's perspective, the differences in US and South Korea foreign policies towards North Korea are evident and a key task is how to exploit them to its advantage.

Overall, South Korea favours a more moderate, long-term transformation in North Korea, whereby economic incentives serve as a means to induce change in North Korea rather than a form of appeasement. Such a stance will also allow moderates in the US to argue more vigorously that taking a harder line against North Korea, by threatening economic sanctions or military action, risks seriously alienating South Korea and weakening the US–South Korean alliance. The key point, from China's perspective, is that any hardline postures adopted by the US towards North Korea can be tempered to some extent by South Korea. At the same time, it must be noted that South Korea's role in the North Korean nuclear issue is fundamentally still a restrictive one, primarily because North Korea still insists on bilateral dialogue with the US and on concluding a peace treaty directly with America.

From the Chinese perspective, the important thing is that the South Korean position on the nuclear issue is still closer to its own. Although the US and South

Korea are formal allies, there are more differences in their approaches to resolving the North Korean issue. In the short term, this is advantageous to China as it means that South Korea is more likely to act in line with Chinese interests with regards to North Korea. It also means that certain US differences with South Korea over North Korea could drive Seoul closer to Beijing in their wider bilateral relationship. The differences in the US and South Korean foreign policies towards North Korea might even increase over time and a key task for China is how to exploit them to its advantage.

South Korea and the Korean peninsula

Apart from its links with the US, South Korea by itself is important to the Chinese grand strategy on the Korean peninsula in the post-Cold War era. In practical terms, establishing formal diplomatic ties with South Korea in 1992 has helped China exert more influence on the entire Korean Peninsula goals, with North Korea already being its client. In the current era, China is the only great power to have considerable influence on both South Korea and North Korea. In terms of Sino-South Korea economic ties, as an economically vibrant state in East Asia, South Korea enhances China's economic security overall. Bilateral trade has increased rapidly, since the establishment of formal ties in 1992: in 2008, South Korea's trade with China totalled US$168.3 billion, with Korean exports accounting for US$91.4 billion. South Korea's role as an important economic partner has meant a degree of trade diversification for China, which aims to counter US dominance in the international economic system. Inadvertently, South Korea contributes to China's economic strength, which in turn provides the basis for China's drive to truly global power status.

At a wider level, South Korea has a role in China's strategy to maintain its influence over the Korean peninsula, which is part of its backyard of Northeast Asia.

From China's perspective, maintaining a peaceful Korean peninsula includes some sort of Chinese influence over the region, and it is precisely this influence that gives Beijing a means to enhance its regional status. Hence, it is possible to argue that China's desire to acquire influence on the Korean peninsula is best seen as the starting point for a return to the Sino-centric world order.[36] The fact is that China was once at the top of the Asian hierarchy and other states, including the Korean kingdom, had to conduct their relations with Beijing in a deferential manner. However, China lost this position as a result of military defeats at the hands of the Western powers and Japan in the nineteenth century. The point is that there are continuities and changes in China's policy towards South Korea if one takes a longer chronological perspective. In the post-Cold War era, South Korea is increasingly important to China's security strategy in East Asia as well as in the grand scheme of strategic competition with the US.

Apart from gaining more influence on the Korean peninsula, China's interest with regard to the task of Korean reunification stems from its goal of engendering a peaceful regional environment. After all, the central challenge for China is to make the external environment safe for its modernisation drive. Therefore, China constantly emphasises that only peaceful means must be used to achieve reunification and South Korea's Sunshine Policy fits in quite well, especially in comparison to the general US approach to North Korea. At a wider level, China promotes regional co-operation, which could induce the opening of North Korea to the rest of the world. Accordingly, together with South Korea, China promotes regional co-operation projects such as the Tumen River Area Development Programme partly with the aim of integrating North Korea into the international community.

On the Korean peninsula, one of the most important issues is the prospect of reunification between the two Koreas. The Korean case parallels the reunification of the two Germanys to a certain extent in that both divisions resulted from the onset of the Cold War. The difference is the Korean peninsula remains divided at the 38th parallel while German reunification has been achieved since the Cold War ended. On this issue, China's key principle is that the two Koreas should resolve the process of reunification by themselves, with outside pressure being kept to a minimum. The point is that China is wary that other foreign powers may get involved on the Korean peninsula again.

In reality, the aim of reducing the probability of other powers getting caught up in Korean affairs has historical roots; regional powers such as Japan and Russia had competed for influence over Korea when China under the Qing dynasty was weak; the Russo-Japanese War 1904–1905 was in part due to competition for influence over Korea. More critically, a key China aim today is to avoid direct American intervention on the Korean peninsula. Hence, if the two Koreas can work out their problems by themselves, that would be more in line with Chinese strategic interests. In this regard, it must be said that the lack of US and Japanese progress in establishing formal links with North Korea has helped to restrict the capacity of Washington and Tokyo to influence inter-Korean relations in a significant manner. In comparison with the US, China enjoys the status of an important middleman between the two Koreas and it wants to prolong this status. Essentially, a two-Korea policy today allows China to wield greater influence on Korean affairs.

The basic Chinese position is that it supports improvement in inter-Korean relations through dialogue and negotiations and eventually a peaceful unification of the two Koreas. In essence, China's longer-term goals on the Korean peninsula, if the nuclear issue can be resolved, are not totally incompatible with that of South Korea. As discussed earlier, South Korea is in favour of engagement with its northern neighbour. The key point is that Seoul's Sunshine Policy is based on a Korean-led – rather than that actively promoted by other great powers – reconciliation in which South Korea plays a key role, although it does recognise the need to maintain good ties with neighbours such as China in order to facilitate the inter-Korean reconciliation process. One premise is that a South Korean-led-reconciliation – as opposed to a US-led or China-led one – would serve to bring North Korea into a more normal relationship with other countries in the international system as well as giving Pyongyang little cause to worry about isolation.

Accordingly, South Korea has the goal of achieving reunification not on the basis of winning the competition for legitimacy but using dialogue, co-operation and persuasion to attenuate confrontation with North Korea. The idea is that this would pave the way for opening up new possibilities and creating conditions for North Korea to reform. This stance has been buttressed by a public consensus among South Korean public for engagement as a way to reducing tensions and promoting co-operation with North Korea.[37] In addition, this public consensus in democratic South Korea has spurred some rethinking on the US–South Korea alliance, especially its linkage to the issue of Korean reunification.

Basically, China aims to ensure that its interests will not be compromised in the event of a concrete outcome. It is clear that South Korea is important to China because it is likely to be the leading party in a reunified Korea. For instance, China will be concerned if South Korea absorbs North Korea; this scenario is unattractive and even threatening to its security interests. South Korea absorbing North Korea, a communist state, can never be a desired outcome as this will indirectly have acute political legitimacy implications for the survival of the communist state system in China itself. More importantly, a reunified Korea sympathetic to the Western powers could over the longer term lead to foreign powers such as the US establishing their influence along the Yalu River. In this regard, the experience of US intervention during the Korean War clearly reminds China of this danger to its military security. In other words, China does not wish to see Korean reunification leading to an enhanced US presence on the Korean peninsula. From a wider perspective, learning from the lessons of history, China aims for a Korean peninsula without other great powers – the US, Japan and Russia – competing for influence on its doorstep.

Conclusion

In this chapter, we have analysed the importance of South Korea in the US's East Asian strategy and the implications for China. South Korea is one of the US's key allies in East Asia and it is also a neighbouring country to China. Hence, the strategic value of South Korea cannot be overlooked by Beijing if it wants to become more influential in regional affairs as well as international affairs. After normalising relations with South Korea in 1992, a key task for Chinese policymakers would be how to make further inroads into Seoul with the aim of strengthening its position there while curtailing US influence.

Today, at a minimum, China wants to encourage South Korea to reduce its dependence on the US. In this vein, it will exploit any differences between the US and South Korea on security issues. Specifically, tensions have increased in the US–South Korean alliance since the ending of the Cold War and this can be better exploited by Beijing to its advantage. At the same time, the extent of the success in China's strategy hinges on South Korea's responses to its overtures as well as the evolution of the general pattern of the US–Korea alliance. Certainly, the North Korean nuclear issue has highlighted certain differences in US and South Korean policies towards the reclusive state. For the purpose of our analysis, China and South Korea are closer in their approaches to the North Korean nuclear issue, which generally focus on inducing North Korea to change rather confronting the isolated state directly.

Overall, a closer relationship with US ally South Korea can serve China's wider goals on the Korean peninsula, beyond the nuclear issue. Since 1992, China has invested heavily in enhancing its bilateral ties with South Korea. Beijing knows that in the longer term, this will serve its goal of maintaining influence over the Korean peninsula as well as in East Asia. Currently, China is the only great power to have considerable influence on both South Korea and North Korea; in this sense, this puts Beijing in a stronger position on the Korean peninsula in relation to Washington. On the wider issue of Korean reunification, China's policies are pragmatic, as its Korean policies in the current era have generally proved to be. Essentially, the Chinese aim is to ensure that its national interests are not compromised in the event of a concrete outcome as well as to ensure minimum intervention from other great powers such as the US. We can now move on from the Korean peninsula to examine the case of Sino-US strategic competition in another region – Central Asia.

8 The US and Central Asia

In this chapter, we look at the ways in which the US challenges China's national interests in Central Asia. Specifically, the aim is to examine the areas of strategic competition between China and the US in Central Asia: the chapter will look at the competition for spheres of influence as well as over ideology and energy sources. At the same time, one must consider the case for mutual shared interests – anti-terrorism and regional stability – between China and the US in this increasingly important region. Overall, it will be argued that China's relations with the US tend towards one of strategic competition; in other words, there is a limit to mutual co-operation, especially if the threat of transnational terrorism gets totally eliminated in Central Asia. We first look at, from China's perspective, the importance of this region, which had previously formed part of empire of another great power, the Soviet Union.

The importance of Central Asia

In terms of military security, Central Asia is important to China's security interests, possibly ranking second after Northeast Asia. In geographical terms, Central Asia includes China's Xinjiang Uighur Autonomous Region, which is predominantly Muslim. For the purpose of our analysis, it is therefore useful to examine Chinese security interests in Xinjiang as this is part of the Central Asia. Currently, it must be stated that China does not face direct military threats on its northwestern flank. This can be contrasted with the past, when Russia and then the Soviet Union frequently threatened China from Central Asia. Basically, China is no different from other states in that it needs to defend its territorial integrity and resist foreign involvement near or in its Xinjiang Uighur Autonomous Region. This enormous region north and west of China's heartlands had historically represented a source of anxiety for Chinese emperors; these emperors expended considerable resources in pacifying Xinjiang and the surrounding border-lands in order to bring under control the ancient oasis cities of the Silk Road. At the same time, it is important to note that China's hold on Central Asia has not been as secure it wished.[1] In the mid-eighteenth century, China was strong and powerful and much of Central Asia came under its influence. However, as the Qing dynasty weakened in the mid-nineteenth century, China's control over Central Asia diminished, primarily due to growing Russian influence and local Muslim-motivated rebellions. One important rebellion took place in the 1860s, in the Ili area that borders present day Kazakhstan. The uprising was led by Yaqub Beg, who managed to set up an East Turkestan government in Kashgar until it was ended by China in 1878. In other words, traditionally, China has to expend military resources to ensure that Xinjiang remains under its control.

In 1884, Xinjiang was formally incorporated into the Qing empire but the Manchu dynasty was weakening during this period and it subsequently collapsed in 1911. The successor Republican government was not strong either; it had to contend with centrifugal tendencies in the form of warlordism and foreign encroachment in the form of Japan. Given this situation, it is not surprising that another great power, the Soviet Union, seized the opportunity to back the Uighurs of Xinjiang in establishing a Kazakh and Uighur East Turkestan Republic in 1933. This attempt was suppressed by the Chinese government, only to be re-established in 1944, and the Soviets managed to control the Ili region until 1946. During the Second World War when China was preoccupied with the war against Japan on the east, Xinjiang was ruled by a Chinese warlord Sheng Shicai, effectively autonomous from Beijing, with Soviet support until 1944.[2] Xinjiang finally reverted to Chinese rule towards the end of the Chinese Civil War and was constituted as the Xinjiang Uighur Autonomous Region of the People's Republic of China (PRC) after the Communists took power in 1949. The point is that from China's viewpoint, control over Xinjiang cannot be taken for granted.

In fact, Chinese control over Xinjiang was tested again during the Cold War, again by the Soviet Union. Following the Sino-Soviet schism, the "social imperialist" Soviet Union became a military threat so China had to station large numbers of troops in areas including Xinjiang during the late 1960s and early 1970s as a defensive line against possible attacks from its northern neighbour.[3] The fact is that the Soviet Union had amassed large number of troops on the western and northern borders as well as in its satellite state of Mongolia so Beijing actually faced a threat to its very existence then.[4] For the purpose of our analysis, the impact of foreign military threats – especially czarist or Soviet – in Central Asia, still influences Chinese security thinking to a certain extent. This is in spite of the fact that the northern threat has diminished since the disintegration of the Soviet Union in 1991. In this vein, it must be pointed out that China's strategy towards Central Asia is today more focused on the US, in particular the lone superpower's entry into this region through the war on terrorism, rather than Russia.

From the perspective of China's political security, control of Xinjiang is vital as this issue relates to the coherence of the Chinese state. In Xinjiang, Uighurs account for about 42 per cent of the population; they are mostly Muslims and are ethnically different from Han Chinese. For instance, during the June 2009 riots, China had to devote resources to bolster security in Xinjiang. The key question today is whether China can dampen the demand for independence by the Uighurs in Xinjiang through offering better material well-being. In general, policies aimed at reducing demand for political change have so far been successfully applied in the country as whole but the issue here is how effective they will be in Xinjiang. Basically, Beijing needs to justify its legitimacy on economic performance in relation to the population of Xinjiang. Hence, it needs to find new substantive validating credentials in economic achievements in Xinjiang order to appease the local population that it rules over and still retains power over.

Accordingly, China plans to develop its northwestern region more and this is in line with the overall national interest. Paralleling relatively successful economic experiments on the east coast, such as the Shenzhen special economic zone (SEZ), China is undertaking several attempts to modernise Xinjiang. The Great Western Development Programme is the most recent large-scale incarnation of several initiatives designed to bring wealth to this poorer region.[5] Such development projects in the northwest bring some economic benefits for the Muslims in Xinjiang and may assuage some of the separatist tendencies, notwithstanding resentment towards such projects by the Muslim population because in general, Han Chinese in the region could get jobs in the state industry more easily and often have a higher standard of living and status. In order to counter any secessionist tendencies, China has often called upon the quasi-military/business conglomerate Xinjiang Production and Construction Corps (XPCC), known colloquially as the *bingtuan*, to crack down on any form of separatist activities. Originally comprising decommissioned People's Liberation Army (PLA) troops who remained as part of the "Xinjiang Wilderness Reclamation Army" after 1949 to perform the role of "economic vanguard", this force has grown in ranks and it accounts for a significant proportion of Xinjiang's economic output.[6]

In general, the erosion of central authority, exemplified by the collapse of the Soviet empire, has forced China to rethink its control over traditionally non-Han areas such as Xinjiang. The comparison with the former Soviet Union and in particular, its policies of dealing with maintaining control over a multi-ethnic empire is instructive. Although the dominance of the Han people in China has been more complete than the ethnic Russians' in their vast empire, Beijing's control of its northwestern frontiers is not as secure as it wishes. Threats of separatism by ethnic minorities these frontiers still exist and China continues to see a long-term threat to its security interests from Islamic fundamentalism and possibly even pan-Turkism.[7] Essentially, China knows that it must learn some critical political security lessons from the disintegration of the Soviet empire and avoid a similar outcome at all costs.

From a wider perspective, in order to continue the modernisation drive, it is clear that China needs a stable and peaceful environment in Central Asia, which forms part of the wider Asian region. Any interstate conflicts or civil wars in Central Asia will impair the regional environment, which will in turn disrupt ongoing economic development programmes there as well as affect China's overall national development plans to some extent. In addition, in relation to raw material reserves, Central Asia is critical to China because it is widely regarded as second only to the Gulf in term of oil resources.[8] The energy security becomes more evident when we examine the case of Sino–US competition for natural resources in a later section. For the purpose of our analysis, the key point is that there is a critical link between economic security and political security, as each reinforces the other to strengthen the Chinese Communist Party's position in China, including in the northwestern regions. Securing key resources such as oil, which is found close to Central Asia, will propel the economic modernisation drive further, resulting generally in a higher standard of living for the masses; the Chinese Communist Party (CCP) hopes that this will assuage calls for political change or in the case of Xinjiang, demand for independence by certain ethnic groups. More importantly, China knows that any instability in Central Asia is bound to invite the intervention of other great powers at its northwestern doorstep.

Competition for spheres of influence

In this section, we explore how the US's entry into Central Asia as key player is deemed as a challenge to China. At the same time, while the US may have occupied the attention of China's strategists today, we also need to include Russia in the analysis of the power structure in Central Asia. In general, the newly independent states in Central Asia are very weak and will not be able to resist the dominance of great powers such as China, Russia or the US, should they chose to exert their influence over the area. From a wider perspective, Central Asia holds an important geopolitical position in the analysis of great power competition in the international system. In the present geopolitical reality, one can turn to Mackinder's Heartland Theory, in which the Heartland includes Central Asia.[9] From China's perspective, although its population, commercial activities and political centre are currently gravitated towards the eastern coast of the Eurasian land mass, population growth may shift the centre of gravity westwards in the future. As early as 1997, Chinese analysts noted that Central Asia has become of greater strategic significance for the US in ensuring Washington's dominant position in leading the world; given that Central Asia links up Europe and Asia via the Caucasus, control over Central Asia could mean the "containment of Europe" and have an impact on East Asia as well as containing Middle Eastern threats.[10] This is accentuated by the economic importance of Central Asia, which will be discussed in the next section.

To a large extent, the US war on terrorism has led to a change in the strategic landscape in Central Asia. There exists now a tripolar structure instead of bipolar one in Central Asia: in addition to Russia and China, the US has made its entrance via Afghanistan primarily and is now regarded as key player in Central Asia geopolitics. Basically, China sees the purpose of US involvement in Central Asia as threefold: to weaken Russian influence in this part of its former empire, to contain the spread of Islamic fundamentalism and to curtail Chinese presence. Although the US generally acknowledges that Central Asia is Russia's traditional sphere of influence, it has partly motivated the North Atlantic Treaty Organisation (NATO) to increase its presence in Central Asia. Under the auspices of

NATO's Partnership for Peace (PfP) programme, the Central Asian Battalion (CentrasBat) – the joint peacekeeping force of Kazakhstan, Kyrgyzstan and Uzbekistan – was established. Some Chinese analysts see the geographical extension of NATO beyond Central Europe, with military force being used for an "out of area crisis response", as foreshadowing a dangerous escalation in Western military alliances and US attempts to dominate the world.[11] In other words, the dangers of US hegemony cannot be underestimated from China's perspective as far as the region of Central Asia is concerned.

At a wider level, a Chinese concern is that NATO will assume a "global mission" and other US allies will become junior partners in this American quest for "security dominance".[12] Traditionally distrustful of multilateral security undertakings, it must be stressed that China has often taken a zero-sum view of alliances, believing that mutual security pacts must have an explicitly identified enemy or they should have no reason to exist. The positive sum notion that an alliance can serve to preserve stability and deter aggression, without identifying specific enemies, is on the whole still rather alien to Chinese security thinking. In this regard, it is natural that China still suspects that most alliances in international system, including NATO's Partnership for Peace (PfP) scheme in Central Asia, are at least partly aimed at itself. In the longer term, Central Asia may become the first major area where NATO, led by the US, poses a direct threat to China. It is also worth noting that, in 2002, the US and India had privately discussed establishing an "Asian NATO".[13] Although nothing concrete has emerged from such discussions, they do demonstrate the complexity of the strategic competition in the region and have implications for China.

Apart from advocating the eastward expansion drive of NATO, the US has actually set up military bases in countries such as Uzbekistan and Kirghizstan to support the waging of the war on terrorism. The Manas air base was regarded as a key to the global war on terrorism, for instance. Basically, if the Central Asian states cannot co-opt the Islamic radical movements from within, the US would have further opportunities to justify any military presence there in the name of fighting terrorists. To some extent, it must be stated that the Central Asian states do value US presence as a bulwark against any Islamic separatist challenges from within.

Undoubtedly, the US's arrival in Central Asia geopolitics was given an impetus by the events of September 11, 2001 which magnified the threat of Islamic terrorism. The US staged a successful military campaign against the Taliban regime in Afghanistan and is still on the hunt for Al-Qaeda in Central Asia. To a large extent, China acknowledges the US's underlying motives but also sees an imperialist logic to such recent American military actions, believing that the war on terror serves as an excuse for American to impose itself in the world in general and Central Asia in particular. Interestingly, such thinking is also evident in certain quarters in Russia.[14] Due to some commonality of strategic interests against the US, China could develop a partnership with Russia, possibly through platforms such as the Shanghai Co-operation Organisation, in order to counter US advancement in Central Asia in particular and American unilateralism in world politics in general.

At the same time, it must be stressed that China also competes with Russia for influence in Central Asia. This competition can be viewed as a continuation of the rivalry that has existed since czarist Russia expanded eastwards from the Urals. In many ways, Russia's current goal is to secure its southern flank, as was case during the Soviet era. From Moscow's perspective, Central Asia complements Russian territory and it is traditionally its sphere of influence. Therefore, Russia had intervened in the Tajik civil war of 1992–1997 in favour of the ruling regime and its interests in Central Asia remain in the post-Cold War era. Given that Central Asia is Russia's traditional stronghold, China would therefore need to invest considerable time and resources to counter Russia's dominance there. For instance, whilst recognising Russian special interests in Tajikistan, China had stressed that the Commonwealth of Independent States (CIS) should be the proper forum for settling issues such as the Tajik civil war. Such security thinking also reflects the fear of further foreign military involvement, especially an American one, in Central Asia, if the region becomes more unstable.

Currently, the general argument is that common perceptions of NATO's policies with regards to Central Asia – driven to a large extent by the US – have helped cement some form of strategic solidarity between China and Russia. Today, both states remain apprehensive about a US-led attempt to dominate Central Asia, a tendency accentuated by American unilateralism in global politics in the light of the Iraqi War and the war on terror. In the short term, aligning with Russia is a sensible option for China as the US is seen as the stronger adversary; in many ways this resembles a return to the global strategic triangle during the Cold War era where these three great powers manoeuvre against one another. Such a phenomenon is now operating at a regional level, where China manoeuvres between the US and Russia in a bid to protect its national interests in Central Asia.

From a wider perspective, in addition to the US and Russia, China could face competition for influence in Central Asia from lesser powers such as Iran and Turkey over the longer term. Iran's influence is not extensive yet and is mainly restricted to Tajikistan, the only Persian-speaking country in Central Asia. In addition, partly relevant to our analysis here is the fact that Turkey was the first state to recognise the independence of the Soviet Central Asian Republics and the first state to open embassies in those states. The first Turkic summit was held in Ankara in October 1992 – attended by the leaders of Turkey, Azerbaijan, Kazakhstan, Kyrgyzstan, Turkmenistan and Uzbekistan. Since then, however, the call for some form of pan-Turkism has petered out. In general, it must be pointed out that Turkey and Iran have up till now not posed a serious threat to China's strategic interests in Central Asia. In contrast, stiff competition for influence has come from the US and Russia. Therefore, China currently formulates its foreign policy in Central Asia primarily with those two great powers in mind.

Another factor in the regional balance of power in Central Asia is the role of the Shanghai Cooperation Organisation (SCO), which came into formal existence in 2001, the very same year that the US came under terrorist attacks on 11 September. The SCO is the successor to the "Shanghai Five" mechanism set up in 1996, five years after the end of the Cold War. This regional organisation has been led by China and Russia with the US remaining as an outsider. In this sense, there is a gross oversight on the part of the US for not diverting sufficient attention to the SCO. To a certain extent, the SCO can serve a means for China to balance against US power in Central Asia, using Russia as an ally in the short term. In this sense, it represents how China can use regional organisations to check the US's power, despite Beijing's traditional aversion to multilateralism in security matters in general. Increasingly, however, the US finds it difficult to separate itself from the SCO, whose initial objective was counter-terrorism. From China's perspective, the danger is that the US's attitude towards SCO may change, that is, from overlooking the regional organisation in the earlier phase of its existence to taking it seriously and eventually becoming a part of it. In that case, China would face a stiffer challenge as it currently enjoys a dominant position in the SCO and generally does wish to see any great power formally becoming part of the regional organisation. Therefore, from China's perspective, there is need to reach out to the Central Asian states ahead of the US as well as maximise its gains from the SCO in the current era.

To a certain extent, involvement in the SCO also enables China to bypass Russia's traditional stake in Central Asia. For instance, promotion of the SCO means the Central Asian states will be less reliant on Russia-sponsored plans for achieving state and regional security. These states will then have more alternatives instead of relying on Russian proposals such as developing rapid deployment forces for co-ordinated regional counter-terrorist actions under the Collective Security Treaty Organisation's (CSTO) framework.[15] Such developments can be regarded as a strategic gain for China over Russia. In general, China aims to pull the former Soviet Central Asian republics further away from the grip of their ex-overlord. In this vein, the SCO has in some ways serve as a device for China to increase its influence over Central Asian states while checking a return of uncontested Russian hegemony in the region. The fact is that China aims not only to actively promote the SCO but more importantly, to lead the regional organisation.

At a wider level, the SCO serves as a platform for China to boost its regional power status and to work more closely with international organisations. For instance, the setting up of a regional anti-terrorist body entails the formulation of legal documents that include working together with the United Nations (UN) Security Council and its anti-terrorism committee. Such actions give China an opportunity to highlight its increasing importance in international affairs. On a positive level, they also raise optimism for the country's further integration into the international society: such further integration can only be beneficial for international community, which generally worries about the implications of China's ascendancy. In the final analysis, it is clear that the China can use the SCO to show the world its credentials as an upholder of peace in Central Asia as well as its commitment to regional security through a proactive regional policy. The point is that through the SCO, China can become more influential in Central Asia than the US over the longer term.

Ideological and energy competition

Apart from the traditional great power competition for spheres of influence, Central Asia also looms large when it comes to analysing China's ideological and energy competition with the US. In ideological terms, essentially, the US advocacy of human rights and liberal democracy is aimed at China as well as the newly independent Central Asian republics. The Soviet Union and the former eastern European states were to a certain extent viewed as having succumbed to the strategy of peaceful evolution; this is a lesson the Chinese have learned and still emphasise today. In Central Asia, Communism has also collapsed but the indigenous states practise authoritarian rule that is congruent with China's illiberal political system. Furthermore, the regimes in Central Asia were previously communist and the relevant point is that Communism still serves as the ideological basis for the current government in China. One might argue that, overall, shared political values have put China in the position as the implicit defender of authoritarian regimes in Central Asia. Basically, China shares with Central Asian states the resentment against the promotion of ideas such as human rights by the Western powers in general and the US in particular. This common interest does constitute some form of unity between China and Central Asian states against the perceived Western strategy of peaceful evolution.

In discussing peaceful evolution, China has naturally highlighted the dangers of foreign powers fomenting internal dissent in Central Asia in order to modify the political systems existent there. The West's and, in particular, the US's criticism of the Andijon event in Uzbekistan was a case in point. In this sense, on an ideological level, Uzbekistan might shift its policy and lean more towards China as its political values are incompatible with Western ones. There is a possibility is that such developments could spill over into other areas such military affairs: instead of continuing military co-operation with the US in the light of criticisms over human rights, for example, countries in Central Asia might even entertain the prospect of Chinese forces on their territories in the longer term. At a regional level, China and the authoritarian Central Asian states are concerned about the spread of liberal values as the abandonment or decreasing relevance of Communism in theory meant such values could dill the void in Central Asia. For example, in the analysis of the fall of the Askar Akayev government Kirghizstan in March 2005, China expressed concern over potential domino effects of more democratic forces in the region.[16] Hence, it is the shared commitment to resist the Western promotion of liberal democracy that binds China and most of the Central Asian states in ideological terms. In other words, China and the authoritarian states of Central Asia bolster it in political security terms in a world where liberal values are increasingly widespread.

Moreover, China has paid a lot of attention to Uighur secessionist movements in Xinjiang and it argues that these are often abetted by the Western powers. The point is that there is a linkage between calls for political liberalisation and independence from Beijing. Certainly, a number of moderate and political organisations and media sources in the West are dedicated to publicising the Xinjiang issue: the Uighur American Association and the East Turkestan National Congress are two such organisations, while the Munich-based Eastern Turkestan Information Bulletin is a key media outlet. In reality, one might argue that such lobby groups in the West have a marginal impact, especially in an age of fighting against terrorism; the US needs tacit Chinese co-operation and is therefore unlikely to pursue the Uighurs' cause in any vehement manner. Nonetheless, the US government has taken an interest in the plight of the Uighurs in Xinjiang at various points in time. For example, US Congress has pressed for the release of a prominent Uighur businesswoman from Xinjiang while she was detained from 2000 to 2005 because of her US-based activist husband.[17] From China's perspective, the West in general and the US in particular support separatist forces in Xinjiang and other border areas with the longer term aim of destabilising China in mind.

In terms of energy competition, Central Asia is set to be the next important arena for China and the US, as well as other states. The competition is given further impetus by ongoing tensions in the Middle East, a traditional supply source, and will intensify if the countries in Central Asia increasingly become the major suppliers of energy resources to the world market. China has become a net importer of crude oil since 1993 and it now relies heavily on the Middle East for its total imports. The basic point is that China and the US are now the world's two largest consumer of oil. China is the world's third largest importer of oil, after US and Japan. In this sense, China is following the footsteps of the US, it is consuming far more oil than it produces.

China knows that economic competition in Central Asia will intensify in the coming years and is worried that more powerful foes such as the US may become more assertive in the search for oil there. The point is that apart from military and political security, economic security is important to China's national interests; this is definitely the case when Chinese strategists examine the case of Central Asia. In addition, China needs access to world markets to achieve economic security and the US holds the key to this because it is the most powerful trading nation and dominates most international economic organisations. In the light of this, the Chinese have often stressed that no country should be allowed to apply economic sanctions – including oil embargoes – to retaliate against the other states. This is especially of its strategic competitor, the US, which had imposed ban on oil exports to Japan during the Second World War. Furthermore, from China's perspective, the US has often tried to impede its economic progress with aim of preventing its ascendancy, as discussed in the earlier chapters.

Above all, China is aware of America's economic motives and they regard US military presence in Central Asia as part of a wider plot to control energy resources in Central Asia as well as the Caspian Sea. The US does seek alternative oil sources to reduce its import dependence on Persian Gulf supplies; a case in point is the pipeline from Baku in Azerbaijan to Ceyhan in Turkey, which was built partly with the aim of avoiding hostile states such as Iran as well as Russia.[18] Given that the US interest in the international politics of the Middle East is very much related to its quest to secure energy resources, the implication is that it will not be long before the lone superpower steps up its influence in Central Asia.

From the US's perspective, China is perceived in a negative light when it comes to energy competition; it is seen as attempting to "lock up" vital energy supplies through a policy of "mercantilism borrowed from a discredited era".[19] Western energy analysts have noted that immense Chinese demand for energy has a major impact in driving global oil prices up and might eventually destabilise the entire market. Furthermore, Beijing's involvement in the global oil sector is often determined by arbitrary and non-market-based administrative decision-making and this worries Western oil experts. At the same time, both China and the US recognise the importance of their economic relationship in general and with reference to energy resources in particular. Such recognition has led to the establishments of bilateral dialogues with the view of managing their energy competition. More specifically, the first meeting of the US–China Energy Policy Dialogue and the establishment of the Department of Energy in Beijing by the US in June 2005 demonstrate the importance of energy issues to both states. Such issues will constitute a significant factor in future Sino–US relations, while having a major impact on economic security, from Beijing's perspective. In this sense, China will seek alternative sources of energy supplies in Central Asia as part of its diversification strategy. Its involvement in African states such as Sudan and Angola are prime examples of such strategic economic thought.

In the current era, China has pursued an active Central Asian policy, partly with the aim of securing energy supplies there in mind. In fact, China has already taken concrete steps to enhance its energy security interests in Central Asia. For instance, Chinese state-owned oil companies took advantage of neighbouring Kazakhstan's incentive to reduce its economic and political dependence on Russia; they are already important entrants in Kazakh energy development, having outbid rivals for controlling interest of several major oilfields in western Kazakhstan. A specific example is the construction of a 2,228 km long oil pipeline from Kazakhstan to Xinjiang.[20] Moreover, China has a stake in the 1,883 km long natural gas pipeline linking gas-rich Turkmenistan to China via Uzbekistan and Kazakhstan. In other words, China is making inroads in terms of securing energy supplies, arguably ahead of its strategic competitor, the US, in Central Asia.

In general, after gaining independence, the Central Asian states want to rely less on Russia's state-owned gas and oil monopolies in developing reserves and marketing their energy products to the wider world; in many cases, clashes over contract terms with Russia have actually pushed these states to try to integrate directly with the global energy markets and to solicit the assistance of international financial institutions. In this regard, China as well as the Western countries have seized the chance to further their economic ties with the Central Asian states and secure further sources of energy supplies, generally reducing the economic influence of the traditional regional power Russia in the process. To a certain extent, the SCO has provided a useful platform for China to negotiate bilateral trade and energy deals with Central Asian states. This is an advantage that China currently enjoys over its strategic competitor, the US, in Central Asia.

In terms of improving indigenous energy supplies, it is important to note that the Xinjiang Uighur Autonomous Region became China's second largest oil production base in 2008 with an output of 27.4 million tonnes, increasing by one million tonnes from the 2007 output.[21] China expects the Tarim Basin in Xinjiang to replace the its northeastern region as the new energy base, possibly supplying over one-fifth of its total oil requirements by 2011, including an output of 35 million tonnes and an import of ten million tonnes of crude oil from Kazakhstan.[22] For China's development programmes, access to global capital markets and international loans is important but so is the security of more energy resources; the main argument is that a strong economic base constitutes the basis for the drive to truly global power status in the twenty-first century.

At the same time, even in cases where energy supplies are guaranteed, China needs to ensure transportation of this supply remains secure. In other words, transportation is an important issue by itself and needs to be more thoroughly analysed in national security planners in general. From the Chinese perspective, there are two options – by sea or land. Given the naval supremacy of the US, it becomes even more pressing for China to secure an overland route for oil imports from Central Asia. For instance, the US navy could block the sea lanes of oil transport to China in the event of bilateral conflict. Currently, the main Chinese desire to build aircraft carriers is for power project capabilities but the heavy responsibility of protecting the country's sea routes for oil imports must not be understated. In fact, there is certain view that the aircraft carriers about to be built by China would have the principal purpose of maintaining maritime transportation security.[23] However, if China does possess aircraft carriers in the future, they would be smaller in tonnage and shorter in cruising range than those of US forces. In this sense, securing overland energy routes would probably be accorded a higher priority in terms of energy security. This is why Central Asia occupies an important place in Chinese economic strategic thinking. The point is that in the event of a Sino-US crisis, China would partially be able to rely on the land route stemming from Central Asia for energy supplies as the sea route may be blockaded by the US.

In order to fuel its modernisation drive, which forms the basis for global power aspirations, China needs a guaranteed supply of economic inputs so energy resources from Central Asia will become more critical in the coming decades. In the energy realm, China competes with the US; the foreign policies of both countries in regions such as Central Asia are driven to a large extent by the quest for the vital resource of oil. At the same time, it must be noted that promoting a balanced energy supply and demand in the world and safeguarding global energy security is a pressing task confronting countries of the world, not just China and the US. In order to safeguard global energy security, China has in fact argued that the international community should embrace and implement a new energy concept that calls for mutually beneficial cooperation, diversified forms of development and common energy security through co-ordination.[24] In short, the basic point is that energy competition is inevitable as fossil fuels are a finite resource and this is evident in Central Asia. If alternative sources of energy may be commercially viable in the long run, the strategic competition between China and the US in this region would be reduced. In other words, in the longer term, technology has the capacity to change the patterns of great power economic relationships and this will apply to Central Asia.

Sino-US co-operation

The above analysis does not suggest that great power co-operation in Central Asia is impossible. There are areas whereby China can find common ground with America – counter-terrorism and regional stability. Firstly, China and the US share the aim of preventing radical Islamic forces from gaining ground in Central Asia. The war against terrorism is one of the many non-traditional security threats that have arisen. China and the US have the opportunity to increase co-operation in this field and further build up mutual trust. Since the events of September 11, 2001, the Islamic movements in Central Asia have gained a global stage as the lone superpower pursues its war on terror. Importantly, China has also used the war on terror to its own advantage. Four months after September 11, China issued an official document that marked its most direct attempt to justify and link its actions against the Uighurs in Xinjiang with the American campaign against Al-Qaeda.[25] At a particular point in time, it was clear that Beijing shrewdly seized the opportunity to link Uighur nationalist movements to Islamic militants pursued by the US, without distinguishing between the violent or non-violent groups in Xinjiang. While the US refused to endorse China's intensified efforts to combat separatist forces directly, it did not highlight the issue specifically. It appears that Washington has recognised the value of having a strategic dialogue with China and a "united front" against terrorists and therefore traded its previous patronage of the Uighur cause for Chinese co-operation on the war on terror to some extent, particularly because of the urgent need to oust the Taliban forces in Afghanistan then. In reality, China knows that defeat of the Taliban regime and other Muslim extremists will bolster its political security in Central Asia and on the whole strengthen its grip on the region. Therefore, some form of tacit co-operation with the US to deal with Islamic extremists seems a good policy in the short term, from Beijing's perspective. In other words, the threat of separatism in Xinjiang remains from Beijing's perspective and coincides with the US global mission of counter-terrorism.

Specifically, from China's perspective, threats on its northwestern flank are represented by the "three evil forces" of terrorism, extremism and separatism.[26] In the late 1980s and early 1990s, the 1989 Tiananmen event and the unfolding of the Tibetan separatist movement as well as former Soviet Central Asia gaining independence have an impact on the Uighurs in Xinjiang. These events in the international sphere help lift their long-cherished hopes to achieve statehood. The disintegration of the Soviet Union has certainly raised political security problems in Central Asia for China as the newly independent Central Asian republics do have at least a modicum of sympathy for the Muslim people in China's westernmost regions. China is aware that the Uighur separatists could receive ideological support and military hardware from neighbouring Central Asian states today; a small number of arms have also flowed from Iran, Afghanistan and sympathetic brethren in Russia to insurgents in Xinjiang in the recent past.

Today, China faces a host of Uighur insurgent groups – United Revolutionary Front of Eastern Turkestan, Xinjiang Liberation Organisation and Uighur Liberation Organisation (ULO), Wolves of Lop Nor, Free Turkistan Movement, Home of the East Turkistan Youth and Organisation for the Liberation of Uighuristan, although how big a political threat they actually pose to Beijing it remains debatable.[27] The important point is that that Xinjiang serves as China's frontline against terrorism in the current era. In this sense, the most dangerous threat posed to China is probably that of the East Turkistan Islamic Movment (ETIM), based along the Afghanistan–Pakistan border. This group, which draws support from Al-Qaeda, has been labelled by United Nations (UN) as a terrorist organisation.

In addition to the US, through the SCO, China has secured the inauguration of a regional anti-terrorist body, which intensifies its co-operation with Central Asian states in the war against the "three forces of terrorism, extremism and separatism".[28] What triggered this deviation from the traditional Chinese policy of non-intervention in a given state's domestic affairs was the fear of a global militant Islam network allying with separatist forces in Xinjiang. At that same time, it must be pointed out that, compared with China, the US is arguably more likely to be directly threatened by such global extremist networks. Nonetheless, China still stresses the need to be vigilant so that extremist and terrorist forces will not take advantage of certain unstable situations in Central Asia. In this sense, what serves the US in its war on terror now coincides with China's predicament on its northwestern front. In this vein, the manipulation of the SCO to serve the cause of eliminating separatism in Xinjiang is indicative of classic Chinese foreign policy manoeuvres, although this is not a difficult task as the other SCO members share similar concerns over separatist threats in Central Asia. For the purpose of our analysis here, the key point is that concerns are also shared by an extra-regional great power, the US.

The second common interest shared by the China and the US in Central Asia is regional stability. This relates to China's desire for quick modernisation and a secure regional environment on its northwestern flank. In fact, this is a more enduring feature and will outlast the US efforts to eliminate terrorism in Central Asia. Overall, it is evident that the US presence in Afghanistan has helped to bolster stability in Central Asia. In this sense, China has actually gained from the US entry in the region after 2001. Even before the events of September 11, 2001, certain US actions had already helped to make the geopolitical situation in Central Asia more stable. In the early 1990s, the US played a role in Kazakhstan returning its nuclear weapons, which was inherited as part of the Soviet Union's nuclear arsenals, and their means of delivery to Russia.[29] The point is that such US activities, in this case relating to a conventional security threat rather than a non-conventional one, serve to bolster stability in Central Asia, which benefits China as well as the region.

In terms of Central Asian stability, one can examine the constructive role of great power management, in this case involving at least Russia and the US. The general argument is that great powers such as China can to a large extent dictate security patterns in Central Asia and more importantly help prevent conflicts between Central Asian countries or even intrastate political violence. In the post-Cold War era, the key is how effectively China, Russia and US can manage their differences and how far they can reach a common ground on Central Asian security issues without sacrificing their own national interests. From the Chinese perspective, consolidating its position in Central Asia and being able to induce a cultural secular, inwardly authoritarian and outwardly moderate Central Asia would be ideal. The question here is how to what degree do Russia or the US share these objectives.

Besides great powers such as the US and Russia, China also needs other partners for maintaining stability in Central Asia – Central Asian states themselves. In this vein, since the end of the Cold War, China has established confidence-building measures with Central Asian states on their land borders. An important agreement on such measures was reached with Kazakhstan, Kyrgyzstan, Tajikistan as well as Russia in April 1996;[30] this far-reaching accord – arguably the most comprehensive arms control agreement in East Asia since the Second World War – restricts deployments and exercises along China's western border region, and was uniquely lengthy and legalistic. The following year, in April 1997, China reached a troops-reductions accord with the aforementioned countries along their common borders.[31] From China's viewpoint, taken together with the 1996 document, this accord made its northern 7,000 km common border "a secure belt of mutual trust".[32] In other words, those moves undertaken by China in the 1990s were aimed at bolster stability on its northwestern flank.

With regards to Central Asian security in the current era, it is evident that China has taken an active role in promoting SCO as a credible regional organisation, although largely out of self-interest. To this effect, China has called on SCO members to step up mutual co-operation, implicitly acknowledging the growing importance of multilateralism and even advocating the replacement of notions of "absolute unilateral security" in favour of some form of co-operative security.[33] In the long run, in addition to great power management, the achievement of Central Asian security must also be underpinned by the indigenous states themselves. These newly independent states must learn to take on more responsibility and act collectively to stabilise the region. An expansion of the SCO to include countries such as Pakistan, Mongolia, India and Turkmenistan in future could be important in this regard. At the same time, it must be noted that China's participation in the SCO does not fully vindicate any strong signs of Beijing embracing multilateralism genuinely; this participation largely represents a means for China to achieve its security goals rather than indicates a radical departure from its preference for bilateralism in international relations. Essentially, China does not want to see a volatile situation in Central Asia and wants to see regional conflicts resolved peacefully. In other words, Central Asia forms part of the wider Asian region and regional stability is vital for China to carry out its economic modernisation goals.

Conclusion

In this chapter, we have outlined the strategic importance of Central Asia to China's national interests. In general, the region has received relatively less attention from those who study China's security strategies, compared with other regions such as Southeast Asia. The argument here is that Central Asia is probably second in importance for China's power projection, after the traditional backyard of Northeast Asia. Essentially, Beijing's aims in Central Asia are threefold: to weed out separatist activities on its northwestern front, to counter US and Russian influence in the region, and to demonstrate to the international community that it can act as a responsible regional power in Central Asia.

From China's perspective, the lone superpower has made an unwelcome entrance in Central Asia since October 2011, primarily via Afghanistan. The competition for spheres of influence today is such that in addition to the traditional overlord, Russia, China has to cope with the US challenge. Currently, the lone superpower is regarded as the bigger threat in Central Asia hence China has aligned itself with Russia to counter the US. At the same time, both China and Russia lead but also compete in the SCO and for influence over the Central Asian states. However, China and Russia share – at least in the short term – a common aim of preventing further US presence in Central Asia. The fact is that the US lead in all realms of international politics is currently unassailable so China and Russia have no choice but to work together – at least tactically.

In bilateral terms, China is engaged in ideological competition with the US in relation to Central Asia. China shares with the indigenous states in the region an authoritarian political system and, therefore, there is a common aim to halt the spread of Western liberal values there. In terms of energy security, Central Asia has attracted the interest of the US and China knows that it needs secure energy supplies to fuel modernisation, which is the springboard for truly global power status. In this sense, China has to compete with the US for access to the region's energy reserves. The overall implication is that economic competition, including over oil, is part of the wider scheme of Sino-US strategic competition in the post-Cold War era.

At the same time, despite the competitive nature of Sino–US relations in Central Asia, there are cases where the two great powers can co-operate. In this regard, the first common goal of China and the US is to eliminate any form of transnational terrorism in Central Asia. For China, this goal also relates to its aim to secure control over the predominantly Muslim region of Xinjiang. The second common interest that China and the US share in Central Asia is maintaining regional stability. This is a more enduring goal compared with the aim of totally eliminating transnational terrorism in Central Asia, which could be achieved in the not-too-distant future. Although China's economic activities are centred in the east, stability on the northwestern front is also important as any signs of instability there would have a negative impact on Beijing's quest to achieve rapid economic modernisation in order to become a truly global power.

9 Conclusions

In this final part of the book, the aim is to identify broader conclusions from the case of Sino-US strategic competition. These broader implications are important for both the academic study of international relations as well as for those involved foreign policymaking. We begin by looking at the main implications of Sino–US strategic competition for both great powers before delving into the notion of reducing the intensity of this strategic competition in the international system.

China's security strategy

From China's perspective, the most important point is to focus on implications of the huge capability gap between itself and the US. In other words, China's comprehensive national strength is far behind that of the US. In effect, the US is far ahead of any other great powers in the international system. Hence, China has no alternative but to basically adopt a strategy of the weak. The ancient Chinese strategy of *taoguang yanghui* is relevant here. Instead of pursuing a strategy of diplomatic activism, China should avoid getting entangled into conflicts where its national security interests are not directly threatened. For a weaker power, compared to the US, extending resources on issues which are outside the perimeter of core national interests is unnecessary. Even if the case is that of a stronger power, focusing too much on other issues that are not directly in the national interest may create extra burdens: in this sense, the case of the US intervention in Somalia in the 1990s would prove instructive for Chinese leaders.

In military terms, the analyses in this book suggest that China should hide its true capabilities and build them up quietly. The ongoing military modernisation efforts, including the aspirations for a blue-water navy, must continue without drawing unnecessary worldwide attention. It is evident that this task is difficult as global attention has already been focused on China's increasing military prowess, which to a large extent is a product of the US-led "China threat" theory stemming from the 1990s. However, unlike the US display of military might in Iraq and Afghanistan, it is important that China has generally strived to keep a low profile as it modernises it military.

Above all, it must be pointed out that the Chinese strategy of *taoguang yanghui* is one tailor-made for ensuring long-term survival in an anarchic international system; the argument is that states employing this strategy is less likely to elicit opposing balancing coalitions and hence able to ensure its continuous accumulation of comprehensive national strength. In the long run, when the capability gap between China and the US has been narrowed, China may then contemplate a slight shift in national security strategy. At that time, confronting the US directly would become a more realistic option. The key point of the *taoguang yanghui* strategy is that a country should only display its comprehensive national strength fully when the time is ripe. In other words, it is a national security strategy emphasising a patient and cautious build-up of comprehensive national strength. Above all, the goal of current strategic thinkers in Beijing is to create a stronger and more powerful China.

Given the complex bilateral relationship with the US, one of the key arguments in this book is that China needs to be constantly aware of ambiguities in US foreign policy and find ways to deal with them. For instance, on the issue of Taiwan, the implications of ambiguity in US policies need to be more worked out more carefully. The US stance of encouraging negotiation between China and Taiwan but not supporting reunification explicitly, to push for peace but not co-operation, and to formally oppose Taiwan's independence but refuse to publicly clarify its position present challenges for strategic thinkers in China in the post-Cold War era. In other words, China must estimate more accurately the complex and double-sided nature of US policies on certain issues.

At present, it is fair to argue that China's international strategy is far from systemic or fully developed. This is especially the case when one compares this with China's domestic policies, where a general blueprint has been formed, such as the irreversible move towards market reforms since 1978. In the current formulation of Chinese foreign policy, a set of existing guidelines – the five principles of peaceful co-existence, anti-hegemonism, and a general posture of independence and self-reliance – exist. However, they are generally too superficial and only offer rough outlines for the action; more specifically, corresponding key links between various issues and specific strategic measures for certain cases are still lacking.

At the same time, it must be noted that China has had a long history of statecraft. In both historical and modern China, concepts of statecraft are found in strategic thought. One of the most famous thinkers in traditional Chinese thinking is Sun Tzu, who lived during the Warring States period; more specifically, the Chinese language has a very rich vocabulary for describing political and military strategies.

Therefore, one can argue that modern Chinese strategic thought consists of an amalgam of traditional Chinese strategic thinking, Marxism and indigenous influences, in addition to military concepts such as the revolution in military affairs. In general, Chinese academic and policy papers on political or military strategy generally contain a unique mix of the modern and the traditional, with discussions of twenty-first century information warfare intermixed with allusions to events in ancient Chinese history, for instance. Moreover, the impact of modern history is important in influencing Chinese strategic thought; the experience of Western and Japanese imperialism since the Opium Wars has left an indelible mark on the Chinese mindset.

In terms of China's approach to Asian security, it must be said the preference is to deal with regional states on a bilateral basis before embarking on multilateral dialogues. In general, Beijing prefers a step-by-step incremental approach whereby it can ensure its security interests will not be compromised in any way. This partly reflects an adherence to a zero-sum view of alliances, in which mutual security pacts must have an explicitly identified enemy – or they should have no reason to exits. The positive-sum notion that alliances can serve to preserve stability and deter aggression, without identifying specific enemies, remains on the whole alien to the Chinese security thinking. Perhaps one main reason for China's reservations in most multilateral security schemes relates to the fact these schemes might simply serve to single out China for criticism, in particular for its military build-up. In this sense, general Chinese suspicions of the Western goal of containment have carried over into regional security discussions such as the ASEAN Regional Forum (ARF). Unfortunately for China, its general unwillingness to subordinate its security interests to regional schemes, has contributed to concerns over the China threat.

At the same time, from the Chinese perspective, one benefit of increasing regional multilateralism in Asian today is that it can serve as a means to exert counter-pressure against US presence. The point is that China has been increasing its involvement in regional organisations but the underlying motive is more to ensure that it gains a stronger position in East Asia in relation to the US rather than an altruistic commitment to regional integration.

In the longer term, it would not be China's interests to remain completely aloof from these regional security activities.

US security strategy

Although this book addresses the case of strategic competition primarily from China's perspective, the analyses here do have important implications for US national security strategy. The US is a Pacific nation and the general argument is that its national interests and ideals alike require stronger engagement in Asia than ever before. In the post-Cold War era, the lone superpower has sought to reinvigorate its alliances and to forge new relationships with countries in Asia that share its values. From the ideological perspective, countries that share US democratic ideals should be Washington's natural partners; in other words, common values help to sustain alliances in general. In terms of Asian security, the basic American premise is that alliances represent the best way to maintain stability and ensure peace there. In this sense, with its allies, the US can confront new security challenges such as transnational terrorism as well as seize new opportunities in this economically vibrant region.

America has five treaty alliances in Asia – Japan, South Korea, Australia, the Philippines and Thailand. From the perspective of its Asian strategy, the US needs to strengthen – if not at least maintain – them. In this book, we have focused on the US's alliances with Japan and South Korea as well as the pertinence of Taiwan, a former US ally, in the scheme of Sino-US strategic competition. At the a wider level, the US's alliances in Asia form part of its global scheme of alliances, which is vital for ensuring American pre-eminence in the international system. In particular, the Atlantic Alliance remains vital, in particular the US–UK "special relationship". The point is that such alliances outside Asia strengthens to the US's overall position in relation to China, even when the case in question is primarily an Asian security issue. Overall, the US, especially through its close alliance with Japan, remains vital for the stability of the Asia-Pacific, which in turn contributes to maintaining international order.

In bilateral terms, the hard strategic choices for the US can be exemplified by the containment and engagement approaches in policy towards China. Essentially, the former approach entails treating China like a major adversary, similar to the former Soviet Union; this means that US must always maintain the huge capability gap between itself and China, in the military, political and economic realms. In other words, the US must not give China any opportunities to achieve parity in any one of these realms. In contrast, the engagement school of thought in the US prefers to treat China as a possible international partner. Here the emphasis is on changing the nature of the Chinese regime, its political system, attendant ideologies and value system. In general, the way to achieve this goal is primarily through increasing economic ties with China as this would enmesh China further into the international capitalist system, which is currently led by the US.

The major strength of the engagement approach is that is the course of economic interactions, China and, in particular, its citizens would become more exposed to Western values and the US would have a better chance of modifying the Chinese political system. In other words, instead of operating strictly on state-to-state basis, the US can indirectly contribute to the enlargement of the Chinese middle class; this middle class will then exert more pressure on the Communist regime in Beijing to contemplate further political liberalisation. The nexus between international relations and domestic politics is vital here as this strategy rests on the assumption that the US could indirectly influence the course of political processes in China through tying it into the international system, especially in the economic realm. In this sense, the strategy of peaceful evolution dating from the Cold War era remains as relevant as ever for US strategic thinkers.

Reducing strategic competition

One of the main conclusions in this book is that strategic competition does not imply the inevitability of military conflict between China and the US. It is true that the emphasis of this book is on structure, rather than agency. In this sense, both China and the US may want to achieve co-operation but they are to some extent constrained by the structure of the international system, more specifically international anarchy. In a world of self-help, it is natural that both states will want to maximise their power – military, political and economic. In the process of power accumulation, both China and the US might come to conflicts over certain issues or in certain regions. Moreover, it is true that both China and the US have divergent worldviews and conflicts are bound to surface, notwithstanding deepening economic integration between the two great powers.

From the Chinese perspective, the defeat of communism has in general meant a global re-assertion of US power and values with a "new world order" proclaimed by America after the demise of the Soviet Union. Basically, since the early 1990s, China has to face the US on its own in the absence of a strategic triangle; it had been able to play one superpower off the other to enhance its security during the Cold War. From the US perspective, it now faces a strategic competitor that is increasing reaching the power of a former adversary, the Soviet Union. Therefore, there is a challenge on how to concoct an effective strategy for the rise of China. From a longer chronological perspective, when the US approached China in 1971–1972, trade was not a non-major consideration in the course of restoring bilateral ties about today the case is different. In other words, this means that range of issues in US–China relations is much greater than in the early 1970s. We have already noted that co-operation is required in nuclear non-proliferation as the dangers of horizontal proliferation increases, for instance.

In the current era, it must stressed that the first common ground for the US and China is that both great powers want to maintain international stability. For China, a developing country, a peaceful environment means that it can carry out modernisation without any major disruptions. For the US, it has taken on the role of guaranteeing international security because this is generally in line with its national interests. In the course of maintaining international stability, the lone superpower is able to assert its dominance in the international system as well as enhancing its global economic interests. Inadvertently, Chinese and US national interests converge on goal of ensuring a peaceful environment, which is beneficial to the international community. Currently, international security has been challenged to some extent by transnational terrorism. Therefore, in the short term, Chinese and US national interests have again converged in that both great powers aim to eliminate this non-conventional security threat. Essentially, the US has led the war on terrorism and China has offered as much support as it could without totally sacrificing some of its cherished principles such as sovereignty and non-intervention in other states.

Second, China and the US find common ground in promoting international economic growth as well as enhancing bilateral trading ties. Since 1978, China has embarked on market reforms and is today an important player in the international economic system. This system is still dominated by the US but both great powers also realise that they have common goals to ensure that the international economic system function smoothly. The prime example is the 2008 financial crisis that emanated from the US. Both great powers as well as the international community know that co-operation is the key to maintaining international economic stability.

More importantly, China and the US know that they have key roles to play in this regard, alongside the major industrialised nations. The fact is that in the economic realm, most of the teething problems can only be resolved through co-operation among states rather than through competition, although the case of fossil fuels competition represents an important exception, given the current stage of technological development in generating power. In the final analysis, the key argument championed by those in the Liberal school of International Relations is that in the long run, great powers such as China and the US will become more interdependent on each other as well as on the international economic system. As a result of closer economic integration, the corollary is that both China and the US know the costs of a major rupture in their relations will be higher than in the previous era. Therefore, they will be more careful in managing their bilateral problems and make all efforts to avoid any escalation of their disputes.

From the above analysis, it is evident that are avenues for attenuating the intensity of Sino–US strategic competition. In this regard, it is hoped that more academic and policy research will be done on the ways to reduce this intensity at all levels – strategic, tactical and operational. From the perspective of the international community, any reduction of the intensity of Sino-US strategic competition can only be positive for the international system as a whole. The crux of the matter is that in the event of a Sino-US crisis, the impact is likely to be global one rather than being confined to a specific region such as East Asia. In this sense, it is in the interest of the wider international community – in particular the other great powers – to invest more efforts in facilitating the continuing Sino-US exchanges and dialogues in all areas of international relations. These other great powers could play the role of a middleman between China and the US, for instance.

In the final analysis, both China and the US do face hard strategic choices in the early twenty-first century: Will they choose co-operation in the new century and build a more co-operative relationship or will they seek to increase competition or even confrontation, following the pattern of traditional relations among great powers in the past several centuries? One thing is certain: the strategic choices that China and the US make will have a major impact on the international system. Accordingly, from the perspective of the international community, it is hoped that both these great powers will make concrete efforts to reduce the intensity of their strategic competition.

Notes

Introduction

1 See Kenneth N. Waltz, *Theory of International Politics* (Reading, MA: Addison-Wesley, 1979), p. 118. See also John J. Mearsheimer, *The Tragedy of Great Power Politics* (New York: W.W. Norton, 2001), pp. 29–54.
2 Kenneth N. Waltz, *Theory of International Politics*, pp. 105–107.
3 Kenneth N. Waltz, *Theory of International Politics*, pp. 118, 124 and 127–128.
4 See, for example, Yu Xintian, "China's strategic culture", *Xiandai guoji guanxi*, vol. 12, 2004, pp. 20–26.
5 See, for example, Yan Xuetong, *Zhongguo Guojia Liyi Fenxi (An Analysis of China's National Interests)* (Tianjin: Tianjin Renmin Chubanshe, 1997).
6 Li Qinggong and Wei Wei, "The world need a news security concept", *Jiefangjun Bao*, 24 December 1997, p. 5.
7 Li Qinggong and Wei Wei, "The world need a news security concept", *Jiefangjun Bao*, 24 December 1997, p. 5.
8 Russell Ong, "Peaceful evolution, regime change and China's political security", *Journal of Contemporary China*, vol. 16, no. 53 (November 2007), pp. 717–727.
9 The primary difference between Marxist and Realist theories centres on whether class interests or national interests drive state behaviour. See Robert Gilpin, *The Political Economy of International Relations* (Princeton: Prince University Press, 1987), pp. 25–64.
10 The notable exceptions are the Mongol and Manchu conquests of China in the thirteenth and seventeenth centuries, respectively.
11 John King Fairbank, (ed.), *The Chinese World Order: Traditional China's Foreign Relations* (Cambridge, Massachusetts: Harvard University Press, 1968); Suisheng Zhao, *Power Competition in East Asia: from the old Chinese World Order to post-Cold War Regional Multipolarity* (New York: St. Martin's Press, 1997), especially Chapter 2.
12 Barry Buzan and Richard Little, *International Systems in World History: Remaking the Study of International Relations* (Oxford: Oxford University Press, 2000), p. 440.
13 David Lake, "Beyond anarchy: the importance of security institutions", *International Security*, vol. 26, no. 1 (summer 2001), pp. 129–160.
14 Mark Mancall, *China at the Centre: 300 Years of Foreign Policy* (New York: Free Press, 1984).
15 Wang Gungwu, *To Act is to Know: Chinese Dilemmas* (Singapore: Eastern Universities Press, 2003), p. 306.
16 The "new security concept" was first proposed at the annual meeting of the ASEAN Regional Forum (ARF) in 1996, reiterated during a visit to Singapore in 1997 and more fully elaborated by former president Jiang Zemin at the United Nations Conference on Disarmament in 1999. See "Roundup comparing security concepts", China

148 *Notes*

Radio International, 29 December 97 in *BBC Summary of World Broadcasts Part 3 Asia-Pacific*, 1 January 98, p. G/2.
17 Information Office of the State Council, *China's National Defense 2000* (Beijing: Information Office of the State Council, 2000), p. 8.
18 See, for example, Liu Zhenmin, "The current international order and China's road of peaceful development", *Guoji wenti yanjiu*, no. 1, 2005, p. 7; Information Office of the State Council of the People's Republic of China, *China's Peaceful Development Road* (Beijing: 12 December 2005).
19 This is the theme of Herbert Butterfield's essay on "The Great Powers" in Herbert Butterfield and Martin Wight (eds) *Diplomatic Investigations* (London: Allen & Unwin, 1967).
20 Hedley Bull, *The Anarchical Society: A Study of Order in World Politics* (London: Macmillan, 1977), p. 207.
21 Hedley Bull and Adam Watson (eds), *The Expansion of International Society* (Oxford: Oxford University Press, 1984).
22 There is a plethora of discussions on prospects of regional institutions in Asia. See, for example, John Ikenberry and Michael Mastanduno, *International Relations Theory and The Asia-Pacific* (New York: Columbia University Press, 2003); Barry Buzan, "Security architecture in Asia: the interplay of regional and global levels", *The Pacific Review*, vol. 16, no. 2 (June 2003), pp. 143–173; Ralph Cossa, "US security strategy in Asia and the prospects for an Asian regional security regime", *Asia-Pacific Review*, vol. 12, no. 1 (May 2005).

1 The US's global supremacy

1 For instance, the Qing dynasty employed the short-term tactic of using Russia to check Japanese encroachment in Manchuria in the 1890s. See, for example, Suisheng Zhao, *Power Competition in East Asia: From the Old Chinese World Order to Post-Cold War Regional Multipolarity* (New York: St. Martin's Press, 1997).
2 The other alternative is bandwagoning, which is not applicable to the Chinese case. See, for example, Randall Schweller, "Bandwagoning for profit: Bringing the revisionist state back in", *International Security*, vol. 19, no. 1 (Summer 1994), pp. 71–107.
3 See, for example, Julian Lindley-French, *The North Atlantic Treaty Organisation: The Enduring Alliance* (Routledge: Abingdon, UK, 2007), pp. 15–16.
4 "US unilateralism is difficult to sustain", *Xinhua news agency*, 17 June 2008.
5 See, for example, Liu Zhenmin, "Current international order and China's road of peaceful development", *Guoji wenti yanjiu*, no. 1, 2005, p. 7.
6 David Shambaugh, *Beautiful Imperialist: China Perceives America, 1972–1990* (Princeton, NJ: Princeton University Press, 1991), pp. 81–82.
7 Anthony Lake, "Confronting backlash states", *Foreign Affairs*, vol. 73, no. 2 (March/April 1994), pp. 45–55. On the Iran–Libya Sanctions Act of 1996 aimed at isolating rogue states, see Michael Mastanduno, "Extraterritorial sanctions: managing 'hyper-unilateralism' in US foreign policy", in Stewart Patrick and Shephard Forman (eds), *Multilateralism and US Foreign Policy: Ambivalent Engagement* (Boulder, Colorado: Lynne Rienner, 2002), pp. 311–317.
8 The "axis of evil" comprises North Korea, Iraq and Iran, as George Bush stated at the State of Union speech in January 2002.
9 George Bush's speech to the Congress on 20 September 2001 states: "Either you are with us, or you are with the terrorists". See text in *New York Times*, 21 September, 2001, p. B4.
10 The strongest statements were made in Information Office of the State Council, *China's National Defence* (Beijing: July 1998).

11 See, for example, John Lewis Gaddis, *We Now Know: Rethinking Cold War History* (Oxford: Oxford University Press, 1998).
12 See, for example, Ma Zhenggang, "The grand transformation of China's diplomacy", *Guoji wenti yanjiu*, no. 4, 2009, pp. 1–6.
13 See, for example, Stephen M Walt, "Alliance formation and the balance of world power", *International Security*, vol. 9, no. 4 (1985), pp. 3–43.
14 Su Ze, "Kosovo War and the new military theory", *Jiefangjun Bao*, 1 June 1999, p. 6.
15 Although Saddam Hussein has been defeated, the challenge of building democracy in Iraq remains. See, for example, David Hendrickson and Robert Tucker, "Revisions in need of revising: what went wrong in the Iraq war", *Survival*, vol. 47, no. 2 (2005), pp. 7–32.
16 US Department of Defense, *Quadrennial Defense Review Report 2010* (February 2010), p. 4.
17 Su Ge, "An assessment of US national security strategy adjustment", *Guoji wenti yanjiu*, vol. 2, 2003, pp. 15–16.
18 US Department of Defense, *The National Security Strategy of the United States of America 2002* (September 2002), p. iv.
19 The US states that it faces four categories of challenges: traditional, irregular, catastrophic and disruptive. See US Department of Defense, *The National Defense Strategy of the United States* (March 2005), pp. 2–3.
20 Benjamin Barber, *Fear's Empire: War, Terrorism and Democracy* (New York: Norton, 2003).
21 US Department of Defense, *The National Defense Strategy of the United States* (March 2005), p. 10.
22 See Michael Walzer, *Just and Unjust Wars: A Moral Argument with Historical Illustrations* (London: Allen Lane, 1977), p. 81.
23 "China's defense spending to increase 7.5 per cent in 2010: draft budget", *Xinhua news agency*, 5 March 2010.
24 Peng Guangqian and Yao Youzhi (eds), *The Science of Military Strategy* (Beijing: Military Science Publishing House, 2005), p. 224.
25 Peng Guangqian and Yao Youzhi (eds), *The Science of Military Strategy* (Beijing: Military Science Publishing House, 2005), p. 224.
26 "China seeks to advance international nuclear disarmament process", *Xinhua news agency*, 23 June 2005.
27 The strategies of the world's five nuclear states can be broken down into two categories: The first includes the US and Russia (Soviet) and it entails a nuclear strategy with both first-strike and war-fighting capabilities. The other category includes China, Britain and France, which is often described as minimum deterrence.
28 Sun Xiangli, "China's nuclear strategy", *China Security*, no. 1 (Autumn 2005), pp. 23–29.
29 US Department of Defense, *Nuclear Posture Review Report 2010* (28 April 2010), p. 51.
30 "Chinese president expressed sympathy to Bush, US government and people for disastrous attacks", *Renmin Ribao*, 12 September 2001.
31 Beijing's ties to the Taliban regime had included providing assistance to build a national telecommunications systems in Afghanistan.
32 China's efforts were, however, rather limited and restrained. China shared some intelligence with the US as well as provided longstanding ally Pakistan with some economic aid and reassurances for Islamabad's support for Washington.
33 Numerous debates exist on the rise of China. See, for example, this special issue: "Contending perspectives on the 'China challenge'", *Journal of Strategic Studies*, vol. 30, Issue 4 & 5 (2007).
34 On the Middle East case, this was also echoed by Palestinian President Mahmud Abbas. See "Palestinian leader urges greater role for China in peace process", *Xinhua news agency*, 16 May 2005.

35 For an account of the failure of the League of Nations as a collective security system, see E.H. Carr, *The Twenty Years Crisis, 1919–1939* (London: Macmillan, 1961).
36 Domestically, China's nuclear export comes under the control of Commission of Science, Technology and Industry for National Defence (COSTIND) in co-ordination with other relevant government departments. See Information Office of the State Council, *China's Endeavours for Arms Control, Disarmament and Non-proliferation* (Beijing: September 2005).
37 Wang Yong, "Using regional co-operation to resolve Sino-Japanese structural differences", *Zhanlue yu guanli (Strategy and Management)*, no. 1, 2004, pp. 41–47.
38 Warren Kimball, *The Juggler: Franklin Roosevelt as Wartime Statesman* (Princeton, NJ: Princeton University Press, 1991), pp. 83–105.
39 See, for example, Henry Nau, *At Home Abroad: Identity and Power in American Foreign Policy* (Ithaca, New York: Cornell University Press, 2003).

2 The US and liberal values

1 Department of Defense, *The National Security Strategy of the United States of America* (September 2002). This ties in with the "democratic peace" theory. See Michael Brown et al. (eds), *Debating the Democratic Peace* (London: MIT Press, 1996).
2 See Immanuel Kant, *Perpetual Peace and Other Essays on Politics, History and Morals* (Indianapolis: Kackett, 1983), pp. 113–115.
3 See, for instance, Michael E. Brown, Sean M. Lynn-Jones, and Steven E. Miller (eds), *Debating the Democratic Peace* (Cambridge, Massachusetts: MIT Press, 1996).
4 See Michael Cox, John Ikenberry and Takashi Inoguchi (eds), *American Democracy Promotion: Impulses, Strategies, and Impacts* (Oxford: Oxford University Press, 2000); Jonathan Monten, "The roots of the Bush Doctrine: power, nationalism and democracy promotion in US strategy", *International Security*, vol. 29, no. 4 (Spring 2005), pp. 112–156.
5 Condoleezza Rice, "Promoting the national interest", *Foreign Affairs*, vol. 79, no. 1 (January–February 2000), p. 49.
6 Charles Krauthammer, "Universal dominion: toward a unipolar world", *National Interest*, no. 18 (Winter 1989/90), p. 47.
7 Tony Smith, *America's Mission: The United States and the Worldwide Struggle for Democracy in the Twentieth Century* (Princeton, NJ: Princeton University Press, 1994).
8 Department of Defense, *The National Security Strategy of the United States of America* (May 2010), p. 8.
9 Department of Defense, *The National Security Strategy of the United States of America* (Sep 2002), p. iv.
10 Joseph Nye, *Soft Power: The Means to Success in World* Politics (New York: Public Affairs, 2004), Chapter 1.
11 Yan Xuetong and Xu Jin, "A comparison of China and America's soft power", *Xiandai Guoji Guangxi*, no. 2, 2008, pp. 16–27.
12 The Four Cardinal Principles are: keeping to the socialist road, upholding the dictatorship of the proletariat, upholding the leadership of the Chinese Communist Party (CCP) and upholding Marxism–Leninism and Mao Zedong thought.
13 "Problems posed by the Soviet Union – a talk given by Gao Di, editor of the Renmin Ribao, to Communist Party editors and cadres on August 30, 1991", *The China Quarterly*, no. 130 (June 1992), p. 483.
14 See Alexander Lukin, "The initial Soviet reaction to the events in China in 1989 and the prospects for Sino-Soviet relations", *The China Quarterly*, no. 125 (March 1991), pp. 119–136.
15 This is a reference to dissidents such as Fang Lizhi and Yan Jiaqi during the "counter-revolutionary rebellion" in 1989. "Chinese paper denounces 'peaceful evolution' approach of US monopoly capitalist class", *Guangming Ribao*, 4 September 1989.

16 "Deng talks on quelling rebellion in Beijing", *Beijing Review*, vol. 32, no. 28 (10–16 July 1989), pp. 14–17.
17 "Chinese agency says 'Western style democracy' not suitable for all", *Zhongguo Tongxunshe*, 4 June 4, 2009.
18 See, for example, David Turnock, *The East European Economy in Context: Communism and Transition* (London: Routledge, 1997).
19 Information Office of the State Council of the People's Republic of China, *Building of Political Democracy in China* (Beijing, October 2005).
20 For a further discussion on state–society relations in China, see, for example, Peter Hays Gries and Stanley Rosen, *State and Society in 21st Century China: Crisis, Contention and Legitimation* (London: Routledge, 2004).
21 "Confucianism and economic modernisation", *Renmin Ribao*, 19 September 94, p. 1.
22 For a further discussion, see Daniel Bell, *East Meets West: Human Rights and Democracy in East Asia* (Princeton, NJ: Princeton University Press, 2000); Michael Freeman, "Human rights, democracy and 'Asian values'", *Pacific Review*, vol. 9, no. 3 (1996), pp. 367–388.
23 Information Office of the State Council of the People's Republic of China, *Progress in China's Human Rights in 2009* (Beijing: September 2010).
24 Nicholas Wheeler, *Saving Strangers: Humanitarian Intervention in International Society* (Oxford: Oxford University Press, 2002).
25 Jeff Holzgrefe and Robert Keohane (eds), *Humanitarian Intervention: Ethical, Legal and Political Dilemmas* (Cambridge: Cambridge University Press, 2003), p. 18.
26 International Commission on Intervention and State Sovereignty (ICISS), *The Responsibility to Protect* (Ottawa: International Development Research Centre, 2001) (www.iciss.ca/report-en.asp).
27 "Chinese agency comments on US House resolution on Tibet", *Xinhua news agency*, 12 March 09.
28 Robert A. Pape, "Why economic sanctions do not work", *International Security*, vol. 22, no. 2 (Fall 1997), pp. 90–136; Robert A. Pape, "Why economic sanctions still do not work", *International Security*, vol. 23, no. 1 (Summer 1998), pp. 66–77.
29 Information Office of the State Council of the People's Republic of China, *Human Rights in China* (Beijing, November 1991).
30 Robert Weatherley, *The Discourse of Human Rights in China: Historical and Ideological Perspectives* (London: Palgrave Macmillan, 1999).
31 Cited in Tang Huihu, "Western media interfering in China", *Dangdai Shijie Yu Shehui Zhuyi*, vol. 3 (1996), pp. 39–42.
32 See, for example, Zhang Jialin, *China's Response to the Downfall of Communism in Eastern Europe and the Soviet Union* (Palo Alto, California: Hoover Institution, Stanford University, 1994).
33 "Problems posed by the Soviet Union – a talk given by Gao Di, editor of the Renmin Ribao, to Communist Party editors and cadres on 30 August 1991", *The China Quarterly*, no. 130 (June 1992), p. 484.
34 Harry Harding, *A Fragile Relationship: the United States and China since 1972* (Washington, DC: The Brookings Institution, 1992), p. 18.
35 David Shambaugh, "Peking's foreign policy conundrum since Tienanmen: peaceful coexistence vs peaceful evolution", *Issues & Studies*, vol. 28, no. 11 (November 1992), p. 68 and pp. 77–80.
36 Liu Keming, "The new thinking of Mikhail Gorbachev's reform", *Soviet Social Science Research*, no. 1 (1992), p. 1.
37 "Chinese paper denounces 'peaceful evolution' approach of US monopoly capitalist class", Guangming Ribao, 4 September 1989.
38 Wang Jiafu, "Strategic analysis of the internal factors affecting traumatic change in the Soviet Union", *Soviet Social Science Research*, no. 1 (1992), p. 2.

39 Steven Levitsky and Lucan Way, "Linkage versus leverage: Rethinking the international dimension of regime change", *Comparative Politics*, vol. 38, no. 4 (October 2006), pp. 379–400.
40 Jon Pevehouse, "Democracy from the outside-in? International organizations and democratization", *International Organization*, vol. 56, no. 3 (Summer 2002), pp. 515–549; Hans Peter Schmitz, "Domestic and transnational perspectives on democratization", *International Studies Review*, vol. 6, no. 3 (September 2004), pp. 403–426.

3 The US and the international economic system

1 Luo Zhaohong, "Disintegration of the Soviet Union and its impact on the world economic and political landscape", *Shijie jingji yu zhengzhi* (World Economics and Politics), no. 10 (1992), p. 5.
2 It was announced at the Pittsburgh Summit on 25 September 2009 that the G20 group will replace the G8 (Group of Eight) as the main council of major economies. China had not been part of the G8, which consisted of the US, Canada, Japan, UK, Germany, France, Italy and Russia.
3 "China uses new programme on using foreign funds", *Xinhua news agency*, 2 August 2006.
4 "Wen Jiabao's speech at evening welcome banquet hosted by US organisations on 22 September 2010," *Xinhua news agency*, 27 September 2010.
5 "China's foreign trade up 34.7 per cent; surplus falls 6.4 per cent", *Xinhua news agency*, 10 January 2011.
6 Robert Gilpin, *War and Change in World Politics* (Cambridge: Cambridge University Press, 1981), pp. 311–312.
7 See, for example, Peter Gowan, *The Global Gamble: Washington's Faustian Bid for World Dominance* (London: Verso, 1999).
8 Robert Keohane, *After Hegemony: Cooperation and Discord in the World Political Economy* (Princeton, NJ: Princeton University Press, 1984).
9 Paul Kennedy, *The Rise and Fall of the Great Powers: Economic Change and Military Conflict from 1500 to 2000* (New York: Vintage Books, 1987).
10 This was suggested by China's central bank governor, Zhou Xiaochuan. "China urges US to evaluate financial crisis policy efficiency", *Xinhua news agency*, 4 December 2008.
11 "China's growth "greatest contribution" to world economy amid crisis – premier", *Xinhua news agency*, 27 September 08.
12 "On meeting the challenges of the warnings the financial crisis brings to the world", *Xinhua news agency*, 13 November 2008.
13 "China becomes second biggest holder of US T-bonds", *People's Daily*, 9 August 2002.
14 "China's average tariff level drops to 9.9 per cent in 2005", *Xinhua news agency*, 28 January 2005.
15 The US–China Business Council, *China's WTO Scorecard: Selected Year-Three Service Commitments* (30 August 2005).
16 "Chinese agency calls 'Buy American' clause 'dangerous precedent'", *Xinhua news agency*, 18 February 2009.
17 Base ourselves on global righteous cause to save Doha Round", *Xinhua news agency*, 30 July 2008.
18 "Wen Jiabao's speech at evening welcome banquet hosted by US organisations on 22 September 2010", *Xinhua news agency*, 27 September 2010.
19 *2005 Report to Congress of the US–China Economic and Security Review Commission* (November 2005)(www.uscc.gov/annual_report/2005/annual_report_full_05.pdf).
20 With the development of the Euromarkets in the 1950s and 1960s, this principle of monetary sovereignty gradually eroded. For instance, the Soviet Union and China

began to deposit some of their US dollar holdings in banks that were beyond the regulatory reach of a hostile US. See Barry Eichengreen and Peter H. Lindert (eds), *The International Debt Crisis in Historical Perspective* (Cambridge, Mass: MIT Press, 1989).
21 "On meeting the challenges of the financial crisis", *Xinhua news agency*, 13 November 2008.
22 "Speech by Wen Jiabao at the seventh Asia–Europe Meeting (ASEM) on 24 October 2008", *Xinhua news agency*, 25 October 2008.
23 "China demands larger quota share of developing countries in IMF", *Xinhua news agency*, 4 October 2009.
24 Chong Zhongying, "Major changes in international relations – East Asian financial crisis", *Shijie Zhishi*, no. 2 (1998), pp. 24–26.
25 China along with Japan leads the way by contributing 32 per cent each. See "South Korea, China, Japan, ASEAN to set up anti-financial crisis fund", *Yonhap news agency*, 24 October 2008.
26 Michael Doyle, "Kant, liberal legacies, and foreign affairs", *Philosophy and Public Affairs*, no. 12 (Fall 1983), pp. 323–353.
27 Dale Copeland, "Economic interdependence and war: a theory of trade expectations", *International Security*, vol. 20, no. 4 (1996), pp. 5–41.
28 Charles Anderton and John Carter, "The impact of war on trade: an interrupted time-series study", *Journal of Peace Research*, vol. 38, no. 4 (July 2001), pp. 445–457; Reuven Glick and Alan Taylor, *Collateral Damage: Trade Disruption and the Economic Impact of War* (Cambridge, MA: National Bureau of Economic Research, 2005).
29 Chinese agency calls for vigilance over "China responsibility theory", *Xinhua news agency*, 18 August 2010.

4 The US and the Taiwan issue

1 "Chinese parliament adopts Taiwan anti-secession law", *Xinhua news agency*, 14 March 2005.
2 They include states such Marshall Islands, Nauru, Palau, Solomon Islands, Tuvalu, Burkina Faso, Chad, Gambia, Malawi, Sao Tome and Principe, Senegal, Swaziland, St Kitts and Nevis, and St Vincent and Grenadines. See "Taiwan thanks allies for UN letter protesting China's Anti-Secession Law", *Central news agency*, 27 July 2005.
3 See, for instance, Taiwan's Ministry of National Defense, *National Defense White Paper 2004* (17 November 2004), part I, chapter 4.
4 "China, Taiwan jointly reduce import tariffs to implement trade pact", *Central News Agency*, 2 January 2011.
5 Hence, the politically charged term "comprehensive economic cooperation agreement (CECA)" had to be dropped in favour of this term.
6 "Taiwan president says economic ties key to cross-strait policy", *Central News Agency*, 21 February 2009.
7 "ECFA would hurt white-collar sector workers: think tank", *Taipei Times*, 16 March 2009.
8 "Taiwan's exports to China rise sharply in 2010", *Central News agency*, 10 January 2011.
9 US General Douglas MacArthur famously depicted Taiwan as "an unsinkable aircraft carrier" and this is still widely acknowledged. See, for example, Robert D. Kaplan, "The geography of Chinese power: How far can Beijing reach on land and at sea?" *Foreign Affairs*, vol. 3, no. 89 (May/June 2010), pp. 22–41; Ministry of Foreign Affairs, China, *What is the Political Intention of the U.S. Congress in Passing the so-called "Taiwan Relations Act?* (15 November 2000)(www.fmprc.gov.cn/eng/ljzg/3568/t17797.htm) (accessed 7 March 2010).

10 "Military experts questions motive behind Rumsfeld's China threat remarks", *Xinhua news agency*, 10 June 2005.
11 This led to the US's US$9.9 million deficit with Taiwan in 2009. Taipei Economic and Cultural Representative Office in the US, *Taiwan–U.S. Relations* (4 March 2010) (www.taiwanembassy.org/US/ct.asp?xItem=11444&CtNode=2297&mp=12&xp1=122010) (accessed 28 April 2010); US Census Bureau, *Trade in Goods (Imports, Exports and Trade Balance) with Taiwan* (www.census.gov/foreign-trade/balance/c5830.html#2009) (accessed 28 April 2010).
12 Craig Addison, *Silicon Shield: Taiwan's Protection Against Chinese Attacks* (New York: Authorlink, 2001).
13 "Text of Taiwan president's 2009 New Year's Day address", *Central News Agency*, 1 January 2009.
14 The Taiwan Affairs Office and the Information Office under the State Council, *The Taiwan Question and the Reunification of China*", (Beijing, August 1993).
15 The Sino-US Communiques of 28 February 1972, 1 January 1979 and 17August 1982 (http://usinfo.state.gov/eap/east_asia_pacific/china/china_communiques.htm).
16 US Department of Defense, *Quadrennial Defense Review Report* (February 2006), p. 6.
17 "China increases missiles pointed at Taiwan to 1,500", *Taipei Times*, 15 February 2009.
18 "Negotiations with China must start from strong position – Taiwan president", *Central News Agency*, 24 December 2008.
19 According to Taiwan's Ministry of Foreign Affairs (MOFA), the deal includes 114 Patriot Advanced Capability (PAC-3) missiles and technical support. "Taiwan welcomes US announcement of arms sales", *Central News Agency*, 30 January 2010.
20 See Kerry Dumbaugh, *Taiwan: Texts of the Taiwan Relations Act, the U.S.–China Communiques, and the "Six Assurance – CRS Report for Congress, No. 96–246 F* (Washington, DC: Library of Congress, 21 May 1998), p. 18.
21 China "strongly" opposes US resolution on Taiwan, *Xinhua news agency*, 24 March 09.
22 "Chen meets delegation of Japanese parliamentarians", *Central News Agency*, 13 January 2006.
23 It must be noted that the Taiwan Strait issue was not explicitly highlighted in that May 2007 meeting. "Taiwan Foreign Ministry says US–Japan security talks serves Taiwan's interests", *Central News Agency*, 3 May 2007.
24 "Taiwan to issue first national security report", *Central News Agency*, 10 November 2005.
25 The limitations of missile defence systems in the Taiwan Strait are discussed in James Lindsay and Michael O'Hanlon, *Defending America: The Case of Limited National Missile Defense* (Washington, DC: Brookings Institution, 2001), pp. 123–130.
26 On the formation of the Democratic Progressive Party (DPP), see Shelley Rigger, *From opposition to power: Taiwan's Democratic Progressive Party* (London: Lynne Rienner Publishers, 2001).
27 For an account of the Tiananmen event, see, for example, Craig Calhoun, *Neither Gods Nor Emperors: Students and the Struggle for Democracy in China* (California: University of California Press, 1994). Elizabeth Wasserstrom and Jeffrey Perry, *Popular Protest and Political Culture in Modern China: Learning from 1989* (London: Westview Press, second edition, 1993).
28 Daniel Bell and Hahm Chaibong (eds), *Confucianism for the Modern World* (London: Cambridge University Press, 2003).
29 For an overview of the "democratic peace" debate, see Michael Brown *et al.* (eds), *Debating the Democratic Peace: An International Security Reader* (Cambridge, Massachusetts: MIT Press, 1996).

30 "Freedom, democracy Taiwan's 'soft power' in ties with China: president", *Central News Agency*, 30 December 2008.
31 Joseph Nye, "Soft power", *Foreign Policy*, no. 80 (Fall 1990), pp. 163–164. Joseph Nye, *Soft Power: The Means to Success in World Politics* (New York: Public Affairs, 2004).
32 "Taiwan willing to share democratisation experience with other nations," *Central News Agency*, 16 November 2005.
33 "President Li says 'peaceful evolution' to continue in mainland China", *Central News agency*, 26 December 97.
34 "Taiwan president believes democracy will defeat China's authoritarian regime", *Central News Agency*, 1 April 2006.
35 Dan Blumenthal and Randall Schriver, *Strengthening Freedom in Asia: A Twenty-first Century Agenda for the US–Taiwan partnership* (Washington: American Enterprise Institute, 22 February 2008), pp. 12–13.
36 "Taiwan to establish 'exclusive' human rights regime", *Central News Agency*, 8 January 2011.
37 On prospects for democracy in China, see Cheng Li (ed.), *China's Changing Political Landscape: Prospects for Democracy* (Washington, DC: Brookings Institution Press, 2008).
38 "Pro-independence scholars: Taiwan should join UN, write new constitution", *Central News Agency*, 4 January 2009.
39 "Taiwan shifts UN bid strategy, targets specialised agencies", *Central news agency*, 17 August 2009.
40 "Fourteen countries support Taiwan participation in UN agencies", *Central news agency*, 30 September 2008.
41 "Puppet of America's double dealing policy", *Renmin Ribao*, 13 June 1995, p. 6.
42 Taiwan party urges US to support "right to self determination", *Central News Agency*, 10 February 2006.
43 "The Taiwan Work Office of the CCP Central Committee and the Taiwan Affairs of the State Council issue a joint statement", *Xinhua news agency*, 28 February 2006.

5 The US and Japan

1 Department of Defense, *The National Security Strategy of the United States of America* (May 2010), p. 49.
2 Department of Defense, *The National Security Strategy of the United States of America* (May 2010), p. 49.
3 Ministry of Defense, *The Defense of Japan 2010* (2010).
4 Japan Defense Agency, *National Defense Programme Guideline for FY 2005 and After* (2004).
5 Ministry of Defense, *The Defense of Japan 2010* (2010), Part I, Chapter 2, Section 3.
6 Richard Samuels, *Securing Japan: Tokyo's Grand Strategy and the Future of East Asia* (Ithaca, NY: Cornell University Press, 2007), pp. 200–201.
7 See, for example, Michael Armacost, *Friends or Rivals? The Insider's Account of US–Japan Relations* (New York: Columbia University Press, 1996), p. 251.
8 Department of Defense, *The National Security Strategy of the United States of America* (September 2002), p. 26.
9 Two important documents were published – *The Council on Security and Defense Capabilities Report – Japan's Visions for Future Security and Defense Capabilities* (October 2004) (better known as the Araki Report) and the *National Defense Programme Guidelines (NDPG) for FY 2005 and After* (December 2004). The tenets of the Araki report were adopted into the *NDPG*, which outlined the official policy.

10 The Council on Security and Defense Capability, *Council on Security and Defense Capabilities Report: Japan's Visions for Future Security and Defense Capabilities* (October 2004); The Council on Security and Defense Capabilities in the New Era, *Japan's Visions for Future Security and Defense Capabilities in the New Era: Toward a Peace-Creating Nation* (August 2010).
11 Japan Defense Agency, *National Defense Programme Guideline for FY 2005 and After* (December 2004).
12 Ministry of Defense, *National Defense Programme Guidelines for FY 2011 and Beyond* (17 December 2010).
13 "Japan develops plans in case of Korean conflict", *Asahi Shimbun*, 12 December 2004.
14 "US think tank report urges Japan to ease ban on collective self-defence", *Kyodo News Service*, 2 December 2008.
15 "US think tank report urges Japan to ease ban on collective self-defence", *Kyodo News Service*, 2 December 2008.
16 Ministry of Foreign Affairs Japan, *Joint Statement of the US–Japan Security Consultative Committee* (19 February 2005).
17 In August 1997, Japanese chief cabinet secretary Seiroku Kajiyama had declared that the "surrounding areas" covered by Japan–US collaboration "should include the Taiwan Strait". See "Comment on Japan–US Defence Co-operation Guidelines", *Zhongguo Xinwen She*, 20 January 1998.
18 This is acknowledged by Japan, see Ministry of Defense, *Defense of Japan 2010* (2010).
19 Ministry of Defense, *The Defense of Japan 2010* (2010), Part I, Chapter 2, Section 3.
20 "Article says plot to contain China lies behind islands dispute", *Zhongguo Tongxun She*, 9 September 1996.
21 "History proves Diaoyu Islands are Chinese territory", *Xinhua news agency*, 8 September 2010.
22 "Opening statement by prime minister Junichiro Koizumi at press conference", *Kyodo*, 19 September 2001.
23 The proposal could win a majority in the General Assembly but probably not the two-thirds vote required to change the United Nations (UN) charter.
24 On the official development assistance (ODA), see Tsukasa Takamine, "A new dynamism in Sino-Japanese security relations: Japan's strategic use of foreign aid", *The Pacific Review*, vol. 18, no. 4 (December 2005), pp. 439–461.
25 Kenneth Waltz, "The emerging structure of international politics," *International Security*, vol. 18, no. 2 (Autumn 1993), p. 66; Chalmers Johnson, "Japan in search of a 'normal' role", *Daedalus*, vol. 121, no. 4 (1992), pp. 1–33.
26 Ian Nish, *The Origins of the Russo-Japanese War* (London: Longman, 1985).

6 The US and North Korea

1 A good account of the Korean War can be founding in Bruce Cumings, *The Origins of the Korean War* (Princeton, NJ: Princeton University Press: 1990).
2 On the other hand, Russia abrogated its 1961 Treaty of Mutual Friendship with North Korea in the 1990s and came up with a new version that does not include military assistance to North Korea if it is attacked by another country.
3 This concept was initially popularised by the Clinton administration as part of a wider effort to identify threats to American security in the post-Cold War era. Robert S Litwak, "What's in a name? The changing foreign policy lexicon", *Journal of international Affairs*, vol. 54, no. 2 (Spring 2001), pp. 375–392. See also Robert S Liwak, *Rogue States and US Foreign Policy: Containment after the Cold War* (Baltimore: Johns Hopkins University Press, 2000).
4 "North Korea terms US rights act an 'open challenge'", *Korean Central News Agency*, 18 October 2004.

5 "North Korean paper supports China's position on US Security strategy report", Nodong Sinmun, 5 April 2006, in *BBC Worldwide Monitoring*, 7 April 2006.
6 Bruce Cumings, *North Korea: Another Country* (New York: The New Press, 2004).
7 Michael Robinson, *Cultural Nationalism in Colonial Korea, 1920–1925* (Seattle: University of Washington Press, 1988), p. 16.
8 "Conclusion of non-aggression treaty between DPRK and US called for", *Korean Central News Agency*, 25 October 2002.
9 "North Korea says inter-Korean relations separate from nuclear dispute", *Yonhap news agency*, 19 December 2009.
10 North Korea reportedly purchased 12 decommissioned Russian Foxtrot and Golf-II class submarines for scrap metal from a Japanese company. See Steven Hildreth, *North Korean Ballistic Missile Threat to the US* (Congressional Research Service: 24 February 2009).
11 North Korea purchased several Soviet-supplied Scud-B missiles from Egypt in the late 1970s and developed them further. See Joseph Cirincione et al., *Deadly Arsenals: Tracking Weapons of Mass Destruction* (Washington, DC: Carnegie Endowment for World Peace, 2002), pp. 250–251.
12 Clark Gibson et al., *The Samaritan's Dilemma: The Political Economy of Development Aid* (London: Oxford University Press, 2005).
13 Nicholas Eberstadt, *The North Korean Economy: Between Crisis and Catastrophe* (New Brunswick, NJ: Transaction Publishers, 2007).
14 Before the Changchun–Jilin–Tumen pilot zone was initiated in 2009, the Chinese part of the Tumen River area cross-border economic co-operation scheme was mainly confined Huichun, a port city in Jilin Province.
15 For further details, see *Changchun Agreement of the Member Countries of the Greater Tumen Initiative* (Changchun, China: 2 September 2005) (www.tumenprogramme.org/news.php?id=500).
16 "North Korean leader 'deeply impressed' by Chinese development", *Korean Central News Agency*, 18 January 2006.
17 South Korean president Kim Dae-jung agreed with North Korean leader Kim Jong-il during their historic June 2000 summit meeting to build this complex, where had envisioned to host 300 South Korean companies by 2006.
18 "South Korea outlines seven projects to help North once denuclearised", *Yonhap news agency*, 28 June 2005.

7 The US and South Korea

1 See Chen Jian, *Mao's China and the Cold War* (Chapel Hill, NC: University of North Carolina Press, 2001), pp. 238–276; John W. Garver, *China's Decision for Rapprochement with the United States, 1968–1971* (Boulder, Colorado: Westview Press, 1982).
2 "USA eases arms sales to South Korea", *Yonhap new agency*, 14 May 2008.
3 "US agrees written nuclear guarantee for South Korea – minister", *Yonhap news agency*, 6 June 2009.
4 *Mutual Defense Treaty between the Republic of Korea and the United States of America* (www.usfk.mil/org/fkdc-sa/sofa/mutdef.htm), accessed on 14 July 2008; "South Paper reports US to maintain troop levels in Korea", *Yonhap news agency*, 24 January 2006.
5 Samuel S. Kim (ed.), *Korea's Democratisation* (Cambridge: Cambridge University Press, 2003).
6 David Steinberg (ed.), *Korean Attitudes Toward the United States: Changing Dynamics* (London: M.E. Sharpe, 2005).
7 Nicholas Eberstadt, *Korea Approaches Reunification* (Armonk, New York: M.E Sharpe), p. 151.

8 See Roh Tae-woo, *Korea: A Nation Transformed* (Elmsford, New York: Pergamon Press, 1990), pp. 11–17.
9 T. J. Pempel, "Northeast Asian Economic Integration: A Region in Flux", *Asia-Pacific Review*, vol. 14, no. 2 (November 2007), pp. 45–61.
10 For ex-president Park Chung Hee's "arms-for-allies" bargaining with the US, see Don Oberdorfer, *The Two Koreas: A Contemporary History* (Reading, MA: Addison-Wesley, 1997), pp. 85–94 and pp. 101–108.
11 National Security Council, *Peace, Prosperity and National Security: National Security Strategy of the Republic of Korea* (1 May 2004).
12 "South Korean leader reiterates 'balancing role' concept", *Yonhap news agency*, 30 March 2005.
13 Jack Levy, "Balances and balancing: concepts, propositions and research design", in John Vasquez and Colin Elman, *Realism and the Balance of Power: A New Debate* (Upper Saddle River, NJ: Prentice Hall, 2003), pp. 139–140.
14 *Sino-ROK (Republic of Korea) Joint Statement*, 28 May 2008.
15 See Samuel S. Kim, "The making of China's Korea policy in the reform era", in David Lampton (ed.), *The Making of Chinese Foreign and Security Policy in the Era of Reform* (Stanford: Stanford University Press, 2001), pp. 371–408.
16 US Department of Defense, *Quadrennial Defense Review Report* (6 February 2006), p. 6.
17 As noted by a National Assembly Legislative Review Committee, see "South Korean Assembly finds US forces plan incompatible with defence treaty", *Yonhap news agency*, 6 February 2006.
18 See, for instance, Li Jun, "The 'strategic flexibility' of US Forces in South Korea: implications and influences", *Xiandai Guoji Guanxi*, no. 4, 2006, pp. 50–54.
19 *Joint Statement on the Strategic Consultation for Allied Partnership (SCAP)*, 20 January 2006. This consultation was launched at the ministerial level.
20 *2007 Diplomatic White Paper* (Seoul: Ministry of Foreign Affairs and Trade, Republic of Korea, 2007), pp. 57–58.
21 *Joint Statement on the Strategic Consultation for Allied Partnership (SCAP)*, 20 January 2006.
22 See The Ministry of National Defense, The Republic of Korea, *2004 Defense White Paper*, chapter 4.
23 This was delayed from earlier agreed 17 April 2012, see "Delay of wartime command transfer to bolster security on Korean Peninsula", *Yonhap news agency*, 26 June 2010. See also *The 39th Security Consultative Meeting Joint Communiqué* (7 November 2007). (www.defenselink.mil/news/Nov2007/39THSCMJointCommunique.pdf).
24 *Sino-ROK Joint Statement*, 28 May 2008.
25 A total of 12 meetings on the Future of the Alliance Policy Initiatives (FOTA) was held from January 2003 to September 2004. FOTA was subsequently replaced by the Security Policy Initiative (SPI) and a total of 13 meetings was held between February 2005 and June 2007. The launch of SPI was agreed at the 36th Security Consultative Meetings (SCM) in October 2004.
26 Guo Xiangang, "South Korea-US alliance seeks new directions", *Guoji wenti yanjiu*, no. 3, 2006, pp. 28–32.
27 See Kenneth Swope, "Beyond turtleboats: siege accounts from Hideyoshi's second invasion of Korea, 1597–1598", *Sungkyun Journal of East Asian Studies*, vol. 6, no. 2 (2006), pp. 177–206.
28 Charles M. Perry et al., *Alliance Diversification and the Future of the US–Korean Security Relationship* (Herndon, Virgina: Brassey's, 2004), p. ix.
29 As expected, North Korea has criticised South Korea's nuclear testing, which it argues adds another obstacle for the smooth procession of six-party talks.
30 "South Korea joins US-led anti proliferation campaign after North's nuke test", *Yonhap news agency*, 26 May 2009.

31 National Security Council, Peace, *Prosperity and National Security: National Security Strategy of the Republic of Korea* (1 May 2004), pp. 32–35.
32 "Full text of North Korea six-party talks chairman's statement", *Yonhap news agency*, 12 July 2008.
33 Kim Dae-jung announced the Sunshine Policy at his inaugural speech as President of South Korea on 25 February 1998. For further details, see Chung-in Moon and David Steinberg (eds), *Kim Dae-jung Government and Sunshine Policy: Promise and Challenges* (Seoul: Yonsei University Press, 1999), pp. 35–36.
34 *North–South Joint Declaration* (15 June 2000).
35 Kim Dae-jung agreed with Kim Jong-il during their historic June 2000 summit meeting to build this complex, where is envisioned to host 300 South Korean companies by 2006. For further details, see Republic of Korea's Ministry of Unification, *2005 White Paper on Korean Unification* (June 2005), pp. 74–84.
36 See, for example, J.K. Fairbank (ed.), *The Chinese World Order: Traditional China's Foreign Relations* (Cambridge: Harvard University Press, 1968).
37 For the impact of public opinion and its relationship to inter-Korean relations during the Kim Dae-jung administration, see Scott Synder, "The end of history, the rise of ideology and the future of democracy in South Korea Peninsula", *Journal of East Asian Studies*, vol. 3, no. 2, pp. 199–224.

8 The US and Central Asia

1 For instance, writing in the 1930s, Owen Lattimore noted that the Chinese had effectively controlled Central Asia for only 425 out of 2,000 years. See Owen Lattimore, *Inner Asian Frontiers of China* (Boston: Beacon Press, 1940), p. 171.
2 Allen S. Whiting, *Sinkiang: Pivot or Pawn?* (East Lansing: Michigan State University Press, 1958), p. 14.
3 The term "social imperialist" was used by the Chinese to categorise the Soviet Union as a socialist country with imperialist ambitions, just like capitalist America. The important point is that China had to face two hostile superpowers in the 1960s.
4 China fought a border war against the Soviet Union along the Ussuri River in 1969. See John. Gittings, *Survey of the Sino-Soviet Dispute: A Commentary and Extracts from the Recent Polemics 1963–1967* (London: Oxford University Press, 1968); Donald Zagoria, *The Sino-Soviet Conflict, 1956–1961* (Princeton, NJ: Princeton University Press, 1962).
5 Nicolas Becquelin, "Staged development in Xinjiang", *The China Quarterly*, vol. 178 (June 2004), pp. 358–378.
6 Abigail Sines, "Civilizing the Middle Kingdom's wild west", *Central Asian Survey*, vol. 21, no. 1 (March 2002), pp. 5–14.
7 See, for example, William Safran, *Nationalism and Ethno-regional Identities in China* (London: Frank Cass, 1998) for a discussion on China's ethnic minorities.
8 For a survey of the oil and gas resources in Central Asia, see, for example, John Roberts, "Caspian oil and gas: How far have we come and where are we going?" in Sally Cummings (ed.), *Oil, Transition and Security in Central Asia* (New York: Routledge Curzon, 2003).
9 Halford Mackinder, "The geographical pivot of history", *Geographical Journal*, vol. 20, no. 4 (April 1904), p. 421. See also G Robbins, "The post-Soviet heartland: Reconsidering Mackinder", *Eurasian Studies*, vol. 11, no. 3 (Fall 1994), p. 35.
10 "Chinese think-tank on Central Asia, NATO", *Zhongguo Xinwen She*, 20 January 1998.
11 See Wang Naicheng and Jun Xiu, "Whither NATO", *International Strategic Studies*, no. 2 (1999), pp. 27–32 and Xie Wenqing, "Observing US strategy of global hegemony from NATO's use of force against the FRY", *International Strategic Studies*, no. 3 (1999), pp. 1–9.

160 *Notes*

12 Dong Guozheng, "Security globalisation is not tantamount to Americanisation", *Jiefangjun Bao*, 24 May 1999.
13 "US dreams of Asian NATO", *China Daily*, 18 July 2003.
14 Interestingly, some Russians also share this view. Although Moscow officially supports the US in the "war on terror", there are Russians who regard this war as outright US imperialism or want support greater integration with the West while remaining still sceptical of then President Vladimir Putin's policies. See John O'Loughlin, Gearoid O Tuathail and Vladimir Kolossov, "Russian geopolitical storylines and public opinion in the wake of 9–11: a critical geopolitical analysis and national survey", *Communist and post-Communist Studies*, vol. 37, No. 3 (September 2004), pp. 281–318.
15 The Collective Security Treaty Organisation (CSTO) aims to build up its military capabilities to cope with new threats such as international terrorism, illegal circulation of narcotics, illegal migration and organised crime.
16 "Chinese agency notes Russia unusually cautious on Kirghizstan crisis", *Xinhua news agency*, 26 March 2005.
17 "China cuts Uighur's sentence", *BBC World News*, 3 March 2004 (http://news.bbc.co.uk/1/hi/world/asia-pacific/3528535.stm).
18 See "Caspian pipeline 'unites nations'", *BBC World News*, 16 October 2004, (http://news.bbc.co.uk/1/hi/world/europe/3749616.stm).
19 Department of Defense, *The National Security Strategy of the United States of America* (March 2006) p. 41.
20 "Kazakhs agree to China pipeline", *BBC News*, 18 May 2004 (http://news.bbc.co.uk/1/hi/world/asia-pacific/3723249.stm).
21 Xinjiang overtook Shandong Province, the previous second largest oil production base. Daqing in the northern Heilongjiang Province leads with annual output of 40.2 million tonnes. "Xinjiang becomes China's second largest crude oil producer", *Xinhua news agency*, 2 January 2009.
22 "China's to increase oil production in Tarim Basin", *Renmin Ribao*, 10 November 2004.
23 "China's military said planning aircraft for protecting oil imports, sea shipping", *Zhongguo Tongxun She*, 6 January 2009.
24 "Chinese vice president Xi Jinping's speech at the international energy conference in Jeddah, Saudi Arabia", *Xinhua news agency*, 22 June 2008.
25 Statement from the Information Office of the State Council, People's Republic of China, *East Turkistan's Terrorist Forces Cannot Get Away with Impunity*, 21 January 2002.
26 "Join hands to build a harmonious region with lasting peace and common prosperity – speech at the eighth meeting of the SCO Council of Heads of State by Hu Jintao, president of the PRC", *Xinhua news agency*, 28 Aug 2008.
27 Dewardic McNeal, *China's relations with Central Asian states and problems with terrorism,"* in *US Department of State – Congressional Research Service Report for Congress* (17 December 2001) (http://fpc.state.gov/documents/organization/7945.pdf).
28 This was achieved at the fourth SCO Summit Meeting in Tashkent. See "Hu's speech at the fourth SCO summit meeting in Tashkent", *Xinhua news agency*, 17 June 2004.
29 Kazakhstan had hosting two strategic missiles launch sites at Derzhavinsk and Zhangiz-Tobe, a nuclear test zone at Semipalatinsk and one strategic bomber airbase.
30 "Five-nation border agreement signed in Shanghai", Xinhua news agency, 26 Apr in *BBC Summary of World Broadcasts Part 3 Asia-Pacific*, 27 April 96, p. G/1.
31 China said it would further cut its troops by 500,000 in three years on the basis of a reduction of one million troops in the 1980s. See "Roundup comparing security

concepts", China Radio International, 29 December 97 in *BBC Summary of World Broadcasts Part 3 Asia-Pacific*, 1 January 98, p. G/2. "Chinese party paper commentary hails Central Asian border accord", Xinhua news agency, 24 April 97 in *BBC Summary of World Broadcasts Part 3 Asia-Pacific*, 26 Apr 97, p. G/1.

32 "Defence minister says China's military diplomacy 'unprecedentedly active' in 1997", Xinhua news agency 26 December 97, in *BBC Summary of World Broadcasts Part 3 Asia-Pacific*, 30 December 97, p. G/112.

33 "Hu's speech at the fourth SCO summit meeting in Tashkent", *Xinhua news agency*, 17 June 2004.

Selected bibliography

Official documents (listed in chronological order)

China

Communique of the Third Plenary Session of the 11th Central Committee of the Communist Party of China (Beijing: 29 December 1978).
Information Office of the State Council of the People's Republic of China, *Human Rights in China* (Beijing, November 1991).
Information Office of the State Council of the People's Republic of China, *Tibet – Its Ownership and the Human Rights Situation* (Beijing: 22 September 1992).
Taiwan Affairs Office and the Information Office under the State Council of the People's Republic of China, *The Taiwan Question and the Reunification of China* (Beijing: 31 August 1993).
Information Office of the State Council of the People's Republic of China, *The Progress of Human Rights in China* (Beijing: December 1995).
Information Office of the State Council of the People's Republic of China, *The Situation of Children in China* (Beijing: April 1996).
Information Office of the State Council of the People's Republic of China, *New Progress in Human Rights in the Tibet Autonomous Region* (Beijing: February 1998).
Information Office of the State Council of the People's Republic of China, *China's National Defence* (Beijing: July 1998).
Information Office of the State Council of the People's Republic of China, *China's National Defense 2000* (Beijing: 2000).
Taiwan Affairs Office and the Information Office under the State Council, *The One China principle and the Taiwan Issue* (Beijing: 21 February 2000).
Statement from the Information Office of the State Council, People's Republic of China, *East Turkistan's Terrorist Forces Cannot Get Away with Impunity* (Beijing: 21 January 2002).
Information Office of the State Council of the People's Republic of China, *China's National Defense in 2004* (Beijing: December 2004).
Information Office of the State Council of the People's Republic of China, *China's Endeavours for Arms Control, Disarmament and Non-proliferation* (Beijing: September 2005).
Information Office of the State Council of the People's Republic of China, *Building of Political Democracy in China* (Beijing, October 2005).
Information Office of the State Council of the People's Republic of China, *China's Peaceful Development Road* (Beijing: 12 December 2005).

Information Office of the State Council of the People's Republic of China, *Progress in China's Human Rights in 2009* (Beijing: September 2010).
Information Office of the State Council of the People's Republic of China, *China's National Defense 2008* (Beijing: 20 January 2009).
Information Office of the State Council of the People's Republic of China, *Development and Progress in Xinjiang* (Beijing: September 2009).

Japan

Japan Defense Agency, *National Defense Programme Guideline for FY 2005 and After* (2004).
Kyushu Economic Federation. *Interaction Transcending National Borders* (no. 24, August 2004).
Council on Security and Defense Capability, *Council on Security and Defense Capabilities Report: Japan's Visions for Future Security and Defense Capabilities* (October 2004).
Japan Defense Agency, *Defence of Japan 2005* (2005).
Ministry of Foreign Affairs of Japan, *Joint Statement of the US–Japan Security Consultative Committee* (19 February 2005).
Ministry of Economy, Trade and Industry of Japan, *White Paper on International Economy and Trade 2005* (July 2005).
Ministry of Defense, *National Defense Programme Guideline for FY 2011 and After* (December 2010).
Ministry of Defense, *Defense of Japan 2010* (2010).
The Council on Security and Defense Capabilities in the New Era, *Japan's Visions for Future Security and Defense Capabilities in the New Era: Toward a Peace-Creating Nation* (August 2010).

South Korea

Korea Institute for Economic Policy, *Regional Integration in Northeast Asia: Approaches To Integration Among China, Korea and Japan* (December 2004).
Ministry of Unification of the Republic of Korea, *2005 White Paper on Korean Unification* (June 2005).
Republic of Korea's Ministry of National Defense, *2006 Defense White Paper* (May 2007).
Republic of Korea's Ministry of National Defense, *2008 Defense White Paper* (July 2009).

Taiwan

Ministry of National Defense of Taiwan, *National Defense White Paper 2004* (17 November 2004).
National Security Council of Taiwan, *National Security Report 2006* (May 2006)
Ministry of National Defense of Taiwan, *Quadrennial Defense Review 2009* (March 2009).
Ministry of National Defense of Taiwan, *2009 National Defense Report* (October 2009).

US

Iraq Liberation Act of 1998 (31 October 1998).
George Bush's speech to the Congress (20 September 2001).

164 Selected bibliography

US Department of State, *Congressional Research Service Report for Congress: China's Relations with Central Asian States and Problems with Terrorism* (17 December 2001).
George Bush's State of Union speech (29 January 2002).
Department of Defense, *The National Security Strategy of the United States of America* (September 2002).
US–China Economic and Security Review Commission, *China's Multilateral Diplomacy in the Asia-Pacific* (12–13 February 2004).
Department of Defense, *The National Defense Strategy of the United States* 2005 (March 2005).
Department of Defense, *The National Defense Strategy of the United States* 2008 (June 2008).
The US–China Business Council, *China's WTO Scorecard: Selected Year-Three Service Commitments* (30 August 2005).
2005 Report to Congress of the US–China Economic and Security Review Commission (November 2005).
Department of Defense, *The National Security Strategy of the United States of America* (March 2006).
Department of Defense, *Quadrennial Defense Review Report* (February 2010).
Department of Defense, *Nuclear Posture Review Report* (April 2010).
Department of Defense, *The National Security Strategy of the United States of America* (May 2010).

Others

Joint Communique of the United States of America and the People's Republic of China (28 February 1972).
Joint Communique of the United States of America and the People's Republic of China (1 January 1979).
Joint Communique of the United States of America and the People's Republic of China (17 August 1982).
Sino-Soviet Joint Communiqué (Moscow: 19 May 1991).
South–North Joint Declaration on the Denuclearisation of the Korean Peninsula (February 1992).
China–South Korea Joint Communiqué (Beijing: 30 September 1992).
Agreed Framework between the United States of America and the Democratic People's Republic of Korea (Geneva: 21 October 1994).
Joint Statement by the People's Republic of China and the Russian Federation (Beijing: 25 April 1996).
North–South Joint Declaration – North Korea and South Korea (June 2000).
Joint Press Statement on the Outcome of ROK–US Bilateral Meeting (20 October 2003).
Text of KMT–Beijing Agreement (29 April 2005).
Joint statement on the Strategic Consultation for Allied Partnership (SCAP) – Japan and the US (20 January 2006).

News agencies

BBC Monitoring
BBC News
Korean Central News Agency

Kyodo news service
Xinhua news agency
Yonhap news agency
Zhongguo Tongxun She

Newspapers

Choson Ilbo
Guangming Ribao
Jiefangjun Bao (People's Liberation Army Daily)
Korea Herald
Korea Times
Nodong Sinmun
Renmin Ribao (People's Daily)
Renmin Ribao (People's Daily) (Overseas edition)
Xinjiang Ribao

Books

Allison, Graham. *Essence of Decision: Explaining the Cuban Missile Crisis* (Boston, Massachusetts: Little Brown, 1971).
Amsden, Alice. *Asia's Next Giant: South Korea and Late Industrialization*, New York: Oxford University Press, 1989).
Armacost, Michael. *Friends or Rivals? The Insider's Account of US–Japan Relations* (New York: Columbia University Press, 1996).
Armstrong, David. *Revolution and World Order: The Revolutionary State in International Society* (Oxford: Clarendon Press, 1993).
Bachman, David. *Bureaucracy, Economy and Leadership in China: The Institutional Origins of the Great Leap Forward* (Cambridge: Cambridge University Press, 1991).
Barber, Benjamin. *Fear's Empire: War, Terrorism and Democracy* (New York: Norton, 2003).
Bell, Daniel. *East Meets West: Human Rights and Democracy in East Asia* (Princeton, NJ: Princeton University Press, 2000).
Brown, Michael, Lynn-Jones, Sean M. and Miller, Steven E. (eds). *Debating The Democratic Peace* (London: MIT Press, 1996).
Bull, Hedley. *The Anarchical Society: A Study of Order in World Politics* (London: Macmillan, 1995, 2nd edn).
Buzan, Barry. *People, States and Fear: An Agenda for International Security Studies in the post-Cold War Era* (Hemel Hempstead: Harvester Wheatsheaf, 1991, 2nd edn).
Buzan, Barry and Waever, Ole. *Security: A New Framework for Analysis* (London, Lynne Rienner, 1998).
Buzan, Barry and Little, Richard. *International Systems in World History: Remaking the Study of International Relations* (Oxford: Oxford University Press, 2000).
Carr, E.H. *The Twenty Years Crisis, 1919–1939* (London: Macmillan, 1961).
Cirincione, Joseph, with Jon B. Wolfsthal and Miriam Rajkumar, *Deadly Arsenals: Tracking Weapons of Mass Destruction* (Washington, DC: Carnegie Endowment for World Peace, 2002).
Cumings, Bruce. *The Origins of the Korean War* (Princeton, NJ: Princeton University Press: 1990).

Cummings, Sally (ed.). *Oil, Transition and Security in Central Asia*, (New York: RoutledgeCurzon, 2003).
Dillon, Michael. *China's Muslim Hui Community: Migration, Settlement and Sects* (Richmond: Curzon, 1999).
Eberstadt, Nicholas. *Korea Approaches Reunification*, (Armonk, New York: M.E Sharpe, 1995).
Fairbank, John King (ed.). *The Chinese World Order: Traditional China's Foreign Relations* (Cambridge, Massachusetts: Harvard University Press, 1968).
Fitzgerald, Charles Patrick. *The Chinese View of Their Place in the World* (London: Oxford University Press, 1964).
Gaddis, John Lewis. *We Now Know: Rethinking Cold War History* (Oxford: Oxford University Press, 1998).
Gills, Barry. *Korea versus Korea: A Case of Contested Legitimacy* (London: Routledge, 1996).
Gilpin, Robert. *The Political Economy of International Relations* (Princeton: Prince University Press, 1987).
Gittings, John. *Survey of the Sino-Soviet Dispute: A Commentary and Extracts from the Recent Polemics 1963–1967* (London: Oxford University Press, 1968).
Gowan, Peter. *The Global Gamble: Washington's Faustian Bid for World Dominance* (London: Verso, 1999).
Gries, Peter Hays and Rosen, Stanley. S*tate and Society in 21st Century China: Crisis, Contention and Legitimation* (London: Routledge, 2004).
Harding, Harry (ed.). *China's Foreign Relations in the 1980s* (London: Yale University Press, 1984).
Harding, Harry. *A Fragile Relationship: The United States and China since 1972* (Washington, DC: Brookings Institution, 1992).
Hsu, Immanuel. *The Rise of Modern China* (Oxford: Oxford University Press, 1990).
Hughes, Christopher. *Japan's Security Agenda: Military, Economic and Environmental Dimensions* (Boulder, Colorado: Lynne Rienner, 2004).
Hunt, Michael. *Ideology and US Foreign Policy* (New Haven, Connecticut: Yale University Press, 1987).
Huntingdon, Samuel. *Political Order in Changing Societies* (New Haven & London: Yale University Press, 1968).
Huntington, Samuel. *The Third Wave: Democratisation in the late Twentieth Century* (Norman, Oklahoma: University of Oklahoma Press, 1991).
Inoguchi, Takashi. *Japan's International Relations* (London: Pinter publishers, 1991).
Inoguchi, Takashi. *Japan's Foreign Policy in an era of Global Change* (London: Pinter, 1993).
Johnson, Chalmers. *Japan: Who Governs? The Rise of the Developmental State* (New York: W.W. Norton, 1995).
Johnston, Alistair Iain and Ross, Robert Ross (eds). *Engaging China: The Management of an Emerging Power* (London: Routledge, 1999).
Kennedy, Paul. *The Rise and Fall of Great Powers: Economic Change and Military Conflict from 1500 to 2000* (London: Unwin Hyman, 1988).
Keohane, Robert and Nye, Joseph. *Power and Interdependence* (Glenview, Illinois: Scott Foresman and Company, 1989, 2nd edn).
Keohane, Robert (ed.) (1986) *Neorealism and its Critics* (New York: Columbia University Press).
Kim, Samuel (ed.), *China and the World: Chinese Foreign Relations in the post-Cold War Era* (Oxford: Westview Press: 1994, 3rd edn).

Kim, Samuel (ed.). *Korea's Democratisation* (Cambridge: Cambridge University Press, 2003).
Lampton, David (ed.). *The Making of Chinese foreign and Security Policy in the Era of Reform* (Stanford, CA: Stanford University Press, 2001).
Lattimore, Owen. *Inner Asian Frontiers of China* (Boston: Beacon Press, 1940).
Lewis, John and Xue, Litai. *China Builds The Bomb* (Stanford: Stanford University Press, 1988).
Lipman, Jonathan. *Familiar Strangers: A History of Muslims in the Northwest China* (Seattle: University of Washington Press, 1997).
Liwak, Robert. *Rogue States and US Foreign Policy: Containment after the Cold War* (Baltimore: Johns Hopkins University Press, 2000).
Mancall, Mark. *China at the Centre: 300 Years of Foreign Policy* (New York: Free Press, 1984).
Mann, Michael. (ed.). *States, War and Capitalism: Studies in Political Sociology* (Oxford: Basil Blackwell, 1988).
Mastanduno, Michael. *International Relations Theory and the Asia-Pacific* (New York: Columbia University Press, 2003).
McSweeny, Bill. *Security, Identity and Interests: A Sociology of International Relations* (Cambridge: Cambridge University Press, 1999).
Mearsheimer, John. *The Tragedy of Great Power Politics* (London: W.W. Norton, 2002).
Moon, Chung-in and Steinberg, David (eds). *Kim Dae-jung Government and Sunshine Policy: Promise and Challenges* (Seoul: Yonsei University Press, 1999).
Nau, Henry. *At Home Abroad: Identity and Power in American Foreign Policy* (Ithaca, New York: Cornell University Press, 2003).
Oberdorfer, Don. *The Two Koreas: A Contemporary History* (Reading, MA: Addison-Wesley, 1997).
Ong, Russell. *China's Security Interests in the Twenty-first Century* (London: Routledge, 2007).
Park, Chung-Hee, Our *Nation's Path: Ideology of Social Reconstruction* (Seoul: Hollym Corp, 1970).
Rigger, Shelley. *From Opposition to Power: Taiwan's Democratic Progressive Party* (London: Lynne Rienner, 2001).
Roh, Tae-woo. *Korea: A Nation Transformed* (Elmsford, New York: Pergamon Press, 1990).
Safran, William. *Nationalism and Ethno-regional Identities in China* (London: Frank Cass, 1998).
Shambaugh, David. *Beautiful Imperialist: China Perceives America, 1972–1990* (Princeton, NJ: Princeton University Press, 1991).
Steinberg, David (ed.). *Korean Attitudes Toward the United States: Changing Dynamics* (London: M.E. Sharpe, 2005).
Stewart, Patrick and Forman, Shephard (eds). *Multilateralism and US Foreign Policy: Ambivalent Engagement* (Boulder, Colorado: Lynne Rienner, 2002).
Task Force on Foreign Relations for the Prime Minister, *The Basic Strategies of Japan's Foreign Policy in the 21st Century: New Era, New Vision, New Diplomacy* (November 2002).
Van Ness, Peter, *Revolution and Chinese Foreign Policy: Peking's Support for Wars of National Liberation* (London: University of California Press, 1970).
Wakeman, Frederic, *The Fall of Imperial China* (New York: Free Press, 1975).
Waltz, Kenneth, *Man, The State and War* (New York: Columbia University Press, 1959).

Waltz, Kenneth, *Theory of International Politics* (Boston: McGraw-Hill, 1979).
Walzer, Michael. *Just and Unjust Wars: A Moral Argument with Historical Illustrations* (London: Allen Lane, 1977).
Wang, Gungwu, *To Act is to Know: Chinese Dilemmas*, (Singapore: Eastern Universities Press, 2003).
Wight, Martin *et al.* (eds), International *Theory: The Three Traditions* (London: Leicester University Press, 1991).
Whiting, Allen. *Sinkiang: Pivot or Pawn?* (East Lansing: Michigan State University Press, 1958).
Woo-Cumings, Meredith (ed.), *The Developmental State* (Ithaca, NY: London: Cornell University Press, 1999).
Wu, Xuewen (ed.). *Shizilukou de Riben (Japan at the Crossroads)* (Beijing: Shishi Chubanshe, 1988).
Yan, Xuetong. *Zhongguo Guojia Liyi Fenxi (Analysis of China's National Interests)* (Tianjin: Tianjin Remin Chubanshe, 1996).
Zagoria, Donald. *The Sino-Soviet Conflict, 1956–1961* (Princeton, NJ: Princeton University Press, 1962).
Zhao, Quansheng. *Interpreting Chinese Foreign Policy: The Micro-Macro Linkage Approach* (Oxford: Oxford University Press: 1997).
Zhao, Suisheng. *Power Competition in East Asia: From the Old Chinese World Order to Post-Cold War Regional Multipolarity* (New York: St. Martin's Press, 1997).
Hedley Bull and Adam Watson (eds), *The Expansion of International Society* (Oxford: Oxford University Press, 1984).

Index

Agreed Framework 99, 120
Anti-Secession Law 59
ASEAN Regional Forum (ARF) 23, 143
Asian Financial Crisis 53–54, 56
Asian values 31
balance of power 1–2
Beijing Consensus 32
Biological Weapons Convention (BWC) 101
bipolarity 10–11
Bretton Woods system 52
Central Asia
 energy competition 133–136
 spheres of influence 129–132
Chemical Weapons Convention (CWC) 22
Chinese Civil War 59
Collective Security Treaty Organisation (CSTO) 132
Communism
 Chinese survival 28, 38
 North Korea 105
 Soviet collapse 28, 37–38, 42–43
Comprehensive Test Ban Treaty (CTBT) 101
Confucianism 31, 36
democracy
 China 29–31
 Taiwan 68–71
 US export of 25–29
democratic peace 25
Democratic Progressive Party (DPP) 73
deterrence 18–19
Diaoyu Islands 83–84
Eastern Europe 30, 37
European Union (EU) 35, 48
Economic Co-operation Framework Agreement (ECFA) 60–61
financial crisis of 2008 52
Five Principles of Peaceful Co-Existence 6

great power management 107
Greater Tumen Initiative (GTI) 105
Group of Twenty (G20) 43, 53
Gulf War of 1991 16, 35
hegemonic stability theory 44–45
hegemony
 concept of 13
 economic 44–47
 US 13–16
human rights
 China 33
 North Korea 95
 US 32
humanitarian intervention 14, 33
imperialism 37, 38
interdependence 55
International Atomic Energy Agency (IAEA) 99, 104, 119
International Monetary Fund (IMF) 5, 52–53
International Security Assistance Force (ISAF) 112
international society 7
Japan
 alliance with the US 79–82
 economic clout 88–89
 Taiwan issue 82–84
 wider role 85–87
Korean Peninsula
 China's influence 97–98
 nuclear issue 99–103
 reunification 123–124
Korean War 93–94, 97
Korean Worker's Party (KWP) 95
Kwangju Incident 112
List, Friedrich 49
Marxism-Leninism 38, 96
Missiles Technology Control Regime (MTCR) 22

most-favoured nation (MFN) 47
multipolarity 12
National Missile Defence (NMD) 19, 102
New International Economic Order (NIEO) 43
Non-Proliferation Treaty (NPT) 22, 77, 102
North Atlantic Treaty Organisation (NATO) 112, 129–130
North Korea
  China's security 93–96
  Communism 105
  nuclear issue 99–103
Official Development Assistance (ODA) 88, 89
peaceful development 7, 118
peaceful evolution
  avenues 38
  concept of 37
  media 39
People's Liberation Army (PLA) 18, 128
Permanent Normal Trade Relations (PNTR) 48
pre-emption 17
Proliferation Security Initiative (PSI) 104, 119
protectionism 49
Realism 1–2
regime change 95, 121
Responsibility to Protect (R2P) 33
Russia
  Central Asia 131–132
  military threat 127
  Soviet collapse 28, 37–38
security
  concept of 6–7
  economic 4, 136
  military 3
  political 3
Security Consultative Committee (SCC) 82
Self-Defense Forces (SDF) 80
Shanghai Co-operation Organisation (SCO) 131–132, 138
Sino-centric 4–5, 122
soft power 27, 69, 70
South Korea
  alliance with the US 115–118
  normalisation with China 122
  nuclear issue 118–122
  sunshine policy 121
Strategic and Economic Dialogues (S&ED) 55
Taiwan
  arms sales 65
  democratisation 68–71
  independence 73–74
  international status 71–72
  US commitment 65–68
Taiwan Relations Act (TRA) 63–64, 66
Taiwan Straits Crises 67–68
Theatre Missile Defence (TMD) 18, 77
Tiananmen event 11, 28–29, 35
Tibet 34
Uighurs 127
unipolarity 9–10
United Nations (UN) 17, 21, 72, 99
United States
  co-operation with China 20–23
  trade with China 50
  East Asian strategy 62–65, 76–79, 110–111
  hegemony 13–16, 44–47
  unilateralism 11
  values 29–32
use of force
  China 18
  US 17, 33
Waltz, Kenneth 1
war on terror 14, 130, 138
Washington Consensus 32
Weapons of Mass Destruction (WMD) 17, 94, 101
World Bank 35, 43
world economy
  China joining 42–44
  US dominance 44–45
World Trade Organisation (WTO) 43, 48–50
Xinjiang 126–129
Xinjiang Production and Construction Corps (XPCC) 128
Yalu River 93
Yellow Sea 106

Taylor & Francis
eBooks
FOR LIBRARIES

Over 23,000 eBook titles in the Humanities, Social Sciences, STM and Law from some of the world's leading imprints.

Choose from a range of subject packages or create your own!

Benefits for you
▶ Free MARC records
▶ COUNTER-compliant usage statistics
▶ Flexible purchase and pricing options

Benefits for your user
▶ Off-site, anytime access via Athens or referring URL
▶ Print or copy pages or chapters
▶ Full content search
▶ Bookmark, highlight and annotate text
▶ Access to thousands of pages of quality research at the click of a button

For more information, pricing enquiries or to order a free trial, contact your local online sales team.

UK and Rest of World: **online.sales@tandf.co.uk**
US, Canada and Latin America:
e-reference@taylorandfrancis.com

www.ebooksubscriptions.com

A flexible and dynamic resource for teaching, learning and research.